THE
STORY OF THE BAPTISTS

RICHARD B. COOK
1838-1916

THE

STORY OF THE BAPTISTS

IN ALL

AGES AND COUNTRIES.

REVISED AND ENLARGED BY A

SUPPLEMENTARY CHAPTER ON THE COLORED BAPTISTS.

BY

Rev. RICHARD B. COOK, D.D.,

Pastor of the Second Baptist Church, Wilmington, Delaware,

AND

Author of "The Early and Later Delaware Baptists."

ILLUSTRATED.

THIRTY-THIRD THOUSAND.

BALTIMORE:
R.H. WOODWARD & COMPANY.
1888.

he Baptist Standard Bearer, Inc.

NUMBER ONE IRON OAKS DRIVE • PARIS, ARKANSAS 72855

Thou hast given a *standard* to them that fear thee;
that it may be displayed because of the truth.
-- *Psalm 60:4*

Reprinted
by

THE BAPTIST STANDARD BEARER, INC.
No. 1 Iron Oaks Drive
Paris, Arkansas 72855
(501) 963-3831

THE WALDENSIAN EMBLEM
lux lucet in tenebris
"The Light Shineth in the Darkness"

ISBN #1-57978-423-2

To his wife
Louisa Love Kerfoot
this volume is
Affectionately Dedicated
by her husband,
the Author.

Sicut lilium inter spinas sic amica mea inter filias

On The Cover: We use the symbol of the "lily among the thorns" from Song of Solomon 2:2 to represent the Baptist History Series. The Latin, *Sicut lilium inter spinas sic amica mea inter filias*, translates, "As the lily among thorns, so is my love among the daughters."

CONTENTS.

ILLUSTRATIONS.

BUNYAN'S STATUE.   See page 170.

CHAPTER I.

AN INTRODUCTION TO THE BAPTISTS.

MR. BRISTOW was the pastor of a Baptist church in a pleasant village near a large city. He felt it to be his duty to attend to the religious and mental instruction of his family, and for this purpose he was accustomed to spend an hour or more each day in their company. These were always occasions of great interest, and their minds had been awakened and were thirsting for knowledge. These hours of home instruction Mr. Bristow occupied sometimes in reading aloud from some instructive book, sometimes in familiar conversation, asking and answering questions, and always seeking to arouse and develop the thinking powers of the children by encouraging them to express their own views and to ask such questions as they desired. Whatever useful information they gained from the books they read, or from what they saw and heard, was thus impressed upon their minds and fixed in their memories by being made the subject of conversation.

On one occasion a question in regard to the Episcopalians, led to a discussion of some of the points of difference between the Baptists and other denominations. Mrs. Bristow

2

suggested to her husband that if he would tell them, in a plain and familiar way, the story of. the Baptists, beginning with their origin, and tracing the course of their history down to the present time, it might be very interesting and instructive to the older children, and that she, herself, and, doubtless, her sister, would be greatly interested in the subject.

"Your suggestion is excellent," said Mr. Bristow. "It is a matter which I have felt to be of the highest importance, that the children of Baptist parents should be thoroughly instructed at home, not only in the principles which distinguish the Baptists as a denomination, but also in reference to the conflicts through which they have passed, and in regard to the n oble men who all along the line of the Christian ages have bra vely maintained these same principles, and in many instances sealed their testimony with their life-blood. According to the plan I have in view, I shall try to show that the Baptists are able to trace their distinctive principles to the apostolic age ; for not only is there a striking correspondence between the Baptist churches of the present day, and those of the New Testament times, but through all the intervening ages, there were people known by various names, and differing in many points, and yet holding, to some extent, the same essential truths and bearing the same general likeness. During the Dark Ages, when, from the union of church and state, Christianity became generally corrupt, there still remained in obscure places, churches and sects which maintained the pure doctrines and ordinances of Christ, and, hence, it is certain that these churches and sects held, substantially, the same principles which are now held as the distinctive views of the Baptists. The Roman Catholic Church claims to be the oldest and the only apostolic church ; but without a shadow of proof. The Papal Church is very old, indeed, but so is Judaism, and so are many of the heathen religions. Age alone cannot establish her claim to be recognized as the true church of Christ. It must be shown that in doctrine and practice she is the same as the primitive church. But this cannot be done. It is a very perverted and corrupt form of Christianity, with a mixture of Jewish ritualism and heathen rites, but also with sufficient gospel truth to give it some resemblance to the true religion. When the Church of Rome departed from the doctrines of the apostles, it ceased to be an apostolic church, and became a political organization. The Baptists claim that their principles are older than the Church of Rome, and they base their claim to being the true church of Christ, not on their age, nor on apostolic succession, traced through the centuries, but mainly on the identity of their doctrines and practices with those of the apostolic churches.

"In reference to some of the great fundamental Christian doctrines, the Baptists agree in the main with all evangelical Christians. The inspiration of the Scriptures; the sinful and lost condition of man; the Deity of Christ; the atoning sacrifice; justification by faith; regeneration by the Holy Spirit; the resurrection of the dead; the general judgment, and the future life, are some of the great truths which we hold in common with them, and in which we delight to have Christian fellowship. But while we rejoice that there is so large a sphere of divine truth in which we can agree with other denominations, yet there are certain great principles of Christian truth, which the Baptists alone maintain. Baptists differ from Pedobaptists,* as we think conscientiously and scripturally. There are certain great and important truths taught in the Bible, which we alone have contended for, and do now practice and defend; such as:

I. The Christian church is designed to be composed of

* Pedobaptists are those who practice the baptism of infants.

regenerate persons, who have professed faith in Christ and have been baptized.

II. The entire separation of church and state.

III. The Bible alone the only rule, or standard, of religious belief and practice.

IV. The immersion of believers, the only baptism of the New Testament.

V. The Lord's Supper, an ordinance committed to the care of the church, to be administered to baptized believers only.

VI. That civil and religious liberty is an inalienable right of man.

" These principles we hold not only to be important in themselves, but they bear such a vital relation to the purity of doctrine and the preservation of the church, that we dare not regard their observance as a matter of indifference. We look upon these principles as a sacred trust, committed to our keeping, and which our fidelity to Christ binds us to guard with the utmost care. If we should be unfaithful, these principles would be lost to the church and to the world. The fact that other denominations either discard or neglect any one of these truths, makes it imperative that Baptists should teach them with special emphasis. Those who accuse us of uncharitableness and bigotry, greatly mistake the spirit that actuates us, and do us great injustice. It is loyalty to Christ and a reverential regard for his word, that make us unyielding in our adherence to what we believe to be the teaching of the New Testament. It is true that Baptists and Pedobaptists are much nearer now than they were formerly, but this is owing mainly to the fact, that the distinctive views of the Baptists have triumphed in a great measure, and other denominations have approached them in many points, by

FIRST BAPTIST CHURCH, BOSTON, MASS. See page 253.

embracing their views. The practice of infant baptism is on the decline, despite great efforts made to hold it up. And according to the great Pedobaptist commentator, Lange, this is as it should be. He says:

'Would the Protestant Church fulfill and attain to its final destiny, the baptism of new-born children must be abolished. It has sunk down to be mere formality, without any religious meaning for the child, and stands in contradiction to the fundamental doctrines of the Reformers on the advantage and use of the Sacraments. It cannot, from any point of view, be justified by the Holy Scriptures, and owes its origin, as well as its retention, by the Reformers to the anti-scriptural and irrational idea, that children, because of original sin, are born under the power of the devil, and exposed to eternal condemnation.'*

"Accepting as a fundamental doctrine, the all-sufficiency of the Scriptures, in matters of faith and practice ; requiring a regenerated church-membership, and the immersion of the believer ; we can readily trace our path through all history, back to the apostolic age. Dr. Hodge in his Theology, says, 'As Paul argued from the faith of the church, we cannot err in following his example. ' If this is true, then we cannot err in rejecting infant baptism, sprinkling, the union of church and state, and other Popish errors, and be safe in adhering to time-honored Baptist principle and practice. But is it a true principle laid down by Dr. Hodge? Not if it stands alone. Error, according to God's word, should never stand, simply because it has been the belief of the church in all ages. The Baptists have both ancient practice and God's word on their side. We do not base our claim on ancient practice alone, for, as Geo. W. Anderson, D. D., forcibly says : ' The Baptists cannot, of course, seek for any

*Dr. R. Fuller on Baptism, p. 148. Charleston, S. C. Edn.

decisive arguments from ancient practice. It matters not how far back a practice may be traced, nor how widely it spreads; it must be rejected if it be opposed to the teachings of the sacred Scriptures. Our great decisive argument is that which is drawn directly from the New Testament.'

Here ended the conversation between Mr. and Mrs. Bristow. Her suggestion, however, was fruitful, and resulted in a course of lectures given to this Baptist circle, in which was told THE STORY OF THE BAPTISTS, and which is here offered to Baptist families everywhere, believing that, as a Hand-Book, it will meet a long-felt want in our denomination.

FIRST BAPTIST CHURCH, PHILADELPHIA. See page 255.

CHAPTER II.

THE BIBLE AND BAPTISM.

THE Bible is God's book. It contains his revealed will to man. Prophets and apostles wrote under the guidance of the Holy Spirit. Jesus is the son of God," Hear ye him." Christ is the head over the church and its Law-giver, and the New Testament contains his law, which is our only infallible guide, and the supreme standard by which all churches and doctrines and rites are to be tried. Those are Christian churches, strictly speaking, that correspond with the New Testament pattern, and the Baptists have ever appealed to the New Testament, as furnishing the only true authority for the faith and practices of the churches.

There are some who regard the church of the first three centuries succeeding the apostolic age, as being the model of what the Christian church ought to be. But they have not the slightest authority. The doctrines and practices of those times are not to be accepted, unless they can be verified by the word of God. The great Erasmus says;—" It is not from human reservoirs, fetid with stagnant waters, that we should draw the doctrine of salvation, but from the pure and abundant streams that flow from the heart of God." So we say it is not from the corrupt pools of early tradition that we receive the doctrines and ordinances of the church, but from the pure fountain of God's word.

It is their adherence to the Bible alone that distinguishes the Baptists from the Roman Catholics, and in a less degree from Protestants. The Papal Church claims the right to change the ordinances, and though this right is questioned by Protestants, generally, yet, practically, they endorse it. Hear Dean Stanley :—" For the first thirteen centuries the almost universal practice of Baptism was that of which we read in the New Testament, and which is the very meaning of the word ' baptize '—that those who were baptized were plunged, submerged, immersed into the water. * * With few exceptions just mentioned, the whole of *the Western Churches have now substituted for the ancient bath, the ceremony of sprinkling a few drops of water in the face.*"*† Which is supreme, Christ or the churches ? Where did the churches get the right to substitute something else, in place of that which Christ ordained?'

In the New Testament, we have all there is upon the subject of baptism. From Christ, then, we are to learn our duty, respecting the ordinances. What he teaches is all-sufficient for all time and all places. What he commands we are to do. From his decision there is no appeal. Apostles, ministers, and churches are not to rule, to alter or amend, but to submit. Since we have the Law-giver and the law, let us ascertain what that law of Christ is. It is found in Matthew 28 : 19, 20 :—" Go ye, therefore, and teach all nations, baptizing them in the name of the Father, and of the Son, and of the Holy Ghost ; teaching them to observe all things whatsoever I have commanded you ; and, lo, I am with you alway, even unto the end of the world : Amen." Also, Mark 16 : 15, 16. We

* Article on Baptism, *Nineteenth Century*, 1879, p. 39.   † Italicized by the author.

J.S.CONANT-SC.BOSTON

"PRAYER MEETING HILL," AND HEATHEN TEMPLE.

p. 18

See page 366.

will not discuss the meaning of the text or of the word—baptize; suffice it to say, that the consensus of Christain scholarship as to what Christ's command means, may be condensed in the concession made by a most distinguished Pedobaptist, —one of the greatest living textual scholars and historians— Dr. Schaff, who says; "There can be no doubt that immersion, and not sprinkling, was the original normal form;"* also, "Baptism * * is * * the sacramental sign and seal of regeneration."†

Dr. Schaff thus places conversion before baptism, *i. e.* immersion, and confirms Baxter, who says; "This * * is the commission of Christ to his apostles for preaching and baptizing. * * My conscience is fully satisfied from this text that it is one sort of faith, even saving, that must go before baptism."‡ Neander, a converted Jew and a Lutheran, who stands in the front rank as a biblical scholar and church historian, and who is regarded as a standard authority in all matters pertaining to the early church, says; "It is certain, that Christ did not ordain infant baptism."§ Christ then commands as baptism, according to these eminent Pedobaptists, the immersion of believers only.

Christ enforces his command by his own illustrative obedience. If John's baptism was immersion then was Jesus immersed. Dean Stanley says; "It is quite correct to translate John the Baptist by John the Immerser."‖ Christ gave both the command and the example to his disciples. How did they understand him? What did they do and teach? Let Pedobaptist scholars testify, as before, as to apostolic preaching and practice, in regard to baptism.

* Church Hist. p. 488. † Dr. P. Schaff on Matt. 28 : 19, in Lange.
‡ Quoted from Dr. Fuller on Baptism, p. 116
§ Christian Religion, p. 360
‖ *Nineteenth Century*, Article Baptism, p. 39, Oct. 1879.

First :—Believers' Baptism.—It is a fundamental belief of Baptists that none but regenerate persons should be received into the fellowship of the churches. Hence they administer baptism only to those who profess faith in Christ. This principal implies the denial of infant baptism. The two stand in direct antagonism. They cannot both be right. Which is scriptural? The baptism of believers, both men and women is spoken of frequently in the New Testament, but the baptism of infants, never. The disciples of the apostolic age did not misunderstand or disobey the teaching and example of Christ To this we have more testimony than we have time to present.

Neander says ;—"Baptism was administered, at first, only to adults, as men were accustomed to conceive of baptism and faith as strictly connected. We have all reason for not deriving infant baptism from apostolic institutions."* Again :—"As baptism was closely united with a conscious entrance on Christian communion, faith and baptism were always connected with one another; and thus it is in the highest degree probable, that baptism was performed only in instances where both could meet together, and that the practice of infant baptism was unknown at this period."† Lange, the great German commentator says ;—" All attempts to make out infant baptism from the New Testament, fail."‡ Says Stark ; "There is not a single example to be found in all the New Testament, where infants were baptized. In household baptism there was always reference to the gospel's having been received."§ Professor Hahn says ;—"According to its true original design it can be given only to adults, who are capable of true knowledge, repentance and faith. Neither

* Church Hist. I. 311.
† Neander, Planting and Training of the Christian Church, Ryland, p. 101.
‡ Baptism, p. 101.
§ History of Baptism, p. 11.

in the Scriptures nor during the first hundred years, is a sure example of infant baptism to be found."[*] These witnesses prove beyond all dispute that infants were not baptized, but that believers' baptism was that of the apostolic age.

In the next place as to the MODE OF BAPTISM. Pedo-baptists speak of the modes of baptism because they adminis-ter the rite in different ways, as sprinkling, pouring, and immersion. But the Baptists hold that there is only one way of administering the ordinance, and that is, immersion.

With Dean Stanley, they believe ;—That "the change from immersion to sprinkling has set aside the larger part of apostolic language regarding Baptism, and has altered the very meaning of the word," because "the ancient rite of im-mersion was properly decided by the usage of the whole an-cient church to be essential to the sacrament of Baptism."[†] Neander says ; "In respect to the form of baptism, it was in conformity with the original institution and the original im-port of the symbol, performed by immersion,"[‡] Mosheim, whose church history is also a standard authority says ; "In this century (first) baptism was administered in convenient places without the public assemblies ; and by immersing the candidate, wholly in water."[§]

Bingham—one of the best of authorities, in his immor-tal "Antiquities of the Christian Church" says ; "As this (dip-ping) was the original apostolic practice, so it continued the universal practice of the church for many ages."[||] Conybeare and Howson, in "Life and Epistles of Paul," say, in Romans 6 : 4 ; "This passage cannot be understood unless it be borne in mind that the primitive baptism was by immersion." Dr.

[*] Theology, p. 556.
[†] *Nineteenth Century* Oct. 1879. Baptism.
[‡] Church Hist. I. 310
[§] Vol. I. 87.
[||] Vol. II, Chapter II.

SPURGEON IN HIS PULPIT. See page 321

Schaff says on the same passage ; "All commentators of note (except Stuart and Hodge) expressly admit or take for granted that in this verse * * the ancient mode of baptism by immersion and emersion is implied, as giving additional force to the idea of the going down of the old, and the rising up of the new, man."* Professor Moses Stuart, in speaking of the Greek word from which "baptism" comes, says; "Baptize means to dip, to plunge, to immerse, in any liquid. All lexicographers and critics of any note agree in this."

And so it appears that all church historians of note are agreed in saying that immersion and not sprinkling was apostolic baptism.

This reference to Professor Stuart reminds us of the following little anecdote that is told of him. The Professor had before him a class, reading and translating from the Greek Testament. When they came to the 16th verse of the 16th chapter of Mark, one of the students translated, " He that believeth and is sprinkled shall be saved."

" Sprinkled," the Professor replied, "is not correct."

"Is it not in accordance with the practice of the denomination ?" asked the student.

" That is not the question," replied the Professor ; "you are now translating the Greek Testament, and the word means, immerse."

If we now compare the Baptist churches with the original pattern given in the Scriptures, we shall find them like the New Testament churches in two important particulars, viz : as to baptism of believers only, and the administration of the ordinance by immersion. This is important, because it is as Christ intended and ordained it, and the baptism of

* In Lange on Romans.

believers only, involves the purity of the churches, and immersion, as Bingham says; "represents the death, burial, and resurrection of Christ, as well as our own death to sin and rising again unto righteousness." To change the ordinance either in regard to its form or subjects, must be attended, as history shows, with the most serious consequences to the purity and life of the church, and renders the innovator liable to the charge of disloyalty to Christ and contempt of his express commands.

A KAREN BAPTIST PREACHER AND HIS WIFE   See page 367.

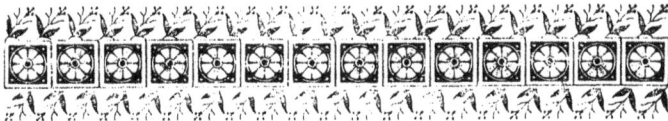

CHAPTER III.

THE FATHERS AND THEIR TIMES.

THE last survivor of the apostles was John, who wrote several books of the New Testament, and closed up the volume of inspiration with that wonderful book, called the Revelation. He lived to be a very old man and died peacefully at Ephesus in the year of our Lord, 100. Thus the apostolic office ceased with the close of the first century of the Christain Era. The opening of the second century introduces us into a new and distinct class of writings, very different from those of the New Testament. They are the productions of men of learning and piety, and from them we learn what were the doctrines and practices of the churches in the time immediately succeeding the apostolic age. Some of these early writers were the companions and associates of the apostles, and, hence, are called the Apostolic Fathers. These were Barnabas, Clement of Rome, Hermas, Ignatius, and Polycarp. The rest of the Fathers lived from A. D. 116 to A. D. 494. They were not inspired men, and therefore their writings cannot be classed with those of the apostles. We must distinguish also between their opinions and their testimony. As men of intelligence and Christian character they are credible witnesses to the *facts* which make up the history of the church in their day, but their *doctrinal opinions* can be accepted only so far as they agree with the Scriptures. They are of no more value than the views of men of equal intelligence and piety in our day. In this way we accept Dean Stanley the *historian,* but we reject Dean Stanley the *theologian.*

We have already seen that the baptism of the New Testament was immersion, and its only subjects, believers. The writings of the Fathers must be accepted as proving what the ordinances were in their day. The testimony of the Apostolic Fathers, shows that baptism was administered as in the New Testament times, by immersion, and that it retained this form for a long time, but it soon began to undergo a change, in reference to the subjects. At first very young children were baptized, and then infants of a few days received the ordinance under the notion that it would save the soul. I shall not call the Fathers themselves to the witness stand, but shall examine learned Pedobaptists, who have made the writings of the Fathers their study, as to the subjects and mode of baptism in the ages immediately following the apostles.

First, as to Infant Baptism. Neander says:—"It cannot possibly be proved that infant baptism was practiced in the apostolic age. Its late introduction, the opposition it met with still, in the second century, rather speak against an apostolic origin."* Towards the close of the second century, says the same author, Tertullian appeared as a zealous opposer of infant baptism; a proof that it was not then customary to regard this as an apostolic institution ; for had it been so he would hardly have ventured to oppose it so warmly.†

* Apostolic Age, I. 140.
† Church History, I. part 2, p. 264.

Curcellæus says;—"Pedobaptism was not known in the world the two first ages after Christ. In the third and fourth, it was approved of by a few. At length in the fifth and following ages it began to obtain in divers places. * * * The custom of baptizing infants did not begin before the third age after Christ, there appears not to be the least footsteps of it in the first two centuries."* The most important recent testimony upon this point is that of Dean Stanley, one of the very best of English authorities. He says; " In the Apostolic age, and in the three centuries which followed, it is evident that, as a general rule, those who came to baptism, came in full age, of their own deliberate choice. We find a few cases of the baptism of children; in the third century, we find one case of the baptism of infants. Even among Christian households the instances of Chrysostom, Gregory, Nazianzen, Basil, Ephrem of Edessa, Augustine, Ambrose, are decisive proofs that it was not only not obligatory, but not usual. They had Christian parents and yet they were not baptized till they reached maturity."†

This is strong testimony against infant baptism in the age of the Fathers. For a long time, allowed occasionally, it was first sanctioned by ecclesiastical law, at the Council of Mileri, A. D. 416, and finally forced by civil law upon the people, when Justinian, A. D. 550, compelled his subjects to renounce Paganism and embrace Christianity. The people were forced then to have their children baptized.

As we have seen that how, in the days of the Fathers, infant baptism was in part substituted for believers' baptism, so I shall now show, upon Pedobaptist authority, as before, that IMMERSION WAS THE ONLY BAPTISM recognized as apostolic by the church during this period and for a long time after-

* Crosby's History Baptists, p. 11.
† In *Nineteenth Century*, October, 1879, p. 39.

wards. Even after the baptism of infants had, by human authority, been introduced into the church, immersion prevailed. And even to this day, the Greek Church adheres strictly to immersion. They have changed the subjects, but not the form of baptism. The Papal Church, and the Protestant churches which sprang from it, have changed both the subjects and the form. The late Bishop B. B. Smith of Kentucky, in a letter to J. L Burrows, D. D , says: " I do fully and unhesitatingly believe that no instance, either of adult or infant baptism, occurred during the first centuries, except by immersion, save only in the few cases of clinic baptism."

In the early ages, sick persons who were unable to receive the regular baptism, which was by immersion, had water poured over them as a substitute. This ceremony received the name of clinic baptism. The custom, no doubt, originated, like infant baptism, in the erroneous view of the saving efficacy of the ordinance. Men who believe that baptism has a saving effect would naturally desire to administer it to infants, and to sick persons who are thought likely to die. At first there were many who considered it unlawful, and they opposed the practice. The clinics were regarded as an exceptional class of Christians and their right to the privileges of the church was often disputed. A notable instance is found in the case of Novatian at Rome, in the early part of the third century. He was elected to the office of bishop, but his ordination was opposed on the ground that he had received only clinic baptism, yet owing to his splendid endowments, this objection was overruled, and he was set apart to the ministry. Knapp says of this period ;

" Immersion is peculiarly agreeable to the institution of Christ, and to the practice of the apostolic church, and so

JUDSON WITH THE LAST LEAF OF THE BURMAN BIBLE TRANSLATED BY HIM

See page 335.

even John baptized, and immersion remained common for a long time after ; except in the third century, or perhaps earlier, the baptism of the sick was performed by sprinkling or affusion. Still some would not acknowledge this to be true baptism, and controversy arose concerning it, so unheard of was it at that time to baptize by simple affusion. Cyprian first defended baptism by sprinkling when necessity called for it, but cautiously and with much limitation. By degrees, however, this mode of baptism became more customary, probably because it was found more convenient ; especially was this the case after the seventh century and in the Western church, but it did not become universal until after the commencement of the fourteenth century."* This testimony of one among the many German scholars, is strengthened by the words of the distinguished Dean Stanley, of England, than whom there is no better authority upon the subject.

"For the first thirteen centuries, the almost universal practice of Baptism was that of which we read in the New Testament, and which is the very meaning of the word—'baptize'—those who were baptized were plunged, submerged, immersed into the water. That practice is still, as we have seen, continued in Eastern Churches. In the Western Church it still lingers amongst Roman Catholics, in the solitary instance of the Cathedral of Milan ; amongst Protestants, in the austere sect of the Baptists. It lasted long into the Middle Ages. Even the Icelanders, who at first shrank from the water of their freezing lakes, were reconciled when they found that they could use the warm water of the Geysers. And the cold climate of Russia has not been found an obstacle to its continuance throughout the vast empire. Even in the Church of England it is still observed in theory. Elizabeth and Edward the Sixth were both immersed. The

* Theology, p. 486, Phila. 1854.

rubric in the Public Baptism for Infants, enjoins that, unless
for special cases, they are to be dipped, not sprinkled. But in
practice it gave way since the beginning of the seventeenth
century. With the few exceptions just mentioned, the whole
of the Western Churches have now substituted for the ancient
bath, the ceremony of sprinkling a few drops of water on the
face.''* The statement made by Archbishop Whateley, is
a very clear and candid testimony. He says; "Except upon
extraordinary occasions, baptism was seldom, or, perhaps,
never, administered for the first four centuries, but by
immersion or dipping. Nor is aspersion or sprinkling ordinarily
used to this day, in any country that was never subject to the
Pope; and among those that submitted to his authority,
England was the last place where it was received, though it
has never obtained so far as to be enjoined; *dipping* having
been always prescribed by the rubric. The Salisbury Missal,
printed in 1530, expressly requires and orders dipping. And
in the first Common Prayer Book of King Edward VI., the
priest's general order is to dip it in water. * * * *
Many fond ladies at first, and then by degrees the common
people, would persuade the minister that their children *were
too tender for dipping.*''*‡ The same author shows how sprinkling was introduced into England from the Continent, and
specially through the influence of Calvin, "so that in the
times of Queen Elizabeth, and during the reigns of King
James and King Charles I., there were but very few children
dipped in the font. But our divines at the Restoration
understanding a little better *the sense of Scripture and Antiquity*, again restored the order for immersion.''†‡ We might
bring forward many other witnesses who would testify to the
same effect, but these are quite sufficient to prove, beyond a

* *Nineteenth Century*, October, 1879.
† Dr. Samson in Appendix to Dagg's Theo.   ‡ Italicized by the author.

reasonable doubt, that during the age of the Fathers, immersion was practiced as the only scriptural form of baptism, while the baptism of infants was unknown in the Christian church on the Continent, until about the middle of the third century, and in England for 1500 years after Christianity was introduced there.

BURMAN MISSIONARY PREMISES AT BASSEIN.

See page 367.

CHAPTER IV.

The Early Christian Sects.

N the next place consider the various bodies of Christians who arose between the age of the apostles and that of the Reformation. Many of them, who, during those times, were stamped as heretics, were noble reformers who sought to resist the progress of apostasy and tried to bring the church back to the simplicity and purity of the Scriptures, or failing in this they separated from that church which had finally become hopelessly corrupt, and established churches of their own, after the gospel pattern. These Christian people furnished the material for the rack, the dungeon, and the stake, during those dark days in which the apostate church took up the bloody sword of persecution, which had been wrenched from the cruel hand of Paganism. Some of these early sects held the divine truths which now characterize us as Baptists. They were not free from error. Some of them had their features greatly marred, but yet, in many respects, they bear a striking resemblance to the Baptists of our day.

They exalted the Scriptures above tradition and church authority ; held to the doctrine that the church should be composed only of regenerate persons ; believed that Christ is the only Head of the church ; baptized believers only ; rejected infant baptism; considered immersion as the baptism of the New Testament; and denounced the union of church and state.

Immersion was not the distinguishing principle of the true churches of those early times, for all the early churches practiced immersion; nor is it the most important doctrine of the Baptists of the present day. None of the early sects are to be claimed as Baptists, except those who held baptism as an ordinance binding on all *believers* and refusing it to all others.

The first of these early Christian sects, of which we have any distinct account, is the Montanists.* They arose about the year 150 A. D., in Phrygia, and continued for five centuries. They were numerous in different parts of Asia, Africa, and Europe. They looked upon themselves, alone, as the genuine Christians †

According to Neander, Tertullian is called "the Montanist," and is said to have belonged to that sect. He is described not only as a zealous opponent of infant baptism, but as one who could not imagine any efficacy of baptism without the conscious participation of the person baptized and his own individual faith.

The Novatians next invite our attention. They derived their origin as well as their name from Novatian of Rome, who lived about the middle of the third century, A. D. 250. He was a man of superior talents, of great excellence of character, and became a bold reformer. He was called the first Anti-pope, and the author of Puritanism, yet we know that Tertullian had quitted the church nearly fifty years

* Mosheim, I. p. 233.

† Neander, Rose Trans. pp. 330—335.

P. 35 **BUNYAN SELLING LACES.** See page 163.

before, for the same reason.* He and his friends set themselves to work to reform the abuses of the church, but finding
their efforts unsuccessful, they separated themselves and organized a new party. They grew rapidly in numbers and strength,
and Novatian churches were formed all over the Roman Empire. They were the Puritans of their day, because they contended for a pure church ; that is, a church composed only of
converted persons. Neander says that they regarded "purity
and holiness as the essential marks of a true church:"† And
Mosheim ;—"They consider the Christian Church as a society
where virtue and innocence reigned universally." They
flourished for about 300 years, and then, probably, became absorbed into other sects holding the same principles, but
bearing different names.

The Donatists and Novatians very nearly resembled each
other in doctrine and discipline, and indeed were charged by
Crispin, a French historian, with holding, in common, the
following things :—

First.—For purity of church members, by asserting that
no one ought to be admitted into the church but such as are,
visibly, true believers and true saints.

Secondly.—For purity of church discipline.

Thirdly.—For the independency of each church ; and,

Fourthly.—They baptized, again, those whose first baptism they had reason to doubt.

They were, consequently, termed rebaptizers and Anabaptists.‡

The Donatists arose about fifty years later than the
Novatians, and continued for many centuries until absorbed

* Robinson quoted by Benedict in Baptist Hist p. 5.
† Neander, Rose Trans. p. 147
‡ Jones' Church Hist., pp. 225, 226

into other churches, and lost under other names. They multiplied rapidly in Africa, in the northern part of which, at that time, there were civilized nations; and nearly equaled in number the so-called Catholic Church. Orchard describes them as correct in morals, simple in spiritual worship, scriptural in faith and practice.* They were professed Ana-baptists. Some of them were distinguished for great learning and talents. One of their peculiar principles was the separation of church and state. When they were called upon to unite with the Catholic Church, and to submit the difference between them and their opponents, to the Roman emperor, they asked, "What has the emperor to do with the church?" "What have we Christians to do with kings, or what have bishops to do at courts?"

At times they were greatly reduced by fierce and bloody persecutions, waged against them by Mitre and Crown. A law was enacted that the person rebaptizing, and the person rebaptized, should be punished with death, in consequence of which, hundreds of bishops, and thousands of inferior clergy, were deprived of churches, while rights of citizenship and the exercise of religious worship were taken from them.† Benedict truthfully says; "For a thousand years after the rise of the Donatists, we find them spread along in all parts of Europe, under different names, but recognized by friends and foes, as substantially the same people, and in the middle of the seventeenth century, Fuller, the English ecclesiastical historian, says of the English Baptists, that they were Donatists, new dipped."

Before the Donatist name disappears from the page of history, another large and important sect makes its appear-ance, called the Paulicians, probably because they gave such

* Orchard's Foreign Baptists, pp. 82, 95.
† Gibbons' Rome, Chapter 23.

prominence to the writings of Paul. About the year 653, Constantine, a young man living in an obscure town in Armenia, received from a traveling stranger, returning from captivity in Syria, whom he had entertained as a guest, the gift of two manuscripts, which were the four Gospels, and the Epistles of Paul. This rare and costly treasure, was highly prized by Constantine, who studied it with great diligence, especially the letters of Paul. Being a man of talent, he taught others the truths which he drew from this pure fountain, and gathered a church founded on New Testament principles. But at length he was arrested by an officer of the Greek emperor, Simon by name, and the members of his church were offered pardon on condition that they would stone their pastor to death. They stood by silent;—silent with horror at the thought of such an act, when an apostate among them, called Justus, like another Judas, became the bloody-handed executioner of his spiritual friend and guide. But the seed had been sown broad-cast, and Paulician churches became very numerous, and existed for a long time, notwithstanding the efforts made to exterminate them.

One of the most distinguished Paulicians was Sergius, a young man of intelligence and education, but without religion, until met by a Paulician woman, in 810, who recommended to him the reading of Paul's writings. He, with others, deemed the reading of the Holy Scriptures not lawful for a layman, but only for the priests. Being convinced by her that he was mistaken, he applied himself to the reading, was converted and spent thirty-four years in preaching the gospel. He traveled all over Western Asia, calling upon the people to abandon a corrupt church and turn to the spiritual worship of God. Multitudes were converted, and to stop the spread of God's work, the severest measures were used. In the reign of Theodore, over one hundred thousand were put to death. Nevertheless, untiring in their zeal, they penetrated into the very heart of Europe with the word.

Of these Christian sects and the causes of their trials, Dr. W. R. Williams writes; "They insisted on the power of the Spirit, as the Great Conservator and Guardian of the life of the Christian church. Now, far back in the days of Montanism, this was offensive to the Christian churches, who became, under power and wealth and fashion, secularized and corrupted. The Compte de Champagny * * has said of the Montanists, that it was hard to find doctrinal error in their views. * * * Out of Montanism came Tertullian, early protesting against the precipitating of Infant Baptism. So the Donatists made in after times, a like testimony against worldliness. Bishop Latimer, himself in later years a martyr, speaking of some Anabaptist martyrs from Holland, who went to the stake in England with heroic cheer and joy, was struck with a parallel of which he does not seem to have discovered all the force; and makes the remark, that these glad sufferers at the stake were like those old heretics, the Donatists of early ages. The Paulicians, a later body, were eminent, especially for their love of Paul's Epistles. For centuries, defamed and pursued, they held their course, testifying and witnessing. Hase, the modern church historian, himself a rationalist, speaks of them as continuing under various names down quite near to our age * * * in Bulgaria."*

* Lectures on Baptist History, p. 120.

SIAMESE PROSTRATING THEMSELVES BEFORE THE SACRED WHITE ELEPHANT. See page 367

CHAPTER V.

THE WALDENSES AND THEIR CONTEMPORARIES.

E have considered, some of the early Christian sects who held Baptist principles, and refused to acknowledge the authority of the Papal Church. We continue the subject. The early history of the Waldenses is very obscure, but it seems to point to the earliest antiquity as the date of their origin. It is probable that the Waldensian churches maintained an unbroken line of succession, apart from the papacy, from the days of the apostles.

Some have ascribed their origin to Peter Waldo; but their existence has been traced back many centuries beyond the time when he lived. He belonged to the sect whose history we are considering, so a brief notice of his character and work will not be out of place. Peter Waldo was a wealthy merchant of Lyons, in France. By the careful study of the New Testament, he became convinced that the system of religion taught and exemplified in the Papal Church was totally different from that which was inculcated by Christ and his apostles. Moved with the true missionary spirit,—an intense desire to make known the truths of the gospel, that souls might be saved, he gave up his business, distributed his goods to the poor, and devoted himself to the work of making known the way of salvation. This was in 1170. He made great efforts to have the Scriptures translated and circulated among the people. His followers became very numerous, and were called "the Poor Men of Lyons," because they renounced the wealth and vanities of the world, and led a life of poverty and humility. Even their enemies concede that they were good people, of honest and upright lives; and yet they suffered cruel persecutions. Peter Waldo, himself, along with many of his followers, was compelled to escape for his life, and fled to Bohemia where he ended his days.

From the statements of their persecutors, we learn that the Waldenses flourished five hundred years before the time of Peter Waldo. They themselves claimed that their doctrines and discipline had been preserved in all their purity, from the days of the primitive martyrs. Under different names they existed in the earliest ages apart from the established Greek and Latin churches. They were the most celebrated body of dissenters who protested against papal corruption during the Middle Ages. Their churches were found widely dispersed through the countries of Spain, France, Germany, Italy, and especially amongst the valleys of Piedmont. An eminent writer says that "it is an error to suppose, that when Christianity was taken into alliance with the State, by the emperor Constantine, in the beginning of the fourth century, all the orthodox churches were so ignorant of the genius of the Christian religion as to consent to the corruption of a worldly establishment." As we have already seen, there were many who maintained the purity of the church from the beginning of the great apostasy.

In times of persecution they sought refuge among the mountains, and dwelt in large numbers in the valleys of the

Alps and Pyrenees, and, hence, received the name of Waldenses, or *the people of the valleys.* This name probably included a number of sects who held different views and practices.

Almost the only account of their early history is derived from the statements of their persecutors, the papists. These are, of course, only partial, but yet when rightly understood they throw a great deal of light on the subject. A Roman Catholic writer says, " their heresy excepted, they generally live a purer life than other Christians." Their enemies generally bear testimony to the simplicity and excellence of their life and manners. They were particularly distinguished from the papists, by their regard for the Bible, and their disregard for the authority of the Fathers and tradition. They translated the Scriptures into the language of the people, and were noted for committing to memory large portions of them. They were specially familiar with the New Testament, and taught its truths with great earnestness and zeal. The early Waldenses therefore held the principles which now distinguish the Baptists. In later times, however, they departed from their primitive simplicity, and about the time of the Reformation many of them embraced the baptism of infants and other errors, probably for the sake of union with the reformers and to escape persecution from them.

Reinerius, a Roman Catholic inquisitor, who was engaged in the persecution of the Waldenses, says, that they affirm these views amongst other things :

" That is the church of Christ which hears the pure doctrine of Christ, and observes the ordinances instituted by him, in whatever place it exists." " The sacraments of the church are two,—baptism and the Lord's Supper." " We consider the sacraments as signs of holy things, or as visible emblems of invisible blessings. We regard it as proper, and even necessary, that believers use these symbols, when it can be done. Notwithstanding which we maintain that believers may be saved without these signs, when they have neither place nor opportunity of observing them." They say that a man is then first baptized, when he is received into their community. Some of them hold that baptism is of no advantage to infants because they cannot actually believe.* If this testimony is to be believed, it is clear enough that the Waldenses held Baptist principles.

The words of the Encyclopedia referring to them are :— "That they understood and practiced immersion as baptism, is evident, but, whether they generally practiced infant baptism has been long a matter of dispute. The words of Reinerius seem to imply that in his time,(1250,) they were of different opinions on this point. The modern Waldenses in the valleys of Piedmont do practice it, but they have so changed in many points since their amalgamation with the Calvinists of the Reformation, having also received their pastors from them since 1603, that nothing decisive can be hence inferred. The only one of their ancient writings which sanctions it is the *Spiritual Calendar*, but this, if it is genuine, is of doubtful date. On the contrary, all their other writings, from the Noble Lesson, in 1100, down to their Confession of Faith in 1655, Dr. Gill affirms, to be in favor of the baptism of believers only. It appears certain that the Cathari, the Paterines, the Berengarians, the Arnoldists, the Petrobrusians, and the Henricians,*i.e.* the earlier Waldenses,so far as history testifies, vehemently opposed infant baptism. That there were, on the other hand, many among them in after years who adopted the practice, is, in view of all the facts, highly probable. Mr. Jones,in the preface to the fifth edition of his History says that the *Waldenses were Anti-pedobaptists*." *

*Encyclopædia of Religious Knowledge—Waldenses.

The Albigenses were named from the place in France where they arose. Benedict collects several authorities to prove that they did hold to believers' baptism. His view is confirmed by more recent investigation. It is said that a million of the Albigenses perished in the fierce persecution waged upon them by the Catholic Church. Men, women and children were put to death, or driven from their homes, and of them and of the Waldenses, it may be said in the language of Scripture, " they wandered about in sheepskins and goatskins, being destitute, afflicted, tormented, of whom the world was not worthy."

There were many more renowned reformers, who led the Reformation in their age, of whom it will be profitable to speak.

Berengarius was principal of the cathedral school at Tours, and afterwards archdeacon of Angers. He was highly renowned on account of his extensive learning, great talents, and the exemplary sanctity of his life and manners. His view of baptism is expressed in these words : "Our Lord Jesus Christ requires of thee that in the faith, that God so loved the world as to give his only begotten son as a propitiation for our sins, thou shouldest submit to outward baptism, to represent *how thou oughtest to follow Christ* in his death and in his resurrection."* His enemies said, "He did all in his power to overthrow the baptism of little children and to pursuade adults to renounce their baptism in infancy." For his teachings he was persecuted, and through fear of death, compelled to recant. He died, A. D., 1088. His followers were called Berengarians, and increased to a great multitude, and spread all over Europe.

Another great preacher and reformer of the Middle Ages was Peter of Bruys, who arose in the south of France about

Neander's, Ch. Hist. III. 525.

p. 46   **EUTAW PLACE BAPTIST CHURCH, BALTIMORE, MD.** See page 258.

1110. He was a priest of the Papal Church, but preached the pure gospel with great power and effect. "He made the laudable attempt," says Mosheim, "to reform the abuses and to remove the superstitions that disfigured the beautiful simplicity of the gospel. Multitudes heard him and followed his teachings."* Peter taught Baptist doctrines. His followers were called Petrobrusians. The same author also calls his followers Anabaptists.† Peter was burned to death A. D. 1130.

He was succeeded by Henry of Lausanne, an Italian monk and hermit, who came to France and preached the gospel with great eloquence and power. Vast numbers flocked to hear him, and embraced his views. Henry following in the footsteps of his predecessor, Peter, rebaptized those who had received the rite without faith, and he organized his followers into churches, or societies. Dr. Wall says of Peter of Bruys and Henry, that "they were the first Anti-pedobaptist preachers that ever set up a church or society of men, holding that opinion against infant baptism and rebaptizing such as had been baptized in infancy."‡ They were far from being the "first." Henry's followers were called Henricians. He was tried and condemned, A. D. 1148, and cast into a dungeon where he languished and died, when and how, nobody knows. They would have burned him had not Sampson, archbishop of Rheims, opposed it, because he did not believe it right to shed blood on account of one's religious belief.

Arnold, of Brescia, was also a noted reformer. He was of Italy, and was condemned by the Pope in the year 1139. He was first hanged, and then his body was burned at

* Vol. I. p. 302. Ch. History
† Vol. IV. p. 428. Ch. History.
‡ Hist. Infant Baptism, II. 250.

Rome, 1155, and his ashes thrown into the Tiber.* He remained in the Catholic Church and there contended for a pure gospel church. He is said by one authority, (Otho of Freising,) to have opposed infant baptism. Other reformers were John de Wickliffe, of whom we shall hear more in connection with the Baptists of England, John Huss, and Jerome of Prague; the latter two, Christian martyrs of the noblest type. In church history we read a great deal about the Manichaeans. They were an early heretical sect, and consequently their name was hurled at others not heretical according to the New Testament, although dissenting from the church at Rome.

*Gieseler's Eccl. Hist. II. 284—nota

GERMAN BAPTIST PUBLISHING HOUSE, CLEVELAND, OHIO.

See page 362.

CHAPTER VI.

THE ANABAPTISTS.

AMONG those who, in the 16th century, gladly hailed the Reformation, inaugurated by Martin Luther, as the dawning of the day, were the so-called Anabaptists, who appeared in great numbers, in almost every country of Europe. The word Anabaptist means rebaptizer, and was given by foes to those who baptized a second time, persons who came to them from other sects. Baptists never admitted that they were rebaptizers. The name was applied, at this time, in derision to those Christians, who, taking the Scriptures as their guide, contended for a converted church membership, and for the baptism of believers only, consequently, rejecting infant baptism, which was the common practice of the Reformed, as well as of the Catholic churches. They therefore held aloof from those churches, and formed societies of their own, and, regarding Catholics, Lutherans, and Calvinists as being unbaptized, baptized all who came to them upon profession of their faith in Christ. In their controversy with opponents the mode of baptism was not discussed, but the subjects of baptism. Hence it is always difficult to determine whether they immersed, or sprinkled, or poured, though in many instances it was immersion, but it is certain that they did believe in a regenerate church membership, were strenuous opposers of infant baptism and strong advocates of believers' baptism.

The Anabaptists re-appeared in great numbers at the time of the Reformation. Dorner, whose language shows how strong, sometimes, are the unjust prejudices, even of good men, testifies to the vast numbers of these Anabaptists, who sprang up all over Europe, out of their hiding places, into which persecution had driven them during the preceding ages. His words are: "This malady of Anabaptism and fanaticism had, in the third and fourth decades—1520 to 1540,—spread like a hot fever through all Germany; from Suabia and Switzerland along the Rhine to Holland and Friesland; from Bavaria, Middle Germany, Westphalia and Saxony, as far as Holstein."* Another writer has said; "In the centuries that preceded, influences were in operation, which, growing in strength, as time rolled on, prepared the way for this wide-spread movement." Mosheim says of their origin: "The true origin of that sect, which acquired the denomination of Anabaptists, by their administering anew the rite of baptism to those who came over to their communion, and derived that of Mennonites from the famous man to whom they owe the greatest part of their present felicity, is hid in the remote depths of antiquity. * * * The various sects were comprehended under the general denomination of Anabaptists, on account of their opposing the baptism of infants, and their rebaptizing such as had received the Sacrament in a state of childhood."†

The Mennonites were a branch of the Anabaptists that originated in Holland, and received their name from Menno

* Benedict's Hist. Baptists, p. 39.
† Mosheim's Ch. Hist. IV, 428.

Simon, a distinguished man to whose earnest labors they owed much of their prosperity. They were the Dutch Anabaptists. Fleeing from Switzerland into Holland to avoid persecution, the Anabaptists soon found a leader, (1536,) in Menno. They spread under this name into other countries of Europe. Rev. J. Newton Brown in his Encyclopedia of Religious Knowledge, says of Menno Simon, called by Mosheim the father of all Anabaptists; "That he believed that immersion was scriptural baptism." It is stated by some that Menno was himself immersed; but this is denied by others. The modern Mennonites, both at home and in America, follow the departure rather than the ancient and scriptural custom of their fathers, and of the apostles. What, on account of persecution, "was done then but of necessity, is now done out of choice as other corruptions are."[+]

Morgan Edwards says : "The Mennonites in Pennsylvania and in other parts of the world have somewhat deviated from Menno, in matters both of faith and practice; and particularly in that of baptism. He, (Menno,) in his declaration concerning Christian baptism in water, printed in 1539, expressly saith: 'After we have searched ever so diligently we shall find no other baptism besides dipping in water, which is acceptable to God, and maintained in his word.' [†] After which he adds; 'Let who will oppose, this is the only mode of baptism that Jesus Christ instituted and that the apostles taught and practiced.' Accordingly, Menno was dipped and did dip others. His successors did the same except where they made proselytes in prisons, or were hindered from going to rivers, and they excused themselves from a consideration of its necessity."[‡] [§]

+ Benedict's Hist. p 132.
† Ibid. p. 24.   ‡ Ibid. p. 39.
§ See *Christian Review*, vol. 26, p. 409-10, for a criticism upon this view.

DROWNING AN ANABAPTIST MARTYR.

See page 60.

Here is an important testimony, regarding the modern Mennonites in Germany, from Lehmann, the late pastor of the Baptist church at Berlin, Prussia, who speaking of how, in 1837, he became a Baptist, says " *that he had learned by a residence of several years in East Friesland, where the Mennonites are numerous and prosperous, that which already caused him to think, concerning the time and manner of baptism, so that at heart he favored the Mennonites.*"† "It may be observed, in the first place, that the Mennonites are not entirely mistaken when they boast of their descent from the Waldenses, Petrobrusians, and other ancient sects, who were usually considered *witnesses of the truth* in the times of universal darkness and superstition. Before the rise of Luther and Calvin, there lay concealed in almost all the countries of Europe, particularly in Bohemia, Moravia, Switzerland and Germany, many persons who adhered tenaciously to the following doctrine which the Waldenses, Wickliffites and Hussites had maintained, some in a more disguised, others in a more open and public manner, viz: 'That the Kingdom of Christ, or the visible church he had so established upon earth, was an assembly of true and real saints, and ought, therefore, to be inaccessible to the wicked and unrighteous, and also exempt from all those institutions which human prudence suggests, to oppose the progress of iniquity or to correct and reform transgressors'. This maxim is the true source of all the peculiarities that are to be found in the religious doctrine and discipline of the Mennonites ; and it is most certain that the greatest part of these peculiarities were approved of by many of those who, before the dawn of the Reformation, entertained the notion already mentioned, relating to the visible church of Christ." *

* Mosheim's Ch. History, IV. pp. 428, 429.

† Unpublished Letters of J. G. Warren, D. D.

By the principle that the church is an assembly of true and real saints, they meant precisely what we mean by a regenerated church membership. This has been the fundamental principle of the Baptists in all ages, that the church should be composed of those only who are born again.

Thomas Munzer has been called an Anabaptist, by many, but the truth is that he was such only in word, and not in deed, for he practiced infant baptism. He was fanatical in religion, and was the leader, with others, in a political revolution that cost him his life, and brought the whole Anabaptist family into trouble because some Anabaptists were among them. Storck, Stubner and Hoffman are classed with him. There are many who regard Munzer as having been in the right in warring against oppression, and think that had he been successful, he would have ranked among the great liberators of the world.

There was another matter that brought the Anabaptists, unjustly, into trouble—the Munster affair. The kingdom established at Munster was one of darkness and not of light, of wickedness, not of righteousness. Many good people were drawn into it unawares. Menno and many other Anabaptists denounced the Munster wickedness. But it was enough that some of them were Anabaptists, to bring the whole body into contempt and expose them to persecution from Romanist and Reformed, from Lutheran and Calvinist. The traveler still beholds, suspended to the tower of the splendid Gothic Church of St. Lambert, three iron cages in which the ring-leaders of the insurrection were encased after a terrible martyrdom. There they hang, high in the air, a warning to all evil-doers, while the whole Anabaptist family are made unjustly to bear the odium, to this day. The late Rev. R. J. W. Buckland, D. D., in a letter published before his death in the "Independent," says ;—"All the ablest historians recognize these differences and absolve the peaceful Anabaptists from all connection with the Munster kingdom. * * * * It was a mere episode of the Reformation, lasting only from February, or more strictly, December, 1534, to the 22nd of June, 1535, or about six months in its full organization. But the peaceful Anabaptists, who made it a religious principle to bear no weapons, use no force, love their enemies, and suffer all things unresistingly, existed by many tens of thousands before, during, and after, this time, in Switzerland, Germany, Moravia, and the Low Countries. In their distinctive principles they were identical with the Waldenses, before them, and the noble Mennonites, after them. Erasmus gave them the highest praise. Wicel, one of the apostles of Lutheranism is quoted as saying; 'If a pastor preaches too fervently of the necessity of returning to God, of living an exemplary life, or seriously correcting one's faults and conforming to the rule of the gospel, he is regarded as an Anabaptist. * * It is no wonder that their history is misread, for it is written by their opponents, and like all the church history of the age, in an intensely polemical spirit.'' But incredible as it seems to us, it is yet too true, that the Protestant reformers did not persecute the Anabaptists and invoke the civil arm against them, alone on account of the Peasants' War, or the abominations at Munster, but in general, solely for their religious opinions and practices.

This statement, the following remarkable words of Mosheim fully sustain; "Certain it is, they were treated with severity; but it is much to be lamented that so little distinction was made between the members of this sect, when the sword of justice was unsheathed against them. Why were the innocent and the guilty involved in the same fate? * * * * Those who had no other marks of peculiarity than their

administering baptism to adult persons, only, and their
excluding the unrighteous from the external communion of
the church, ought, undoubtedly, to have met with a milder
treatment than what was given to those seditious incendiaries,
who were for unhinging a government and destroying all
civil authority.   It is true, indeed, that many Anabaptists
suffered death, not on account of their being considerd as
rebellious subjects, but merely because they were judged to
be incurable heretics, for in this century the error of limit-
ing the administration of baptism to adult persons, only, and
the practice of rebaptizing such as had received that
sacrament in a state of infancy, were looked upon as most
flagitious and intolerable heresies. * * *   Neither the
view of the flames that were kindled to consume them, nor
the ignominy of the gibbet, nor the terrors of the sword,
could shake their invincible constancy, or make them
abandon tenets that appeared dearer to them than life and
all its enjoyments.''*

"The time will probably arrive," says Spurgeon,
" when history will be re-written, and the maligned Baptists
of Holland and Germany will be acquitted of all complicity
with the ravings of the insane fanatics, and it will be proved
that they were the advanced-guard of the army of religious
liberty, men who lived before their times, but whose influence
might have saved the world centuries of floundering in the
bog of semi-popery, if they had been allowed fair play.   As
it was, their views, like those of modern Baptists, so com-
pletely laid the axe at the root of all priest-craft and
sacramentarianism, that violent opposition was aroused, and
the two-edged sword of defamation and extirpation was set to
its cruel work and kept to it, with relentless perseverance,
never excelled, perhaps never equaled.   All other sects

Mosheim's Ch. Hist. Vol. IV. p. 435.

p. 57 PRESIDENT FRANCIS WAYLAND, D. D., L L. D. See page 373

may be in some degree borne with, but Baptists are utterly intolerable to priests and Popes ; neither can despots and tyrants endure them.''*

* Metropolitan Tabernacle—its History &c., by Rev. C. H. Spurgeon, p. 13.

IMMANUEL BAPTIST CHURCH, CHICAGO, ILL.

See page 265.

CHAPTER VII.

HERE were many Anabaptists, who suffered for the truth's sake at the hands of Papists and Protestants in the Netherlands, Germany and Switzerland. In the *Martyrs' Mirror*, and the *Baptist Martyrology*, there are hundreds of cases recorded.

In all of these places the persecutions were legalized both by civil enactment, and by ecclesiastical sanction. In Germany, by the edict of King Ferdinand in 1527, death was the penalty for Anabaptism. The Emperor Charles V. caused them to be hunted down and put to death. In 1529, at the Diet of Spires, it was ordained that death should be visited upon every Anabaptist. There also met at Homburg in 1536, a Diet composed of the Reformers of Germany and their followers in church and state. Luther and Melancthon were among the number. That body sanctioned the punishment of Anabaptists, even by death, by the civil authorities. At the beginning of the Reformation, the first to suffer martyrdom in Germany were Hans Koch, and Leonard Meyster, who were put to death at Augsburg in 1524. They were said to have been descendants of the Bohemian and Moravian Waldenses, and were placed at the head of the list of Anabaptist martyrs. Michael Satler, who had been a monk, was put to death in 1527, for uniting with the Anabaptists, and marrying a wife. He was executed in a most barbarous manner. His tongue was cut out, his flesh torn with red hot pincers and his body finally burned.

Leonard Schoener, a barefooted monk, growing disgusted with the hyprocrisy and wantonness of the monastic orders, became an Anabaptist under the ministry of Hubmeyer. He was an educated man. Having preached throughout Bavaria, he was beheaded, and then burnt at Rottenburg, in 1528. Hans Schloffer was tortured with great cruelty, and questioned by the priest upon the subject of infant baptism. He answered, "that we must first preach the word, and baptize those only who hear, understand, and believe and receive it. This is true Christian baptism and no infant baptism. The Lord has nowhere commanded to baptize infants."

At Alzey there was a wholesale slaughter of Anabaptists in 1529. Three hundred and fifty were confined in prison and literally dealt out to the executioner like sheep to the slaughter, as fast as the executioner could dispatch them. In whose body, then, was the cruel soul of Nana Sahib? Those who were waiting their turn to die, sang until the executioner came for them. It was at this same place—Alzey—that nine brethren and three sisters were imprisoned, and when they refused to renounce their faith, were put to death, the men by the sword and the woman by drowning. A sister came to comfort the female prisoners while they were yet in prison and exhorted them to be true and firm, despite their sufferings, and for the sake of the eternal joy to come to them. For this visit—for comforting and strengthening these suffering saints—she was burned to death.

Two young girls were arrested at Bamberg, snortly after their baptism, and after being cruelly tortured to make them recant, were burned to death. While going to the stake their tormentors put upon their heads, in derision, crowns of twisted straw, when one of the girls said to her companion ; "Our Saviour wore a crown of thorns for us, and shall not we wear these harmless crowns for him? and, besides, we shall soon be crowned by him with glorious crowns of gold."

Among many Christians condemned to be burned at Saltzburg, there was a young and beautiful girl of sixteen. Even the hearts of her persecutors were moved, and after vainly trying to persuade her to recant, the executioner took her in his arms to a trough for watering horses, that was near by, and thrusting her head under the water, held it there until she was dead. Wolfgang Brand-Hueber was an Anabaptist preacher, who was put to death at Lintz. This was one hundred years before Roger Williams' celebrated proclamation of civil and religious liberty in Rhode Island, and yet this martyr expressed the same sentiments when he taught that obedience and submission should be rendered to magistrates in all things not contrary to God. This has ever been Baptist belief. And to this day, there is not full liberty in Germany for our brethren.

The Anabaptists appeared in Switzerland in 1523. According to Erasmus, they were numerous there in 1529.[*] They suffered there at the hands of the Reformed. The first decree against them imposing a fine, was passed by the Senate at Zurich, one of the Cantons, in 1525. In 1526, another decree was passed, making the penalty for Anabaptism—death. It forbade believers' baptism, and compelled the baptism of infants. And these laws were made

* Orchard's Foreign Baptists, p. 346.

with the full approbation of the reformers, who were intensely active in securing their execution. And yet, Bullinger, one of the reformers, testifies ; " For the people said, ' Let others say what they will of the Dippers, we see in them nothing but what is excellent, and hear from them nothing else but that we should not swear, or do wrong to any one, that every one ought to do what is right, that every one must live godly and holy lives. We see no wickedness in them.' "*

Still, for a long period, the persecutions continued throughout all Switzerland, which so far from checking Anabaptism, seemed to stimulate its growth. It was either, go to the Reformed Church, or die. They preferred death. Here are a few instances out of the many. Balthazar Hubmeyer was one of the most distinguished Anabaptists who felt the severity of the laws and the persecuting spirit of the Swiss reformers. Hubmeyer was a learned and eloquent Catholic priest, and was called Doctor, by the Romanists. He was born in Bavaria, in 1480. In 1516, we find him preaching in the cathedral at Ratisbon to great crowds of people, at which time he began to take sides with the reformers, preaching against many Romish errors. He soon fully embraced the Reformed doctrines and practices, and became the friend of the Swiss reformers, and with Zwingle, lived in the most intimate intercourse. *He had translated the Gospels and the Epistles into the language of the German people*, to whom he now also preached the gospel. He came, finally, to regard infant baptism as a popular error and renounced it. After pleading in vain with his friend Zwingle, and his associates to do the same, he was baptized, with over one hundred others, by William Roubli.

Hubmeyer, himself, soon after baptized three-hundred upon profession of their faith. He was siezed and impris-

* Martyrology.

P. 63

HOWLAND N.Y.

WRITING AND SELLING PRAYERS IN CHINA.

See page 365.

oned at Zurich. It was said by his enemies that he recanted, but on one occasion when a large concourse of people were collected in the great church by the leaders, and Zwingle and his companions were there to hear the recantation, he disappointed them. They waited in breathless silence to hear him condemn Anabaptism. When he did break the silence with his voice, it was to re-assert that infant baptism was without the authority of God. His voice was drowned in the uproar of the horrified people, and above the din was heard the voice of Zwingle. They had argued with him in prison, and (these Protestant reformers!) had even applied the tortures of the rack, to convince him that he was wrong, but he would not deny the truth, so he was hurried back to prison. It is said that he made a recantation afterwards, and was released from prison, but he was still confined to the city of Zurich, from which he soon escaped. He was not long allowed the liberty of preaching Christ, for he was again arrested, and taken to Vienna, where he was burned to death, March 10, 1528 ; and at the same time his devoted wife was drowned in the Danube, by the same unpitying hands. His last words were ; "With joy I die that I may come to the Lamb of God, that taketh away the sin of the world." His wife urged him to constancy. He has left many writings to live after him.

Previous to the execution of Hubmeyer, Felix Mantz, a native of Zurich was drowned at that city. This was in 1527. Like Hubmeyer, he was at one time a friend of the Swiss reformers, but when he began to preach to crowds upon the unscripturalness of infant baptism and an unregenerated church membership, and to baptize believers, he was imprisoned by them. His last words were, "Into thy hands, O Lord, I commend my spirit."

Louis Hetzer was another intimate friend of Zwingle, until he adopted Anabaptist principles. He translated a portion of the Scriptures. He was beheaded at Constance in 1529. His death was glorious. Even his enemies were surprised at his calmness, his charity, his courage, his faith, and remarked, never was there such a death seen at Constance. Many more cases of oppression and cruelty could be related. The effort was to exterminate. Even as late as 1671, seven hundred persons, homeless and destitute, were driven out of Berne. Great was the suffering of old and young. From Switzerland, the Anabaptists fled in great numbers to the Netherlands, to escape persecution. Previously (1510) great numbers passed into Holland and the Netherlands and coalesced with the Dutch Baptists. Papist and Protestant persecuted them there as elsewhere.* The Emperor Charles V., (1535,) and his son and successor, Philip II. of Spain, (1556,) issued their imperial bloody edicts, against them, and the terrible Spanish Inquisition was brought, at length, to help the magistrate to discover and punish the so-called heresy.

The Lord soon raised up for them, in the country of their adoption, a leader in Menno Simon, from whom they have been given the name of Mennonites, and by whose labors they were greatly increased in numbers. He was born in the year 1492, at Witmarsum, Friesland. He was, at first, a Catholic priest and preached in his native village, was a man of great ability, and, evidently, of extensive learning. He was then ignorant of the Scriptures, however, and knew nothing of experimental religion. When first awakened to the errors of popery, and upon searching, was unable to find infant baptism in the Scriptures; he went to Luther and to other reformers for conference, but they gave him no light. He united with an Anabaptist church, in 1536, and retired

* Orchard's Foreign Baptists, p. 330

from public life, but his brethren recognizing his humility and talents, brought him forward as a leader and teacher among them. At their earnest solicitation, and his own feeling: "Woe is me, if I preach not the gospel," he gave himself up to the work of the gospel ministry, knowing full well that bonds and imprisonments awaited him.

" From the commencement of his ministry among the German Anabaptists, to the end of his days, that is, during the space of twenty-five years, he traveled from one country to another, with wife and children, exercising his ministry under pressures and calamities of various kinds, that succeeded each other without interruption, and constantly exposed to the danger of falling a victim to the severity of the laws. East and West Friesland, together with the province of Groningen, were first visited by this zealous apostle of the Anabaptists; from thence he directed his course into Holland, Gelderland, Brabant, and Westphalia, continued it through the German provinces that lie on the coast of the Baltic Sea, and penetrated as far as Lavonia. In all these places his ministerial labors were attended with remarkable success, and a large number of believers were added to the church. Hence, he is deservedly looked upon as the common chief of almost all the Anabaptists, and the parent of that body that still subsists under that denomination. The success of this missionary will not appear surprising to those who are acquainted with his character, his spirit and talents, and who have a just notion of the condition of the Anabaptists at the period of time now under consideration."*

The martyrdom of Sicke Snyder was the means of awakening Menno, himself. "He was beheaded in Lewarden,

*Mosheim's Church History.

in 1531. The constancy of this man to his views of
believers' baptism, preferring even an ignominious death to
renouncing his sentiments, led Menno to inquire into the
subject of baptism. Menno could not find infant baptism
in the Bible; and on consulting a minister of that persuasion,
a concession was made *that it had no foundation in the Bible.*
Not willing to yield, he consulted other celebrated reformers,
but all these he found to be at variance, as to the grounds of
the practice, consequently he became confirmed that the
Baptists were suffering for truth's sake. In studying the
word, convictions of sinfulness, and of his lost condition
became deepened ; and he found God required sincerity and
decision. He now sought new spiritual friends, and found
some with whom he, at first, privately associated, but afterwards became one of their community." *

In 1539, when pursued by enemies, Menno took refuge
in the house of his friend and brother Tiaert Keynerts.
Menno escaped but his friend was arrested. It was a capital
offence to give shelter to a heretic, in those days. He was
cruelly tortured to make him reveal where Menno was
concealed, but he refused to tell, and died for his brother.
In 1543, Menno was hunted through all West Friesland and
a price was set upon his head. Even malefactors and
murderers were offered pardon, the freedom of the country,
the favor of the emperor, and a hundred carlgulden to deliver
him to the criminal judge. On one occasion, a traitor had
promised, for a certain sum of money, to deliver him to his
enemies. He tried to betray him at a meeting, but Menno
escaped in a wonderful manner. Not long after, the traitor
with an officer, and in search of Menno, passed him in a
boat on a canal. The traitor said not a word, but let him
pass on to some distance, and escape upon shore. Then he

* Orchard's Foreign Baptists, p 342.·

E

THE COLUMBIAN UNIVERSITY BUILDING.

WASHINGTON, D. C.

See page 375.

exclaimed, "The bird has escaped us." "Why," said the officer, "did you not inform us?" "I could not speak," said the man, "for my tongue was tied." Whereupon the officer, calling him a villian, severely punished him.

By the kind intervention of Providence, he was permitted to escape the vigilance of his pursuers and finally, to die in peace. A kind nobleman, the lord of Fresenburg, Holstein, beholding the sufferings of the Anabaptists, and observing the true nobility of their character, invited them to settle upon his estates, where he would extend to them his protection. Many accepted his generous offer, and before long whole churches were living there in prosperity and peace. Here, Menno lived the latter part of his life, sending into the countries around the written word of life, and here he died, January 13th, 1559.

Anneken Von de Hove was an Anabaptist and was buried alive at Brussels, in 1597. The high court, in company with some Jesuits, (members of the so-called Catholic Society of Jesus,) went with her to the hole dug outside of the city. When they had covered her lower extremeties with earth, the Jesuits called upon her to recant. She refused to deny her Lord, so the work went on, they still calling upon her to renounce her faith, until they threw the earth upon her face, and heaped it over her head and finally with deadly hate stamped upon it with their feet.

The time came, however, when civil and religious liberty was granted the Anabaptists in the Netherlands. They found a friend in William, Prince of Orange, "the glorious founder of Belgic liberty."* "He resolutely stood out against all meddling with men's consciences, or inquiring into their thoughts. While smiting the Spanish Inquisition

* Mosheim's Church History.

into the dust, he would have no Calvinistic Inquisition set up in its place. Earnestly a convert to the Reformed religion, but hating and denouncing only what was corrupt in the ancient church, he would not force men, with fire and sword, to travel to heaven upon his own road."*

* Motley's Rise of the Dutch Republic, II. pp. 362, 206.

FIRST BAPTIST CHURCH, PROVIDENCE, R. I.

T. E. BROWN, D. D., PASTOR.

See page 205.

CHAPTER VIII.

EARLY ENGLISH BAPTISTS.

ISTORY and geography are very intimately associated, and should be studied together. Let us trace the growth and spread of Baptist principles. Look on the map. There is Palestine, on the eastern border of the Mediterranean sea. There is the river Jordan, flowing down through the land, in whose waters Jesus was "buried in baptism,"by John the Baptist. There is the city of Jerusalem, where the first Christian church was formed, composed of immersed believers only, and separate from the state. From this land of small dimensions, but distinguished above all others, as the birth-place of the Son of God, and of Christianity, Baptist churches spread through the surrounding countries ; around the Mediterranean sea, as along two arms into Africa and through Asia Minor ; and across the Egean sea to Athens and Corinth and "round about into Illyricum;'' across the Adriatic sea into Italy, and over unto Spain, and up through Germany and France; and then, crossing the British Channel, the standard of the cross was planted in the midst of those islands of the sea, where a pure Christianity has always found a congenial soil, and

flourished with peculiar vigor. Here, in this land of our fore-
fathers, we shall find the history of the Baptists invested with
peculiar interest.

It is not known at what period the gospel was introduced into Great Britian. It is certain, however. that
Christianity was carried into England at a very early period,
probably as early as the close of the first, or beginning of the
second century, and as far as baptism is concerned it must
have been at that time scriptural. The " Nonconformist,"
an English paper, says : " In England there can be no doubt
that Baptists existed so early as the third century. We are
warranted in saying that the early British Christians
held the distinctive principles of Baptists. Austin, in
Canterbury, in the sixth century, had great trouble with a
colony of Baptists, in Wales, and used such repressive
measures against them as to load his name with infamy.
Toward the close of the seventh century, 692, Ina enacted a
law, that all children should be baptized within thirty days of
their birth, thus indicating that Baptist ideas largely prevailed." Infant baptism was introduced into Britian at an
early date, but immersion was the prevailing mode, from the
first until the Reformation. There are some well-authenti-
cated accounts of wholesale baptisms there in early ages.
Augustine baptized 10,000 converts in the river Swale, in
Kent, A. D. 597, in one day, among whom was King Ethel-
bert. At Easter, 627, Paulinus baptized in England 3000
souls. Some Pedobaptists deny the possibility of immersing
even the three-thousand, converted at Pentecost, in one day.
Yet, there are several undoubted instances of the immersion
of a large number, within the same period of time. The
celebrated Chrysostom, Bishop of Constantinople, immersed
in one day, in 404, with the assistance of his Presbyters, about

BAPTISTERY OF BISHOP PAULINUS

See page 298.

3000 persons; and in July, 1878, J. G. Clough, D.D., Baptist missionary in India, with five assistants, two baptizing at the time, immersed 2,222 believing Telugus, converts from heathenism, in six hours.

Mr. Spurgeon has expressed himself upon English Baptist history. He says; " It would not be impossible to show that the first Christians who dwelt in this land were of the same faith and order as the churches now called Baptist. * * All along our history from Henry II. to Henry VIII. there are traces or the Anabaptists, who are usually mentioned either in connection with the Lollards or as coming from Holland. All along there must have been a great hive on the Continent of these 'Reformers before the Reformation'; for despite their being doomed to die, almost as soon as they landed, they continued to invade this country to the annoyance of the priesthood and hierarchy." Spurgeon quotes the following statement from W. J. E. Bennett, of Frome, a ritualist, whose hatred of the Anabaptists rendered him least likely to manufacture ancient history for them. Mr. Bennett says; "The historian Lingard tells us, that there was a sect of fanatics, who infested the north of Germany, called Puritans. Usher called them Waldenses; Spelman, Paulicians,(the same as Waldenses.) They gained ground and *spread all over England*; they refused all Romish ceremonies, denied the authority of the Pope, and more particularly, *refused to baptize infants.* Thirty of them were put to death for their heretical doctrines, near Oxford; but the remainder still held on to their opinions in private, until the time of Henry II. 1158; and the historian Collier tells us that wherever the heresy prevailed, the churches were either scandalously neglected, or pulled down, and *infants left unbaptized.* " " We are obliged to Mr. Bennett for this history,

which is in all respects authentic, and we take liberty to
remark upon it, that the reign of Henry II. is a period far
more worthy of being called remote, than the reign of Henry
VIII., (the founder of the Episcopal Church,) and if Baptists could trace their pedigree no farther, the church of
Thomas Cranmer, (the Episcopal,) could not afford to sneer
at them as a modern sect. Concerning the poor, persecuted
people that are referred to in this extract, it seems that under
Henry II. they were treated with those tender mercies of
the wicked, which are so notoriously cruel. 'They were
apprehended and brought before a council of the clergy, at
Oxford. Being interrogated about their religion, their
teacher, named Gerard, a man of learning, answered in their
name, that they were Christians and believed the doctrines of
the apostles. Upon a more particular inquiry, it was found
that they denied several of the received doctrines of the
church, such as purgatory, prayers for the dead, and the
invocation of saints ; and refusing to abandon these damn-
able heresies, as they were called, they were condemned
as incorrigible heretics, and delivered to the secular arm to
be punished. The King, (Henry II.) at the instigation of
the clergy, commanded them to be branded with red hot
iron on the forehead, to be whipped through the streets of
Oxford, and having their clothes cut short by their girdle, to
be turned into the open fields, all persons being forbidden
to afford them any shelter or relief, under the severest penalties. This cruel sentence was executed with its utmost
rigor, and it being the depth of winter, all these unhappy
persons perished with cold and hunger.' '' *

Usher says ; '' The Berangarian or Waldensian heresy,
had, about the year 1180, generally infested France, Italy,
and England. Not only the weaker sort in the country vil-

*Spurgeon in Met. Tab. History, pp 10, 11.

lages, but the nobility and gentry in the chief towns and cities, were infected therewith, and therefore, Lanfranc, Archbishop of Canterbury, who held this See, both in the reigns of William the Conqueror, and of his son William Rufus, wrote against them, in the year 1087. The Arch-bishop adds from Poplinus' History of France, ' that the Waldenses of Aquitain, did, about the year 1100, during the reigns of Henry I., and Stephen, kings of England, spread themselves and their doctrines all over Europe', and mentions England in particular. ''*

In the fifteenth century, John de Wickliffe, a Roman Catholic priest of remarkable talents and learning, born in England, in 1324, appeared. He was the greatest among re-formers. He remained in the Papal Church, but he attacked her errors and preached the doctrines of the New Testament with such clearness and power, as to bring upon him the hatred of the Pope and clergy. His great work was to trans-late the Scriptures into the language of the English people, so that, for the first time, they had the Bible in their own tongue. Wickliffe escaped the many schemes of the Catholics to pun-ish him for such wickedness, and died in peace, under the protection of the Duke of Lancaster, in 1384. Forty years after his death, his bones were dug up by his enraged ene-mies and burned with his books, and the ashes cast into the Swift. Many accuse Wickliffe of rejecting infant baptism. He did hold opinions which would have legitimately led him to reject this, among other popish errors, and many of his followers did refuse to baptize their new-born children, rightly contending that unbaptized infants would be saved. †
His followers increased in number and were said, at one time, to have reached 100,000, in England alone, and to have taken

*D'Anvers on Baptism, pp. 275, 278. Ivimey's History of English Baptists, I. p. 55.
‖Martyr's Mirror, p. 275.

the lead there, among evangelical reformers. Severe measures were adopted to suppress them, and foreign Rome, in 1400, induced English rulers, for the first time, to impose the death penalty upon dissenting Englishmen.*

This law was made to suppress the Wickliffites or Lollards. The first martyr under this law, was Sir. William Sawtre, who held Baptist sentiments. Sir. John Oldcastle, or Lord Cobham, was also arrested for his religious sentiments, and cruelly put to death. In the reign of Henry V. multitudes were committed to the flames, and the Lollard's Tower was prepared. This was a tower fitted up at the Lambeth palace at Canterbury. It still stands. The huge rings and staples to which the suffering Christians were fastened before being taken to the stake, are now preserved in the lumber room of the palace. These, with the tower, itself, are silent witnesses of suffering patience and cruel wrongs. The exalted character of these sufferers is well attested to. When Bonner asked; "Where was the church, before the time of Luther ?" Fox answered ; "Among the Lollards in the diocese of Norwich."†

Robinson describes a Baptist congregation existing in Chester, in 1457. "I have seen enough to convince me, that the present English Dissenters, contending for the sufficiency of Scripture, and for primitive Christian liberty, to judge of its meaning, may be traced back * * * to the Apostles. One branch *uniformly denied the baptism of infants*; all allowed Christian liberty, and all were enemies to the established hierarchy reigning over the consciences of their brethren. I have now before me a register of Gray, Bishop of Ely, which proves that in the year 1457, there was

* Orchard. Hist. Baptists in Britain. pp 4,6.
† Orchard

McMASTER HALL, TORONTO, ONTARIO.

See page 290.

a congregation of this sort in this village of Chesterton."*

" In 1534, Henry VIII. assumed the headship of the English church, throwing off the dominion of the Pope. A convocation of the national clergy declared, in 1536, that the doctrines of the Baptists were detestable heresies, to be utterly condemned. In 1538, Cranmer was ordered to proceed against them, and burn their books, and instructions were sent to magistrates *throughout* England to execute the laws against them. Several were burned to death at Smithfield, and some, fleeing the country, were martyred in their land of refuge. Thirty-one Baptists were put to death in Holland, in 1539, who had fled from England. (Baptist Jubilee Memorial.) Bishop Latimer, in a sermon preached before Edward VI., referring to events in the reign of Henry VIII., said; ' Baptists were burned in different parts of the kingdom, and went to death with good integrity.' "†

Edward VI. carried on the reformation begun by Henry VIII. but while favoring the papists and others with pardon, the Baptists were deemed unworthy of the king's clemency. A royal commission was created, called, sometimes, " the Protestant Inquisition," to proceed against the Baptists, and under this commission the celebrated Joan of Kent, or Boucher, and many others, were burnt to death. Joan was a pious woman, well known at the court of Edward VI. Taylor claims in his general history, that she was a Baptist. She was an earnest distributor of Tyndale's New Testament, and was a great reader, herself, of the Scriptures. She was accustomed to tie the books under her apparel, with strings, and in this way, take them into the palace. Many persons were blessed by the perusal of the word of life, she gave them. Archbishop Cranmer was clamorous for her death. He was

* Benedict 309, quoting notes on Claude's Essays II, pp 53, 55.
† Spurgeon in Ford's Repository.

moved when the young king turned to him and said ; "If I do wrong, since it is in submission to your authority, you shall answer for it before God." She was burned to death, May 2nd, 1550. George Van Pare, a Dutch Baptist, was burned at the same place in 1551. Cranmer, Ridley, Latimer, and John Rogers, who all approved the executions, were, themselves, martryed in the next reign, that of " Bloody Mary."

Dr. Cramp gives an account of the discovery of congregations at "Bocking, in Essex, at Feversham, in Kent, and other places," in the reign of Edward VI., that existed about 1548. There were four ministers apprehended among them, from which he infers that their number must have been large. These ministers, Humphrey Middleton, Henry Hart, George Brodebridge and Coal, and about 160 members of the congregation, were arrested. " It is clear that they were Anabaptists," remarks Dr. Cramp, who also quotes Strype as saying that "they were the first that made separation from the Reformed Church of England, having gathered congregations of their own."* This was before Presbyterians or Independents were known in England. Middleton was kept in prison, and afterward burned in the reign of "Bloody Mary," who succeeded to the throne, upon the death of Edward VI. She was a papist and sought to re-establish in England, the dominion of the Pope. Among the martyred in her reign were many Baptists.

* Strypes Memorials II. p 381. Baptist Magazine, Feb. 1866, pp 113, 115.

CHAPTER IX.

FROM ELIZABETH TO CHARLES.

N the 17th of November, 1558, Queen Elizabeth ascended the throne of England. Marsden, as quoted by Spurgeon, says that; "In her reign, the Anabaptists were the most numerous, and, for sometime, by far, the most formidable opponents of the Episcopal Church. They are said to have existed in England since the early days of the Lollards."* Dr. Some, a churchman of great note in her days, in a book written against the Puritans, complains of the Baptists, that they had "several conventicles in London and other places ; and that some of their ministers had been educated at the university, and that they held heretical opinions."†

Elizabeth had no patience with those of Baptist sentiments. She was a Protestant and favored the established church, but was intolerant with dissenters. The " Baptist Memorial " says, that a royal proclamation was issued, in which it was ordained that all Baptists and other heretics should leave the land, but they seemed to gather fortitude ;

* Spurgeon in Met. Tabernacle History, p. 14.
† Ivimey, I. p. 108.

for some formed themselves into separate societies, and in 1575, the seventeenth year of Elizabeth's reign, a congregation of them was formed without Aldgate, London, of whom some were banished, twenty-seven were imprisoned, and two were burnt to death, in Smithfield.‡   This was a company of German Anabaptists, and the two, mentioned as having been burned to death, were John Pieters, and Henry Terwoort.

John Fox, the author of the "Book of Martyrs," took compassion on them, and wrote the queen a truly pathetic and eloquent letter, entreating her to spare them. Even Fox thought they deserved some kind of punishment for being Baptists, only he begged the queen not to be so cruel as to roast them alive. But his petition was of no avail, except he was allowed a month's time to convert them from their dangerous errors. Fox used every effort to induce them to renounce their faith, in order to save their lives. But they replied, "We are sorry that you do not understand our matter. We seek with our whole heart to serve the one God and Christ, in a good conscience, and to edify our neighbor, as far as possible in us lies. Therefore we gladly receive what the Holy Scripture testifies, and wish to be permitted to adhere to the plainness and simplicity of the word of God." They also sent to the queen, from their prison, a confession of their faith, and asked to be released. But it was all in vain. They could no more move the queen to give up her cruel purpose than Fox could induce them to renounce their faith.

Terwoort was a young man about twenty-five years of age, and had been married only a few weeks. Pieters was aged, and had nine children dependent on his daily labor for support. His first wife had been martyred at Ghent in Flanders; and his second wife was the widow of a martyr.

Crosby, I. p. 79. Ivimey, I. p. 102.

BELFRY OF A TEMPLE AT OSAKA, JAPAN   See page 367.

F

These facts were made known to their persecutors, and permission was asked that Pieters and his family might leave the country. But in vain. On Friday, July 22nd, 1575, they were led forth to be executed. As they were bound to the stake, Pieters said; "The holy prophets, and also Christ our Saviour, have gone this way before us, even from the beginning until now." One of the Protestant preachers, "would that I could write it—Popish Priests"--who stood by, said, "These men believe not on God." Pieters replied, "We believe in one God, our heavenly Father Almighty, and in Jesus Christ, his Son." Before the fire was kindled they were offered life and pardon if they would renounce their faith; but they answered, "You have labored hard to drive us to you, but now, when placed at the stake, it is labor in vain." Finding that they would rather die than renounce their faith, the fires were kindled and these two faithful witnesses for the truth, were burned to ashes. The queen's advisers were perhaps more to be blamed for these cruel persecutions than Elizabeth herself. Sandys, Bishop of London, Whitgift, and, perhaps, other leading Protestants, influenced the queen against the Baptists. They, by their action, said; "Their blood be upon us and upon our children." And it was required at their hands.

Elizabeth died in 1603, and was followed in succession by James I., and by Charles I. James united Scotland and England in one kingdom. While in Scotland, James was a strict Presbyterian, but when he ascended the English throne, he became an Episcopalian, and an intolerant bigot. It was soon apparent that the dissenters were to gain no advantage by the change of rulers. They were persecuted as hotly as ever, and many left the country, while those who remained were obliged to hold their meetings in out of the way places, going into the woods, or meadows, or assembling for worship in private barns, stables or haylofts. On the 11th of April, 1612, Edward Wightman was burned to ashes, at Litchfield, for saying that the baptism of infants is an abominable custom, and that Christianity is not wholly professed and preached in the Church of England, but in part. He is known to have been a Baptist, and is supposed to be the progenitor of a large family of this name, in England, having among them many Baptist ministers. He was the last one of the large number who were put to death in England, about 1400 in all, for their religious opinions. Of this great number who were burned at the stake, the name of William Sawtre stands first, and that of Edward Wightman closes the long list, in a period of 212 years, and both of these were Baptists.

This was not, however, the end of the persecutions ; for the Baptists and other dissenters still suffered, multitudes dying in prison, and from other methods of cruelty; but no more were burned to death. For seventy years, until William III., in 1689, they suffered from imprisonment, fines, stocks, stripes, and exile. It was about this time that the struggle for religious freedom began, and it will be interesting to observe the part which our Baptist ancestors took in the inauguration of the great conflict, which has ended in the triumph of civil and religious liberty. We shall find that the noble tree, under whose spreading branches, we now worship God, "with none to molest or make us afraid," was planted and protected by Baptist hands, and often watered with their tears and their blood.

The Baptists have always been the champions of religious liberty. *The union of church and state has been the great enemy of freedom of conscience,* and this they have always opposed. In the year 1614, a treatise on religious freedom, was published by Leonard Busher, entitled "Religious Peace, a plea for liberty of conscience," and was the earliest published work, in the English language on this subject. It will be interesting to observe some of the sentiments contained in this work, which in those times were new and strange, but in our day, are accepted as self-evident truths. "Christ's Kingdom," says Busher, "is not of this world, therefore, it may not be purchased nor defended with weapons of this world, but by his Word and Spirit. It is not only unmerciful, but unnatural and abominable, yea, monstrous, for one Christian to vex and destroy another for difference and questions of religion. It is not the gallows, nor prison, nor burnings, nor banishing, that can defend the Apostolic faith. * * * They cannot be Christ's bishops and preachers, that persuade princes and people to such anti-christian tyranny and cruelty. And it is very evident that these bishops and ministers, who give over men and women to the magistrates, to be persuaded by persecution, do show clearly that their doctrine is not good." Again, he uses these prophetic words, which have a glorious fulfillment in our day; "I do verily believe, that, if free liberty of conscience be granted, that the spiritual kingdom of these idol bishops will in time fall to the ground, of itself, as the idol Dagon fell before the Ark."*

Another treatise was published about this time, 1615, entitled "Persecution for Religion, Judged and Condemned," by the same author who was a member of Mr. Helwys' church. He denounces interference by the magistrate in the affairs of religion, and expresses his abhorrence of *all* persecution, and advances the true idea of religious liberty, for he " would grant religious freedom even to the

*Tacts on Liberty of Conscience: Hanserd Knolly's Society.

RICHMOND COLLEGE, RICHMOND, VIRGINIA

See Page 376.

Papists.'' In this respect he is far in advance of all the teachers of his time. In the year 1620, a tract was published in behalf of religious freedom, entitled ; " A Most Humble Supplication of many of the king's majesty's loyal sub- jects, ready to testify all civil obedience by the oath of allegiance or otherwise, and that of conscience, who are persecuted (only for difference in religion) contrary to divine and human testimonies.''* The book was written in prison, by a man, who was denied the use of pen, ink and paper. The account is given by Roger Williams, who says, "The author * * being committed by some, then in power, close prisoner to Newgate, for the witness of some truths of Jesus, and having not the use of pen and ink, wrote these arguments in milk, on sheets of paper brought him by a woman, his keeper, from a friend in London, as the stop- ples of his milk bottle. In such paper, written with milk, nothing will appear, but the way of reading it by fire being known to this friend, who received the papers, he transcribed and kept together the papers, although the author could not correct nor review what himself had written.''†

It was during the reign of James, that the first regularly organized English Baptist church, of which we possess any detailed account, was formed in Amsterdam in 1607, by John Smyth, formerly a clergyman of the Church of England. He became a dissenter, in the beginning of the reign of James I., and fled, with others, from England to Holland to escape persecution. Here he joined a pious company of English fugitives, who had preceded him. He and some others, upon the examination of the Scriptures, without out- side influence, became Baptists, discovering that there were no scriptural grounds for infant sprinkling. One of their number, probably Mr. Helwys, baptized Smyth, who then baptized the others. This was the first General Baptist church, composed of Englishmen, after the Reformation, of which we have knowledge. Baptist churches, in time of persecution, were mostly held in private houses, and hence, difficult of discovery. The first Particular Baptist church was not formed till 1633. Thomas Helwys, who succeeded to the pastorate of the church, upon the death of Smyth, in Holland, in 1611, returned to London, accompanied by his church, about 1612. Smyth is regarded as the founder of the "General" Baptist churches of England, which are Arminian in doctrine, and "close," or restricted in communion; while the "Particular" Baptists are, for the most part, Calvinistic in doctrine, and open in communion. In 1691, many of the General Baptist churches adopted Unitarian views, and the orthodox formed, in 1770, what is known as the "New Connection."

The Rev. John Morton was a fellow-laborer with Smyth and Helwys, and probably returned to London with the latter. He suffered in the cause of believers' baptism, and wrote a book in defence of the General Baptists, a copy of which was found in the beginning of the civil wars, in demolishing an old wall near Colchester, and was entitled "Truth's Champion." The names of the ministers which next appear in the history of the General Baptists are Thomas Lamb, Henry Devine, E. Barber, William and David Jeffery and Thomas Grantham. The latter was, during a long and active life, a distinguished leader and promoter of the Baptist cause. In 1625, Charles I. came to the throne. He was a weak man, and a tyrannical ruler. The "Protestant Inquisition" was revived, and Presbyterians and Baptists, alike, suffered for nonconformity to the Episcopal Church. It was in this reign that the first Particular or Calvinistic Baptist

WORSHIPING JUGGERNAUT.

See page 367

church was formed. It arose out of a division that occurred
in an Independent church, which was gathered in 1616.
Some of the members believed that baptism was not rightly
administered to infants, and so looked upon their own baptism received at that age, as invalid.   They asked for
dismission to form a Baptist church, and the church, believing that they were acting from a principle of conscience,
and not from obstinacy, granted it.   They were immersed
and formed into a Baptist church, September 12, 1633.   As
to their number, after giving the names of about twenty men
and woman, it is added, "with divers others."   It met in
Broad Street, Wapping, London.   Their minister was John
Spilsbury. Soon afterwards, in 1638, William Kiffin, Thomas
Wilson, and others, were dismissed at their own request, to Mr.
Splisbury's congregation.* A question here arose, as to "the
propriety of suffering ministers to preach among them, who
had not been baptized by immersion."   Mr. Kiffin, who
"opposed this principle", withdrew, with others, and helped
form, about 1640, the Devonshire Square church, of which
he became and remained pastor, till 1701.†

Rev. Francis Cornwell, A. M., was educated at Cambridge.   While undergoing imprisonment in the reign of
Charles I., for refusing to perform some of the ceremonies
connected with the Episcopal service, a woman came to him,
who had some doubts as to whether infant baptism could be
proved from the Scriptures.   Mr. Cornwell, who considered
the Scriptures the only rule of faith, made diligent search,
but was unable to find the doctrine of infant baptism in the
Bible, and was convinced that believers, only, were the proper
subjects of baptism.   After this he was baptized by Rev.
William Jeffery, became a zealous Baptist, and made an

* Ivimey's History Baptists, I. p. 138.
† Ivimey's History Baptists, II. p. 297.

appeal to the Westminister Assembly of divines, then sitting, in a work he published, entitled ; " The Royal Commission of King Jesus." In it he says ; " How shall I admit the infant of a believer to be made a visible member of a particular church, and be baptized before it be able to make confession of its faith and repentance ?" This book was distributed among members of the House of Commons, and produced great excitement. Before this, Mr. Cornwell made known his change of sentiment, in a sermon at Cranbrook, in Kent, 1644, in the presence of a body of ministers, several of whom were greatly startled when in preaching from Mark VII. 7 ; " In vain do ye worship me, teaching for doctrines the commandments of men ;" he boldly declared that Pedobaptism was an anti-christian innovation, a human tradition, and a practice for which there was neither example, precept, or the direction of the word of God. One of the minitsers present, Christopher Blackwood, an able preacher and a graduate of Cambridge, who took notes of the sermon to reply to it, was convinced by it and baptized. "There is in this parish church, (Cranbrook,) at present, a baptistery, built for the purpose of immersion. It is a brick cistern, placed against the wall within the church, above the floor. There are steps, both outside and inside, for the convenience of the persons baptized, while the administrator stands by the side of the baptistery, to immerse the person, without going into the water. It is supposed that this was built by the vicar, a Mr. Johnson, at the beginning of the last century. Since the memory of a person now living at Cranbrook, it has been twice filled with water for Mr. Johnson to baptize adults."* Mr. Cornwell collected a company of baptized believers in Kent, who formed themselves into a church, " according to the pattern of the first churches of

*Ivimey's History of Baptists, II, 227 note.

Judea,'' and of which he became, and remained, the faithful pastor, until his death. He was succeeded in the pastorate by his son. Neal calls the father '' one of the most learned divines that espoused the cause of the Baptists.'' An ardent advocate of religious liberty, he was also a strenuous opposer of persecution for conscience' sake.

JOHN de WICKLIFFE.   See page 76.

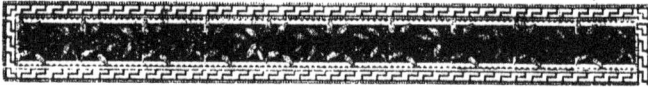

CHAPTER X.

PRIEST AND PRESBYTER.

URING the contest between King Charles and the Long Parliament, the Baptists were forgotten, and the persecution of them discontinued, so that they rapidly increased in numbers. When King Charles I. had the power, the Presbyterians suffered persecution along with the Baptists. But as soon as the Presbyterians gained the control of the government, they persecuted the Baptists, who, just before, had been their companions in suffering. Milton, who lived at that time and took part in the discussion in favor of religious liberty, wrote;

"New Presbyter is but old Priest, writ large."

The leading men of that day among Presbyterians were bitterly opposed to religious liberty. Dr. Featley, one of their most distinguished men, wrote a book entitled; "The Dippers Dipt, or the Anabaptists ducked and plunged over head and ears, at a Disputation in Southwark." He says; "This fire, which in the reigns of Queen Elizabeth and King James, and our gracious sovereign [Charles I.] till now was covered in England under the ashes; or, if it brake out at any time, by the care of the ecclesiastical and civil magistrates, it was soon put out. But of late, since the unhappy distractions which our sins have brought upon us, the temporal sword being other ways employed, and the spiritual locked up fast in the scabbard, this sect, among others, has so far presumed upon the patience of the State, that it hath held weekly conventicles, re-baptized hundreds of men and women together in the twilight, in rivulets, and some arms of the Thames, and elsewhere, dipping them over head and ears. It hath printed divers pamphlets in defence of their heresy, yea, and challenged some of our preachers to disputation. Now, although my bent has always been hitherto against the most dangerous enemy of our Church and State, the Jesuit, to extinguish such balls of wild fire as they have cast into the bosom of our Church, yet, seeing this strange fire kindled in the neighboring parishes, and many Nadabs and Abihus offering it on God's altar, I thought it my duty to cast the water of Siloam upon it to extinguish it." After quoting these words, Spurgeon remarks; "The waters of Siloam must have been strangely foul, in Featley's days, if his 'Dippers Dipped', is to be regarded as a bucket full of the liquid. The neighboring region which was so sorely vexed with 'strange fire', was the borough of Southwark, which is the region in which the church, now meeting in the Metropolitan Tabernacle, was born. We are not aware that any of its pastors, or indeed any Baptist pastor in the universe, ever set up for a priest, and therefore the Nadabs and Abihus must be looked for elsewhere, but Dr. Featley, no doubt, intended the compliment for some of our immediate ancestors."*

Dr. Featley further said ;—"Of all heretics and schismatics, the Anabaptists, should be the most carefully looked into, and severely punished." Richard Baxter, the author of that excellent book, "The Saint's Rest," wrote, "I abhor unlimited liberty and toleration of all, and think myself easily able to prove the wickedness of it."

*History Metropolitan Tabernacle, p. 15.
†Ivimey p. 169.

The Presbyterian ministers of London, about that time, declared it to be "a great wrong that men should have liberty to worship God in that way and manner as shall appear to them most agreeable to the word of God, and no man be punished or discountenanced by authority for the same. We detest toleration so much pursued and endeavored in this kingdom, accounting it unlawful and pernicious."* "Laws were actually passed by Parliament, forbidding Baptists to preach or write, or speak, against the established Presbyterian church. And many of them suffered imprisonment, because they could not comply with such laws. But they were not persecuted so severely as in former times, because the popular feeling was beginning to be averse to such cruel persecutions, and the intolerance of the Presbyterian party, excited general disgust."†

The difference between Presbyterians and Baptists is not great in reference to the doctrines of grace, but they differ very widely in reference to the nature of the Christian church, and the ordinances, and these are by no means unimportant. The difference of views on these points are just as great between them now, as they were in the 17th century, but the feelings with which Christians regard those who differ from them, have greatly changed. In the year 1644, the Baptists of London published a Confession of Faith, "which shows that in all important points of theology, Christian ordinances and church government excepted, the Baptists agreed with all other evangelical Protestants."‡ It was their opposition to infant baptism that made the Baptists particularly offensive to the Presbyterians, though the latter also disliked their scriptural form of baptism by

*Neal's History of Puritans, III. 300.
‖Crosby I. 192.
‡Confessions of Faith, p. 13.

SPURGEON'S METROPOLITAN TABERNACLE

See page 321.

immersion. They were not willing that the Baptists should believe and practice what the Scriptures teach on these points. One of the Baptist ministers of that day, Samuel Richardson, says, "We had as good be under the Pope, as under your Presbyterian check. You would all be tolerated, and would have none tolerated but yourselves. You would suffer none to live quietly and comfortably but those of your way. Is this to do as you would be done by ?"*

Richard Baxter argued that Baptist ministers ought not to be tolerated in England, any more than highway murderers, because baptizing over head in cold water, is likely to result in the death of the person baptized, (so he said,) and, therefore, is a violation of the commandment, "Thou shalt not kill."

A Baptist minister, living in Baxter's time, whose name was Samuel Oates, while engaged in a missionary tour in the county of Essex, England, in the year 1646, baptized several hundred persons who had been converted under his preaching. One of the converts having died a few weeks after, Mr. Oates was actually committed to prison, put in irons, and indicted for murder. Fortunately, however, it was proven on the trial that the young woman, who had died, was in good health for some time after her baptism, and the jury returned a verdict of not guilty.†

One of the most important events of this period, was the framing of the great Presbyterian Confession of Faith, known as the Westminister Confession, by an assembly of divines, convened by order of Parliament for the purpose, and which sat from 1643 to 1649. Neal says ; " There was not one professed Anabaptist in the (Westminister) Assembly,"‡ and it is a cause for astonishment that a single member

---

* Tracts on Liberty of Conscience; Hanserd Knolly ⸱ Society, p. 284.
† Crosby I, 236.
‡ History of Puritans, III. 116. Dublin, 1755.

of it should advocate the Baptist and apostolic practice of dipping. The celebrated Dr. Lightfoot says; "*So many were unwilling to have dipping excluded, that the vote came to an equality within one, * * * twenty-four for the reserving of dipping and twenty-five against it.*" In the final vote a few more names were added to the majority. Dr. Lightfoot was himself a Presbyterian and a member of the Westminister Assembly. According to him, this company, *not of divines, but of uninspired men*, by a majority of *one*, and then of a few more, rejected the mode of baptism prescribed in the inspired word of God, and refused to permit its use in the Presbyterian church. This is still the law among Presbyterian churches of British origin to-day, in Scotland, Ireland and England, and in all American Presbyterian churches. And according to the law established in that human council, by a small majority, a Presbyterian minister can be deposed from the ministry for immersing persons, even though he may believe it to be scriptural baptism.

About this time, Baily, of Glasgow † said, that in "number", the Baptists were above all sects in the land, and had forty-six churches in and about London. About the year 1650, the Baptist churches began to form themselves into associations, and the Baptist churches of England, Ireland, Scotland, and Wales, began to correspond with each other.

On the 30th of January, 1649, Charles I. was beheaded, and the Commonwealth was established. Soon after this, Cromwell was created, by Parliament, Lord Protector. Such a title was very offensive to the Baptists, who had fought for the liberties of England, and they were greatly disappointed when Cromwell was clothed with arbitrary power.

†Baptist Jubilee Memorial.

During these times, the Baptists prospered, but they were by no means unmolested. Numbers of Baptists were found in Cromwell's army, and were pious, orderly and brave. But when Cromwell became Protector, his friendly feelings toward the Baptists changed. It was quite natural that Cromwell should fear them, on account of their well-known republican sentiments. Hence, he was anxious to get rid of all Baptists who occupied any office or position of influence. He removed many of them from the army, and dismissed the principal officers of his own regiment, because they were of that denomination. Some of them, however, were still allowed to remain. W. R. Williams, D. D., in the "Christian Review," as quoted by Benedict, says; "The period of the Commonwealth and the Protectorate, was the season in which our distinguishing sentiments * * * became the property of the people. * * * Now, they began rapidly working their way, and openly, into the masses of society. The army, that won for Cromwell his 'crowning mercies,' as he called those splendid victories which assured the power of Parliament, became deeply tinged with our views of Christian faith and order. They were not, as military bodies have so often been, a band of mercenary hirelings, the sweepings of society, * * but * * men who entered the ranks from principles rather than gain, and whose chief motive for enlistment was, that they believed the impending contest one for religious truth, and of national liberties. * * * In this army the officers were, many of them, accustomed to preach; and both commanders and privates were continually busied in searching the Scriptures, in prayers, and in Christian conferences. The result of the biblical studies and free communings of these intrepid, high principled men, was, that they became, a large portion of them, Baptists."

TREVOR HALL, ROCHESTER THEOLOGICAL SEMINARY, N. Y.   See page 373.

Dr. Williams names some distinguished Baptists of the period of the Commonwealth and the Protectorate : Major-General Harrison; Colonel Robert Lilburne, brother of John Lilburne; General Lambert, nearly related to Cromwell ; Overton, the friend of Milton, and second in command in Scotland ; Colonel Mason, the Governor of Jersey; Vice-Admiral Sir John Lawson, who brought over the navy at the Restoration to the Stuarts, as Monk did the army; Colonel Hutchinson ; John Milton, the immortal poet, and a host of others. To this list may be added the name Richard Deane, Major-General and General at Sea. He was in supreme command in Scotland, and at his death was accorded a public funeral in Westminster Abbey.

"The ministry of our denomination," continues Dr. Williams, " comprised, too, men of high character. * * * Tombes, the antagonist of Baxter, Bamfield, Gosnold, Knollys, Denne, and Jessey, all Baptist preachers, had held priestly orders in the English established church. Gosnold, [the Spurgeon of his day,] being one of the most popular ministers in London, with a congregation of three thousand; and Jessey * * whose acquirements and talents, piety and liberality, won him general respect. Kiffin, a merchant, whose wealth and * * private character had given him influence among the princely traders of London, and introduced him to the court of the Stuarts, was pastor of a Baptist church in that city. Cox, another of our ministers at this time, is said by Baxter, to have been the son of a bishop; and Collins, another pastor among us, had in his youth been a pupil of Busby. Du Veil, a convert from Judaism, who had * * * been applauded by no less a man than the eloquent and powerful Bossuet, became a Baptist preacher, and closed his life and labors in our communion."

It was in Cromwell's time that the Baptists, in latter days, secured a foothold in Ireland. Rev. Thomas Patient, the assistant of Mr. Kiffin, went with General Fleetwood to Ireland, and preached in Dublin Cathedral. He had much success, and baptized many throughout the country. He signed letters as minister of a church in Dublin, in 1653, and is said to have organized the church at Clough Keating, which numbered between 200 and 300 members, in 1740. One of the most remarkable men the Baptists ever produced, was Rev. Alexander Carson, LL. D., who was born in county Tyrone, in 1776. One of his books, "Carson on Baptism," is still a standard work on that subject.*

Baptist sentiments were introduced into Scotland by Cromwell's soldiers. Probably a church was formed at Edinburg, in 1765, under the pastoral care of Mr. Carmichael and Archibal McClean. The church at Leith was the first. There have been few more distinguished men, for piety, learning, and benevolence, than the eminent Scotch Baptists, Robert and James Haldane. The Baptists in either Ireland or Scotland, have never been numerous, but many men of note, from both places, have figured in Baptist history, everywhere. The first church in Wales, that admitted none but baptized believers to fellowship, was gathered at Ilston, through John Miles and Thomas Proud, who came to London in 1649, seeking the truth.† But it is claimed that, from the earliest times, Baptist sentiments have prevailed there.

*Ivimey I, 235.
†Ivimey I, 240.

p. 104 RICHARD FULLER, D. D. See page 255

CHAPTER XI.

BAPTISTS OF CROMWELL'S TIME.

MAJOR-General Harrison was one of Cromwell's ablest generals, and, at one time, one of his most confidential friends. When Charles I. was removed from the Isle of Wight to Hurst Castle, he commanded the troop of horse in that expedition, and also commanded the grenadiers when Cromwell dissolved the Long Parliament. He was one of the judges who condemned the king, and was active in bringing him to execution. He was a member of the Council of State under the Commonwealth. But he did not conceal his opposition to Cromwell's assumption of the Protectorate. On this account, and for other reasons, he was degraded and imprisoned in the same castle whence he had brought the king. When the monarchy was restored, he was condemned as a regicide, and sentenced to be hanged, drawn, and quartered. His trial and execution were both conducted in a barbarous manner. In giving voice to condemn the tyrannical king, he thought he was serving the best interests of his country, and promoting the cause of liberty. He was a man of great integrity during his life, and met his death with calmness and true Christian heroism.

Colonel Hutchinson was another distinguished Baptist, well known to history. He was governor of Nottingham during the time of the civil wars, and afterwards a member of the House of Commons. In the field and in the senate, he distinguished himself as a person of great courage, and as a man of learning and eloquence, and his speeches always commanded attention. He was, also, one of the judges who condemned Charles I., but on account of his great moderation and kindness when in office and in power, he had so gained the esteem, even of his enemies, that when the other judges were executed, his life was spared. After having been arrested on suspicion of treason, he was sent to the Tower, and finally to Sandown Castle, where, without a trial, he was confined until his feeble health gave way, and he died in 1644 from the hardship and exposure of imprisonment. The circumstances which led him to become a Baptist are very remarkable. While Colonel Hutchinson was governor at Nottingham, the Presbyterian minister, in the great church there, who was very bitter against his brother ministers, urged him to suppress the meetings of the Baptists. The Colonel at first invited the persecuted chaplains to hold meetings in his house, where the people flocked in great numbers, and excited the envy of the Presbyterians. Yielding at last to their solicitations, he broke up a private meeting in the cannoniers chamber, where some notes against pedobaptism were found and brought to the governor. These notes were examined by his wife, who, having more leisure then, than he, read them and compared them with the Scriptures. She was convinced that the practice of baptizing infants was not to be found in the Bible. Having communicated her doubts to her husband, he examined the subject to satisfy her. He first searched the Scriptures alone. Then he read all the eminent writers on both sides of the question. After a

thorough and impartial investigation, he was fully convinced
that infant baptism was without scriptural authority. After
the birth of their child, he invited the Pedobaptist ministers
of the place, to a dinner. Here he frankly told them his doubts
in regard to the baptism of infants, and asked them, if they
could give any scriptural reason for the practice. After hearing their arguments, Colonel Hutchinson and his wife both
declared themselves to be dissatisfied with the practice,
believing it to be contrary to the word of God. They then
asked the ministers, what, in view of their doubts, it was their
duty to do with their own child. Most of them said that
they ought to conform to the general practice of other
Christians, even if it were not clear to themselves. One,
of them, however, Mr. Foxcraft, said that unless they were
convinced that the word of God warranted the practice, it
would be sin for them to conform to it. Colonel Hutchinson
and his wife, concluded not to have their child baptized.
This was in 1647. From this time, ministers and people re-
viled them and treated them with malice, although the Colonel
and his wife still attended their meetings and did not with-
draw their benevolences and civilities from them. His wife
remarked that he might have said to them as his master said
to the old Pharisees ; " Many good works have I done among
you : for which of these do you hate me ?"

Dr. W. R Williams speaks thus of Colonel and Mrs.
Hutchinson : "'The English matron, whose *Memoirs* form one
of the most delightful narratives of that stirring time, and
who, in her own character, presented one of the loveliest
specimens of Christian womanhood, Lucy Hutchinson, a
name of love and admiration, wherever known, became a
Baptist. She did so together with her husband, one of the
judges of Charles I., and the governor of Nottingham Castle,
for the Parliament, from the perusal of the Scriptures. Of

SHORTER COLLEGE, ROME, GA.

See page 377.

no inferior rank in society—for Hutchinson was a kinsman of the Byrons of Newstead, the family whence sprung the celebrated poet,—their talents and patriotism and christian grace, and domestic virtues, throw around that pair, the lustre of a higher nobility than heralds can confer, and a dignity, compared with which, the splendor of royalty and the trappings of victory, are poor indeed.''

Colonel Henry D'Anvers was an officer in the Parliamentary army. He became a Baptist, and was an elder in a Baptist church, in London, while governor of Strafford. He held to the laying on of hands after baptism. The laying on of hands, except in the case of ordination, is generally regarded as a sign of the communication of the Holy Spirit, by the apostles. And since none but the apostles had the power of communicating the Spirit, none but they have a right to use the sign which indicates that power. D'Anvers was a man of learning, and the author of a '' Treatise on Baptism,'' which is said to be the most scholarly and complete work on the subject which had then been published. He was a person of great note among the Baptists, having descended from very reputable parents, and being of considerable learning, of great piety, and extensive usefulness. As an official he was well beloved among the people, being noted for not taking bribes. He suffered imprisonment in the Tower, after the restoration, but was released through the intervention of a friend at court, and died in 1686.

Henry Jessey was one of the chief men of Cromwell's time, and was a man of learning, having graduated at Cambridge University. He was converted while at college, and served for some time as an Episcopal clergyman, but was dismissed for nonconformity, and became pastor of an Independent church, in London. His congregation became agitated on the question of baptism, and some of them,

remarkable for piety and judgment, left and joined the
Baptists. This led him to study the subject for himself.
He was first convinced, that baptism ought to be performed
by immersion, and that sprinkling was a modern corruption
brought into use without just reason, either from Scripture
or antiquity. He announced to his people, that all the
children brought to him, he would baptize by dipping, according to the scriptural form of the ordinance. And this
he did. A controversy on the subject of baptism, in 1644,
led him into continued investigation, and he began to see
that none but believers should be baptized. But before an-
nouncing his sentiments on the side of believers' baptism, he
consulted with Dr. Goodwin, Philip Nye and others, upon
the subject. Their arguments for infant baptism failed to
satisfy him, and following his convictions, he was immersed,
June 1645, and became the pastor of a Baptist church in
London, where he remained nearly twenty years, until his
death. Much of his time was spent in translating the Bible
into English, a work for which he was well qualified by his
familiarity with the original languages in which the Bible
was written. His habit was to carry about with him his
Hebrew and Greek Testaments, calling the one, his " sword
and dagger," and the other, his " shield and buckler." He
enlisted the aid of other men of learning, both of his own and
other countries, and so anxious was he for the completion of
the work, that he would often exclaim, " O that I might see
this done, before I die!" But in this he was disappointed.
The restoration of the monarchy and the changes which
followed, interfered with the completion of the work, and
he died without seeing it published.*

Henry Denne was also a graduate of the University of
Cambridge, and spent ten years in the ministry of the

*Ivimey's Baptist History, 1. p. 179 ; Crosby, 1. p. 313.

Episcopal Church.   He was an earnest, faithful, and fearless
preacher.   In the year 1641, he preached a sermon at a
visitation meeting at Baldock, at which a large number of
the clergy and ministers from the neighborhood were present.
He denounced the vices of the clergy, and the corruptions
in doctrine and worship.   He condemned persecution as a
sin and a wrong, and declared if those in authority were as
diligent freeing the church from the unworthy among themselves, as they were in discovering and persecuting noncon-
forming ministers, it would be much better.   This sermon
made a profound impression and created for him a great
reputation as a preacher.   The opposition of his enemies
tended to drive him out of a church, where he saw so many
evils, while the plain teachings of Scripture led him to the
Baptists.   He was baptized in the year 1643, by Thomas
Lamb, a Baptist minister of London, and, having preached
with great success, formed many churches.   He was arrested
and imprisoned for preaching against infant baptism, and
immersing believers.   On being released, he went about
preaching and baptizing, in various places, with like success.
To escape the persecution of his enemies, he entered the
army, where he was known as "Parson Denne."   At one
time, he came near losing his life.   Having become, in some
way, implicated with a mutiny of some soldiers, he was
sentenced, along with several others, to be shot.   When he
stepped out, expecting to be executed, he was told that
mercy had been extended to him.   On hearing this announce-
ment, he wept, and declared himself unworthy of such a favor,
and that he was more ashamed to live than afraid to die.
He was pardoned in this case, because he had been esteemed
for his piety, and had received his sentence with such a
manly acknowledgment of its justice, together with such an
humble confession of his fault.*

*Fenstanton Records, as quoted by Dr. Cramp.

His after life, at least, proved that he was worthy of the favor shown him. In the year 1653, he left the army. Full of missionary zeal, he went about preaching the gospel in destitute towns. He was a man of note and a leader among the Baptists of his day. He wielded the pen with ability, and wrote a reply to Dr. Featley's book, "The Dippers Dipt." He first met Featley in prison, where both were suffering for conscience' sake. He also held a discussion with the doctor, himself, and engaged in a public disputation with Dr. Gunning, a celebrated minister, who afterwards became a bishop. This controversy was listened to by thousands of people, and the lady, at whose suggestion it was held, was afterward baptized by Mr. Denne. After an active and useful life, he died, sometime after 1670.* It is remarkable, how many ministers and laymen left the Pedobaptist ranks in those trying days, to join the Baptists.

*Ivimey, I.

TREMONT TEMPLE BOSTON.

See page 253.

PLACE WHERE BOARDMAN WITNESSED THE BAPTISM OF 34 KARENS JUST BEFORE HIS DEATH.
TAVOY DISTRICT.

See page 337.

CHAPTER XII.

THE RESTORATION.

HERE were doubtless many in the age that followed the death of Cromwell, 1658, who sincerely loved the Bible and ever practiced its precepts, but Charles II., was not one of them. He was a bad man and a despotic ruler, and seems to have learned nothing from the misfortunes of his father and his family. While still at Breda, before his return, he promised as one condition of his restoration to the throne of England "liberty to tender consciences," and that no man should be disquieted or called in question for differences of opinion in matters of religion, which did not disturb the peace of the kingdom.* This promise he did not keep. It is computed that 70,000 persons suffered for religion, 8,000 of whom were destroyed, during the period from the Restoration to the Revolution of 1688. Many of these were Baptists and among them the famous names of Bunyan, Kiffin, Keach, Knolly, and Hewling.

"The Baptists," says Sir James Macintosn, the English historian, "suffered more than others under Charles II., because they had publicly professed the principle of religious liberty."† Henry Jessey writes of "The imprisoning,

*Ivimey's History Baptists, I. p. 272.
†Benedict's History Baptists, p. 324.

plundering, and barbarous inhumanity and cruelty, that hath lately been practiced toward several ministers of the gospel and other peaceable people, in Wales, Lincolnshire, Gloucestershire, and other places."* Thomas Grantham petitioned the king for the Baptists in Lincolnshire. They say : " We have been much abused as we pass in the streets, and as we sit in our houses ; being threatened to be hanged if we but be heard praying to our Lord in our families, and disturbed in our so waiting upon him, by uncivil beating at our doors, and sounding of horns ; yea we have been stoned when going to our meetings, the windows of the place where we have met have been struck down with stones ; yea taken as evil doers and imprisoned when peaceably met together to worship the Most High in the use of his most precious ordinances."†

A declaration of faith was presented at the same time, signed, as Crosby says, by more than 20,000 General Baptists. The king promised relief. From Reading prison several peaceable Baptists petitioned the king in 1660. They complained of being despoiled of their goods, and imprisoned, and yet they bore all patiently, rejoicing in their suffering for Christ's sake. In November of this year, John Bunyan was imprisoned for preaching the gospel. It was by a law passed in the reign of Elizabeth, to suppress the Puritans. It imposed imprisonment on those who refused to attend the Episcopal Church, or who held worship of their own. When Charles II. was crowned April 23, 1661, a great many prisoners were released and all who had been imprisoned on account of religion since his return were included in the general pardon ; but Bunyan did not share this favor, he was kept in prison. In 1661 " Venner's Rebellion" occured. Thomas Venner held to Fifth Monarchy

---

*† Ivimey, I. 275, 276.   II

principles and with fifty·of his flock, all armed, marched
out of his little meeting-house, in London, to overthrow the
existing government, and establish the kingdom of Jesus
Christ by the sword. He and his followers were defeated
and those not killed in the strife were executed. But the
king made this trifling affair a pretext for a proclamation
forbidding the assembling of Baptists and others for religious
worship. The Baptists disclaimed all sympathy with Venner,
and presented to the king an address signed by William
Kiffin and some other Baptist ministers and laymen, in which
they say, "That such evil opinions and practices are not a
natural or necessary consequence of the doctrine of baptism,
* * * yet by the like mistake we now suffer under
jealousies, through the wicked treason, rebellion and murder
of a few heady and distempered persons pretending to introduce a civic and temporal government of Jesus Christ by
their swords, and to subvert all civil government and
authority. Yet we cannot imagine a reason why their bloody
tenets and tragical actions, should reflect on those of our
persuasion, the persons not being of our belief or practice
about baptism." They asserted their loyalty and prayed to
be judged by their own principles and actions and not by
those of others, and to be permitted to worship God in
peaceful freedom according to their faith. It was all of no
avail. According to Crosby, over 400 were crowded into
Newgate prison, while in and out of London other prisons
were full. Among them were the distinguished ministers,
Hanserd Knollys and Vavasor Powell.

Many petitions of the Baptists to the king show
their principles and their sufferings. One, March 8, 1661,
came from George Hammon, William Jeffery and other
ministers in Maidstone jail, Kent county. It reminds the
king of his promise made at Breda, of the unjustness of

their detention and of the danger of their own lives and the
threatened destruction to their wives and little ones. Another
was sent by ten Baptists imprisoned at Dover, among whom
was supposed to be Samuel Taverner, formerly governor of
Dover Castle, but then a Baptist preacher. A pamphlet
written at this time states: "In June, 1661, there came
divers rude soldiers, wicked, swearing, and debauched persons
to the meeting house in Brick lane, near Whitechapel, and
laid hands on several men to the number of more than
twenty, who in a peaceable manner demanded of them their
warrant for so doing. But they would not show any authority ; which one William Caswell seeing, he said to this
purpose ; that if they had warrant he would obey it, but if
they had none they should carry him for he would not go.
With that they beat him with their hangers about the head
and pulled him along by force, sometimes taking him up
between three or four of them and then letting him fall with
violence in the dirt, brushing with great force his stomach
and breast against the rails, in so much that with blows and
falls he is deprived of health to this day." Several of the
soldiers were afterward arrested and suit commenced against
them according to law, but were rescued by John Robinson
keeper of the Tower, who was in a fury at the arrest of his
men. He issued a warrant for William Caswell, and had
Thomas Hull, his defender, cast into Newgate prison, with
another person who accompanied and tried to bail him.

But a worse fate than imprisonment awaited some of
them. On the 19th of October 1661, John James, a Sabbatarian Baptist, and pastor of a church in London was dragged
by force out of his pulpit to prison. He was charged with
uttering treasonable language against the king. His accuser
was a man of vile character, by the name of Tipler, whose
testimony the magistrate refused to receive. But other wit-

CALVARY BAPTIST CHURCH
FIFTY-SEVENTH STREET.

118   CALVARY BAPTIST CHURCH, NEW YORK CITY.

See page 258.

nesses were brought forward on whose false testimony he was condemned. When the lieutenant of the Tower, (Robinson) read to Mr. James' congregation the words of which their pastor was accused, they all declared that they had never heard him speak such words. But all this testimony was outweighed by that of the degraded men who had been bribed to testify to a falsehood. Only one month after his arrest, Mr. James was tried, condemned and sentenced " to be hanged, drawn and quartered on the next day." The poor broken hearted wife went to the king with a petition, presenting the facts of the case and entreating that her husband's life might be spared. When the king knew who she was he held up his finger in derision and said : " O ! Mr. James, he is a sweet gentleman." While she continued to plead for mercy the door was shut in her face.

Notwithstanding her rude repulse, she sought the presence of the king again in the morning, and with true womanly courage begged him to spare the life of her husband. The king replied, that he was a rogue and should be hanged. One of the lords present asked of whom she spoke, and Charles answered ; " Of John James, that rogue ; he shall be hanged." His death was a glorious one. Dragged on a hurdle to Tyburn, where he was executed, he was calm, patient and forgiving, and exhorted those around him. His last words were ; " Father into thy hands I commend my spirit."*

Some laws that were passed were oppressive to Baptists. The first was a bill passed in 1662, to enforce uniformity in religion and to eject all the ministers from established churches who could not give unfeigned assent and consent to the articles of the Church of England, and of everything contained in the Book of Common Prayer, and also that

*Ivimey, I. pp. 324, 325.

would not declare upon oath that it was not lawful on any pretense whatever, to take up arms against the king. By this act many of the godliest men in England were driven from the established church, and among them were some Baptists who it seems had retained churches belonging to the establishment from the time of Cromwell. Their places were given in many instances to bad men. The Baptists, people as well as ministers, suffered under this law. At Aylesbury, persecution raged and two large houses beside the jail were full of imprisoned dissenters. Ten men and two women, Baptists, were arrested at their meeting and required to conform to the Church of England, or leave the realm. In case of refusal they were threatened with death. They refused to do either, so sentence of death was passed upon them, and they were remanded to prison to await the execution, and all their property seized. At this juncture, Thomas Monk, son of one of the condemned, rode at once to London to Mr. Kiffin, who went in great haste to Chancellor Hyde and entreated him to lay the matter before the king. The king seemed surprised that any of his subjects should be put to death for religion only and promised pardon. This however would take time, and prompt action was necessary, so the king was again sought for a reprieve which was granted. The condemned were overjoyed and their persecutors dismayed when Monk arrived with the reprieve, but they kept the Baptists in jail until the pardon of the king arrived.

Another one of these laws was the "Conventicle Act" of 1664. This law prohibited any person, over sixteen years of age, from being present at any meeting for religious worship, in any other manner than is allowed by the liturgy of the Church of England. The penalty for the first and second offenses was imprisonment or a fine. For the third offense, a heavy fine or banishment to the "American Plantations";–the name by which the American colonies were then known ; and in case of their return from banishment before the expiration of their term they were to suffer death without the benefit of the clergy. It was a most wicked law and its cruelty was very greatly intensified by the fact that those who were accused of violating it were denied the right of trial by jury. Any magistrate could fine, imprison, or banish without restraint and from his decision there was no appeal. Under this law many persons were fined, imprisoned or banished because of their fidelity to their religious convictions.

Another was called the " Five-Mile Act," Oct. 31 1665. It required all nonconformist ministers to take oath declaring it to be unlawful under any pretense to take up arms against the king, and that resistance to the king, or his officers was treasonable, and that it was unlawful at any time or in any manner, to seek to alter the government in church or state. Many ministers refused to take the oath, and as a penalty, they were forbidden to go within five miles of any city, or town, that sent members to Parliament, or within five miles of any place where they had formerly exercised their ministry. For every offense they were fined two hundred dollars. They were also prohibited from teaching any private or public schools. The object of this act was to compel these ministers to conform to the Church of England from fear of starvation. But rather than sacrifice their religious convictions, many submitted to be exiled from home and friends, suffering the loss of property, and in many cases languishing in prison till death came to their release. Some ministers managed to elude their enemies by traveling long journeys by night, and lying concealed by day, and thus preaching to their flocks at great personal risks.

Observe particularly the circumstances that seem to have given rise to this persecuting law. London was visited by the plague. It extended into the surrounding country. In London alone about one-hundred thousand fell victims to its ravages in less than a year. The greatest part of the clergy of the established church, fled and the nonconformist ministers remained and attended the deserted parishes, preaching the gospel to the living of to-day who became the dead of to morrow, and administering to the sick, dying and bereaved. They thought themselves exempt from all laws of conformity at such times. "But it will amaze all posterity," says Neal, "that at a time both of war and of the plague, and when the nonconformist ministers were hazarding their lives in the service of the poor distressed congregations of London, the prime minister, Lord Clarendon and his creatures, instead of mourning for the sin of the nation and meditating a reformation of manners, should pour out all their vengeance upon nonconformists in order to make their condition insufferable."*

In 1670 a second conventicle act was passed. It imposed a heavy fine on both minister and people who were found engaged in religious worship, and the owner of the place where the meeting was held, whether house, barn or yard, was subjected to a fine. One-third of these fines went to the informer, and of course this made every knave an interested spy, anxious to make money out of the sufferings of his pious neighbors. Urged on by men in high authority in church and state, the informer and the constable vigorously prosecuted their infamous work, and many pious people became the victims of their cruelty and injustice. Still another persecuting act was passed in 1673, called the "Test

*Ivimey, 1. pp· 357, 358.

THE UNIVERSITY AT LEWISBURG, PA.

See page 376.

Act." The year before Charles II. had issued his " Declaration of Indulgence," by which he suspended during his pleasure, the punishment imposed for nonconformity. The king's design, according to Ivimey, was to secure toleration for the Roman Catholics, with whom he sympathized.

This measure was unpopular with the nation, who feared the return of the Roman Catholics to power. To satisfy the popular demand, the "Test Act" was passed. It provided that no one could hold any office of honor or profit under the government, unless he partook of the Lord's Supper according to the rites of the Church of England, and declared his disavowal of the doctrine of transubstantiation. In order to keep out the Catholics, many of the dissenters bound themselves to take communion at the hands of the Episcopal clergy, or to hold no office within the gift of the English government. They thought soon to remove the test for themselves, and let the one applying to the Catholics remain ; but in this they were disappointed, for it remained in force 152 years, not being repealed until the year 1828. This law was very injurious to the morals of the nation, tending to corrupt the consciences of men, and make them hypocrites. Persons of the worst character would not hesitate to come to the communion table, in order that they might be eligible to office, while men who were conscientious and worthy, would refuse to submit to such an unjust requirement.

CHAPTER XIII.

ENGLISH BAPTIST MARTYRS.

EFOE, Delaune, and other illustrious men suffered during the reign of the Stuarts for being Baptists. Thomas Delaune, a man of great ability as his works clearly show, was imprisoned. Daniel Defoe, the author of "Robinson Crusoe" was a man of eminence, and in sentiment a Baptist. He was born in London in the year 1661, and is the author of a number of books both of prose and poetry. His "Robinson Crusoe" was by no means the ablest of his literary productions. One of his works, published in 1702, is entitled: "The shortest way with Dissenters." It is written in an ironical style, and attacks with severe sarcasm those who persecuted others for conscience' sake. This book the House of Commons declared to be a seditious libel. The author was sentenced by the court to be fined, imprisoned and pilloried. He bore this punishment with meekness and cheerfulness, knowing that it is only crime, and not the prison or the scaffold that causes shame, and remained in prison two years. In the reign of Queen Ann, he was again imprisoned for writing another book of the same character.

Defoe was a man of a very superior natural abilities, possessing a vivid imagination along with a sound judgment.

He was a vigorous writer and he wielded his pen in defense of the Baptists and in advocacy of human liberty, and for this he suffered.

Thomas Delaune whom Ivimey calls the "Champion of Nonconformity," was another sufferer for conscience sake. His parents were Baptists and very poor. He was educated near Cork, by Squire Riggs, whose tenants his parents were. At sixteen he became the clerk of Mr. Bamfield, at Kingsale, and was converted through the instrumentality of his employer. He became at once, an earnest active christian, and his zeal for the truth soon brought upon him persecution, on account of which he came to London, where he taught a grammer school and also served as pastor of a Baptist church. About this time Dr. Calamy, a clergyman of the Church of England, published a sermon entitled: "Scrupulous Consciences;" in which he challenged the nonconformists to a fair and honorable discussion of the points at issue between themselves and the Church of England. Thomas Delaune who was a learned man, accepted the challenge, and replied in a most effective manner, in a work entitled; "A Plea for Nonconformists;" justifying the separation. This book passed through twenty editions, and was never answered, except by abuse and stripes. Defoe, says: "The book is perfect of itself. Never author left behind him a more finished piece, and I believe the dispute is entirely ended. If any man ask what we can say why the dissenters differ from the church of England, and what they can plead for it I can recommend no better reply than this, Let them answer in short, Thomas Delaune, and desire the querist to read the book."*

Yet for publishing this book, Delaune was cast into Newgate prison, where he was placed among the vilest wretches. At the same time that the author was arrested, his work was seized while passing through the press. This was

*Ivimey I. p 403.

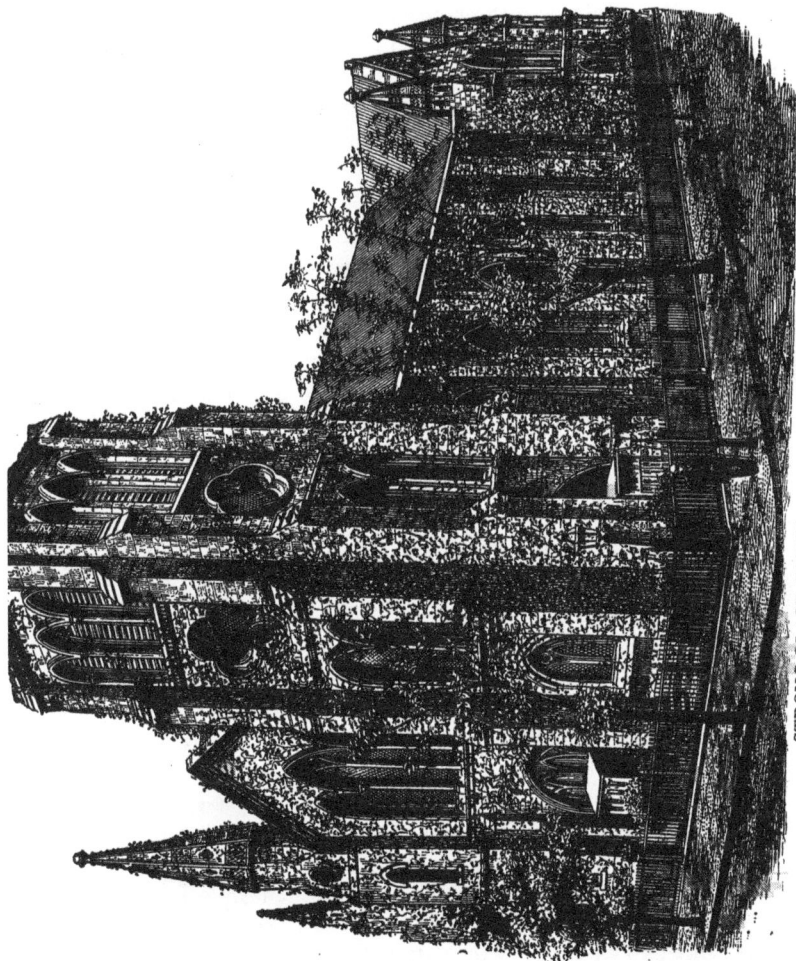

STRONG PLACE BAPTIST CHURCH, BROOKLYN, N. Y.

See page 326

in the year 1683, and in January of the next year he was brought from prison to be tried on the charge of "false, seditious, and scandalous libel, against the King and the Book of Common Prayer." He offended against the latter by pointing out its errors, and by showing that it contains many things that are unscriptural, and therefore to be rejected by Christians who are bound only by what is taught in the word of God. This was considered a great offense. At his trial Mr. Delaune, said to the court ; "If what I have written be true, it is no crime, unless truth be made a crime. If false, let Dr. Calamy, or any of the guides of your church, confute me as he promised in his sermon aforesaid, by good Scripture and good reason, then will I submit. If the latter method be not taken I must repeat it, 'tis very hard, my lord, 'tis very hard."

But the court refused to listen to any appeals of reason, and he was condemned to pay a fine of one hundred marks, and to give bail for his good behavior for one year. His books were to be burned before the Royal Exchange, London. The sentence meant that he was to suffer in prison till death came to his release. Dr. Calamy approved, at least he refused to use his influence to prevent it, although he was appealed to by Mr. Delaune, who reminded him that he professed to be a Christian minister and that he had invited the discussion. "This is not the treatment," said he, "which one scholar deserves of another." He told Dr. Calamy that he wanted to be convinced by something more like divinity, than Newgate prison, and said ; "You would have performed the office of a divine, in visiting my place of confinement, to argue me out of my doubts, which you promised *Scripture* and *reason*, not a *mittimus*, or *Newgate*, could easily do. To the former I *can* yield, to the latter it seems I *must*. This is a severe kind of logic and will probably dispute me out of the world." *

*Ivimey I. p. 397. *

Defoe, who wrote the preface to the seventeenth edition of Delaune's work, gives us the following sad account of his imprisonment: "His expensive prosecution, depriving him of his livelihood, which was a grammar school, and long imprisonment, had made him not only unable to pay his fine, but unable to subsist himself and his family. He continued in close confinement in the prison at Newgate, about fifteen months, and suffered there great hardships by extreme poverty, being so entirely reduced by this disaster, that he had no subsistence but what was contributed by such friends as came to visit him. His behavior in this distress, was like the greatness of mind he discovered at his trial. And the same spirit which appears in his writings, appeared in his conversation, and supported him with invincible patience under the greatest extremities. But long confinement and distress of various kinds, at last conquered him. He had a wife and two small children, all with him in prison, for they had no subsistence elsewhere. The closeness and inconvenience of the place first affected them, and all three by lingering sorrow and sickness, died in the prison. At last, worn out with trouble and hopeless of relief, and too much abandoned by those who should have taken some other care of him, this excellent person sank under the burden, and died also. I cannot refrain saying, such a champion of such a cause deserved better usage. And it was very hard such a man, such a Christian, such a scholar, and on such an occasion, should starve in a dungeon, and that the whole body of Dissenters in England, whose cause he died for defending, should not raise him *sixty-six pounds, thirteen shillings and four pence* to save his life!" "I am sorry to say," continues Defoe, "he is one of near 8000 Protestant dissenters, who perished in prison in the days of that merciful prince, King Charles II."

Another martyr for the truth was Francis Bamfield. He was a learned and excellent man. Ivimey gives a full account of him.*   He was educated at Oxford University, and entered the ministry of the Church of England. But he became dissatisfied on account of the corruptions and errors which he found in the establishment.   The "Act of Uniformity" proved the occasion, and he left his growing congregation at Sherborne and became a nonconformist minister.   A short time after, he was preaching in his own house, when he was arrested with his assistant and twenty-five of the principal persons, and thrown into prison.   On the Lord's day he preached in the prison yard, and numbers of the town's people assembled to hear him.   Afterwards he suffered for eight years in Dorchester jail, where he preached almost every day to the people who resorted to the jail to hear him.   During this time a church was organized of those who were converted under his preaching.   After his release in 1675, he went from county to county, preaching the word, for which he was again imprisoned at Salisbury.   In the year 1676, he became pastor of a Sabbatarian Baptist church, which he formed in London at Pinner's Hall.   His congregations were frequently broken up by officers of the law. On one occasion while preaching, a constable entered the room and interrupting him, said : "I have a warrant from the Lord Mayor to disturb your meeting."   "I have a warrant from the Lord Jesus Christ ; who is Lord Maximus, to go on ;" replied the courageous preacher, and he proceeded with his discourse. But he was seized and taken off, with six of his members, who were fined ten pounds each.   They met again and resumed their services in the afternoon of the same day, but their meeting was again broken up.   They then went to the house of the pastor where they concluded the religious exer-

* I. II. Volumes, History Baptists.

CHICAGO BAPTIST UNION THEOLOGICAL SEMINARY.

See page 376.

cises of the day. But on the following Sabbath he was again arrested, and as he refused to sign the oath of conformity, he was declared out of the king's protection, sent to prison for life, or during the king's pleasure. After enduring the hardships of Newgate prison for about a year, he died, adding another noble name to the list of Baptist martyrs.

Another victim of the persecutors of those times, was Vavasor Powell, who is called the "Whitefield of Wales." He was born in 1617, was learned in the languages, and while a young man received ordination as a minister of the Episcopal Church and for awhile officiated at Clem. He confessed afterwards his unfitness for the sacred office, because he slighted the Scriptures and was a stranger to secret and spiritual prayer, and a great profaner of the Sabbath. One day as he was preaching on the Sabbath, a Puritan rebuked him which led him to be concerned for his soul. He was afterward converted and joined the nonconformsits, being baptized on profession of his faith in 1636, and finally became a Baptist minister. His eloquence and zeal made him very popular as a preacher and at the same time exposed him to the hatred and malice of his enemies. He was imprisoned thirteen years, or nearly all the time from the restoration to his death. On one occasion while preaching, he was seized along with sixty or seventy of his hearers. As it was too late to take them to the magistrate, the mob who made the arrest placed their prisoners in the church. Here in the midst of the night, Mr. Powell preached a sermon to his fellow prisoners from Matthew 10 : 28 ; "And fear not them which kill the body, but are not able to kill the soul, but rather fear him who is able to destroy both soul and body in hell." The next day they were taken to the office of the magistrate who was not at home when they arrived. While they were waiting for his return Mr. Powell again preached, having among his hearers the family of the magistrate, who on his return home, was not a little annoyed at finding his house turned into a conventicle. But his daughter, who had been deeply impressed by the sermon, pleaded for the preacher's release, which was reluctantly granted.

In 1642, he was compelled to leave home in order to escape persecution, and came to London where he preached with great acceptance, he being equally fluent in English and in Welsh. Afterwards he went into Kent, where he preached and labored with great success. After three years he returned to Wales, where he remained fourteen years, going about from place to place, preaching and planting churches. Often he would ride a hundred miles in a week, preaching at every place where he could gain admittance by night or day. There was scarcely a church, chapel, or town hall, in all Wales, in which he had not preached. In the year 1660, he was again persecuted and thrown into prison. Fortunately he had been in prison only nine weeks, when, at the coronation of Charles I., a general pardon and jail delivery were proclaimed, and he was released. At another time he was confined in a loathsome prison in London for two years. Here his health was permanently impaired by the noisome effluvia to which he was exposed. He was removed to South Sea Castle where he was confined for five years longer. After his release he returned to Wales, where he resumed the work of preaching.* But here he was again arrested on the charge of an Episcopal clergyman, who accused some of his hearers of going to their place of meeting, armed to resist the authorities in case of interference. Although this charge was false, and could not be proven, Mr. Powell was still retained in prison. By the intervention of his friends, he was taken to London for trial. The court decided that the

* Ivimey; and Davis' Hist. Welsh Baptists.

proceedings by which he was imprisoned, were illegal, yet the magistrate committed him in defiance of law and justice, to the Fleet prison, where he remained until he died, in the year 1670.

His sufferings were great but he bore them all with patience. During his last illness, which continued about a month, his physician forbade much talking, but so great was his zeal, that he could not refrain from speaking and singing and praising God, until he was exhausted. Thus his last days were spent in rapturous praise and joyous worship, so that his gloomy prison became to him a palace of beauty and delight, where he waited till death came and "dissolved the earthly house," and the ransomed spirit took its flight to the mansions on high. Mr. Powell was one of the many Baptist preachers who from the earliest period down to the present day, have become famous for piety, eloquence, and suffering for Christ in the principality. The name of Christmas Evans, born in 1766, stands among the illustrious preachers of the world.

The accession of King James II., in 1685, brought no relief to the persecuted flock of Christ. His reign was marked by the same cruel excesses, as characterized the latter part of the reign of Charles II. James was an avowed papist and tried to restore to power the Papal Church. The nonconformists were obliged to hold their meetings in the night, often assembling at midnight, or just before the break of day. Sentinels were stationed outside of the building in which the flock was gathered, in order to give warning of the wolf's approach, which often came suddenly in the shape of the mercenary spy and informer. In these meetings singing had to be omitted and even the voice of the zealous preacher was likely to attract the vultures of prey. The buildings where they met were sometimes provided with places of concealment, or a trap door, in order that the minister, who was always a special object of vengeance, might make his escape. But notwithstanding all their precaution it was often impossible to escape the malicious vigilance of the informers, who like a pack of hungry blood-hounds were set upon their track. No dissenting minister was safe. No matter how blameless his life, no matter how eminent for learning and piety a man might be, if he dared to preach the gospel, or worship God in any way different from that which the ecclesiastical law prescribed, he was exposed to insult and abuse, even in the streets, and liable to arrest and fines and imprisonment. These penalties were inflicted upon vast numbers, both ministers and others, who suffered untold agonies on account of their fidelity to the truth and the rights of conscience.

METROPOLITAN TABERNACLE

OPENED MARCH 25 1861

p. 136   SPURGEON'S CHURCH.   See page 321

CHAPTER XIV.

THE DAWN OF FREEDOM.

UR history now reaches a period which may be called "The Dawn of Freedom," because the dark times of persecution begin to give place to the increasing light of religious liberty, but deeds of darkness were still committed. King James II., who had been engaged in bitterly persecuting the dissenters, suddenly changed his policy.

In 1687, his "Declaration of Indulgence" was issued, removing all restraint on nonconformists, whether Papists or Protestants, at the royal pleasure. His object was to secure supreme power for himself, and toleration for papists.

While some of the Baptists were deceived by this seeming conversion to the doctrine of religious liberty, many of them were shrewd enough to see that it was only in the interests of the papists, to give them relief, that this stretch of kingly power was hazarded. Whatever was his motive, yet he did grant them enlarged liberties. The churchmen he oppressed. In order to win their favor and secure their aid in his designs, special favors were bestowed on the dissenters, and civil honors were even thrust upon them. But

Dr. Cramp says; "Every one knows what followed. The English were not to be cajoled. They had no taste for popery and arbitrary power. The deliverer came. The tyrant fled. Persecution ceased. Thanks be to God for the Revolution of 1688!"

We give an account of some of the distinguished and noble men who suffered during the reigns of Charles II., and James II., and yet lived to see the dawn of religious freedom.

One of these was William Kiffin, who though a most faithful subject and law abiding citizen, was compelled to feel the heavy hand of these monarchs simply because he was a Baptist. We have some account of his life from his own pen. He was a merchant prince of London, and at the same time a prince among preachers. Ivimey calls him, "The Father of the Particular Baptists." His fortune was gained honestly by trade with Holland, and not as many were gained in his day, as well as in ours, by dishonest means.

Mr. Kiffin was born in London, in 1616, and was converted in early life. He had the plague when 9 years old. At first joined the Independents, but afterward withdrew, along with many others, and united with the First Particular Baptist church, Mr. Spilsbury's people. Soon after 1640, he withdrew from this church, because he would not agree with them as to the propriety of suffering ministers to preach amongst them who had not been immersed.*

Mr. Kiffin was instrumental in forming, along with others, the Devonshire Square church, of which he was chosen pastor, in which position he remained for sixty years, to the time of his death.

*Ivimey, Hist. Baptists, I, pp. 296, 297.

It was his to be tried both by adversity and prosperity, having not only riches, but the honors of the world bestowed upon him. He was well known to kings James and Charles. On one occasion, Charles sent to borrow of him, $200,000. Mr. Kiffin knowing well the unprincipled character of the king, sent word that he had not so much money at his command, but if his majesty would accept it, he would make him a present of $40,000. Charles accepted the gift, and Mr. Kiffin in referring to the transaction, said that he had saved $160,000. Possessed of great influence at court, he used it, as well as his wealth, for the protection of his oppressed brethren. Lord Arlington told him that his name was in every list of disaffected persons fit to be secured; "yet the king would never hear anything against me," he remarked. This did not save him, however, from frequent arrest and imprisonment. But the Lord always raised up friends for him, and Mr. Kiffin regarded his deliverances, as merciful providences. Soon after he was converted he was stoned as he was leaving church; but some time after, he was called upon to visit a dying man, who sent for him to confess that it was he who had stoned him.

He was arrested while attending meeting at Southwark, charged with preaching treason from the pulpit. This was before the differences arose between the king and the parliament. During his imprisonment, some brutal prisoners were hired to kill him, but were diverted from their purpose by his kindness to them. Again he was charged with conspiring with others to overthrow the state. At another time he was charged by the Duke of Buckingham with hiring two men to assassinate the king. He had some difficulty to establish his innocence, but he finally did. After his affliction in the death of his sons the laws were put into execution against dissenters, and Mr. Kiffin was arrested, and prosecuted by persons who were anxious to secure the fine, which was two hundred dollars. He put this sum into the hands of an officer, but succeeded through some errors in the proceedings in defeating the informers on the trial. The trial cost him one hundred and fifty dollars, but he did not have to pay the fine. This result discouraged the informers from proceeding against other brethren. But his enemies were determined to entrap him. They attended his meetings and secretly kept a record of them, and finally prosecuted him for them all at once, attempting to have him fined $1,500.00. But he again defeated them at law through errors in the records, and they were compelled to abandon the suit.

In addition to these troubles and in the midst of them, Mr. Kiffin was called to pass through deep afflictions in his family. His oldest son, who was about twenty years of age, was called away from earth to heaven. His obedience to his parents and forwardness in the ways of God, were such as made him very amiable in the eyes of all who knew him. His death was a great affliction to his parents. His second son, who possessed a feeble constitution, was sent abroad to travel according to his desire. The father engaged the services of a young minister to accompany his son, and especially to guard him against the corrupting influences of the popish religion. This young minister, though his expenses were paid, deserted his charge, who soon after, at Venice, got into a dispute with a Romish priest. The priest for revenge destroyed him with poison. Mr. Kiffin felt himself greatly supported and comforted by his heavenly Father and ever acknowledged God's providence and mercy.

Dr. Cramp says, " Here is a fine trait of the good old Protestantism. William Kiffin would not have acted like some of the moderns who send their children to Roman

MEMORIAL HALL, ERECTED IN 1878, AT BASSEIN, IN HONOR OF KO-THAH-BYU, THE FIRST KAREN CONVERT, BAPTIZED 1828.

See page 367.

Catholic schools. So solicitous was he for his sons preservation from the insidious error, that he was content to incur a double expense on his tour, rather than risk his spiritual safety. All honor to him."

Only three years after this, he was called to bear a still greater affliction. His wife died October 2, 1682. His own words show how noble a woman she was, and how highly he esteemed her. He says : " It pleased the Lord to take to himself my dear and faithful wife, with whom I had lived forty-four years ; whose tenderness to me and faithfulness to God, were such as cannot by me be expressed, as she constantly sympathized with me in all my afflictions, and I can truly say, I never heard her utter the least discontent under all the providences that attended myself or her. Eying the hand of God in them she was a constant encourager of me in the ways of God. Her death was the greatest sorrow to me that I ever met with in the world."* But a two-fold sorrow came upon him only the next year, and that too without his wife to help him bear the crushing weight. Two of his grandsons, Benjamin and William Hewlings, who with their widowed mother had found a home in Mr. Kiffin's family, joined the ill-fated expedition of the Duke of Monmouth, who claimed the throne of his father Charles II., and as King James was a tyrant and a papist, these young men, who loved liberty, were induced to join the duke's ranks. But the enterprise ended in disaster and ruin. The two Hewling brothers were taken prisoners and condemned to death. They were both young men of great beauty and grace of person, heirs to a large fortune and the last male descendents of their family. But better than all this they possessed superior talents, excellent moral character, eminent piety, and were

* Ivimey's II. 318.

devoted Baptists. Earnest petitions from their mother and from Mr. Kiffin were presented for their lives, but in vain. King James would not be moved.

They were executed separately. But the bearing of both the young martyrs, was characterized by a sublime heroism. Both lay down their lives with heavenly resignation and joy. The people and officers who witnessed their triumphant death, were convinced of their piety and were deeply affected. Some of the officers were heard to say, that they would have been glad to change conditions with those young men. Many persons who witnessed the scene said ; it both broke and rejoiced their hearts. From the noble bearing of these and other Christian young men who died as martyrs for liberty it became a common saying, "If you would learn how to die, go to the young men of Taunton."

In carrying out his purposes the king sought to gain the good graces of Mr. Kffiin by appointing him, under the new charter, to the office of alderman of the city of London. He sent for Mr. Kiffin to attend him at court. When he went thither in obedience to the king's commandment he found many lords and gentlemen. The king came up to him and addressed him with all the little grace he was master of. He concluded by telling Mr. Kiffin that he had put him down as alderman. This would have been regarded by most men as a great honor, but Mr. Kiffin replied ; "Sire, I am a very old man, and have withdrawn myself from all kind of business for some years past, and am incapable of doing any service, in such an affair, to your majesty in the city. Besides Sire," the old man went on, fixing his eyes steadfastly on the king, while the tears ran down his cheeks, "the death of my grandsons gave a wound to my heart which is still bleeding, and will never close but in the grave." The king was deeply struck by the manner, the freedom, and the spirit of this unexpected rebuke. A total silence ensued, while the fallen countenance of James seemed to shrink from the horrid remembrance. In a minute or two, however, he recovered himself enough to say: "Mr. Kiffin, I shall find a balsam for that sore," and immediately turned about to a lord in waiting.* Mr. Kiffin at first declined to accept the appointment, because he believed that the king's design was to overthrow the Protestant religion. But he was induced afterward to accept it in order to escape the severe penalties to which he would have subjected himself by an absolute refusal. After fulfilling the duties of his office for about nine months, he was discharged, very much to his relief. He lived to an honored and useful old age, and died in the year 1701, in his eighty-sixth year.

Another of the illustrious men who suffered for conscience' sake during the persecuting reign of Charles II., was Benjamin Keach. He was born February 29, 1640, and was one of the most celebrated Baptists of that day. He suspected the validity of infant Baptism because of the silence of the Scriptures about it, and was converted and baptized at the age of fifteen.

The church discovered his talents, piety, and consecration to the service of God, and called him to the work of the ministry in his eighteenth year. He became pastor of a church for the first time when 28 years old. His first church was in Southwark, London. For four years they were obliged, for concealment, to meet in a private house in Tooley street, but in 1672, they were permitted, by the Act of Indulgence, to build a house of worship. Mr. Keach was so successful in

* Ivimey's I. 473.

his ministry, that the house was frequently enlarged to accommodate the growing congregation until it was capable of holding nearly 1000 persons.

Mr. Keach, in leaving Buckinghamshire in 1680, sold all of his property. On his way to London with his wife and three children, the stage coach was beset by highwaymen, who robbed the passengers of every thing of value. The robbers left him without money, with wife and children among strangers, but he found friends who relieved his immediate necessities. The plainness and fearlessness of Mr. Keach as a preacher exposed him afterward to persecution. Once he was seized by four dragoons, who bound him and laid him on the ground, intending to trample him to death with their horses. But just as they were about to put spurs to their horses to execute their murderous design, a humane officer rode up and ordered them to desist. The historian, Crosby, who was a member of his church, says of him, however, that he aimed to avoid hard censures of those differing from him, and was of a peaceful disposition.

Mr. Keach was a voluminous writer and his works are classed by Crosby as "practical, polemical and poetical." Some of his books are still held in high esteem. One of the least of his publications brought upon him a great deal of suffering. It was written by him at the age of 24, and was called "The Child's Instructor; or a New and Easy Primer." This little book contained an exposition of Baptist views, and was declared to be "Seditions and venomous," and "contrary to the Book of Common Prayer and the Liturgy of the Church of England."*

The Chief Justice, Hyde, afterwards Lord Clarendon, pronounced sentence, as follows, against him: "That you

*Ivimey's History Baptists, I. 351.

CROZER THEOLOGICAL SEMINARY, UPLAND, PA.

P. 146

See page 377.

shall go to gaol for a fortnight without bail mainprize, * *
and to stand in the pillory at Aylesbury in the open market
* * from eleven o'clock to one. * * And the next Thurs-
day to stand in the same manner, and for the same time in the
market at Winslow; and there your book shall be openly
burnt before your face, by the common hangman. * * And
you shall forfeit to the king's majesty the sum of twenty
pounds, shall remain in gaol until you find sureties for your
good behavior, and appearance at the next assizes, there to renounce your doctrines, and make public submission as shall
be enjoined you.''

The pillory was a very cruel mode of punishment, and
was usually inflicted only on the vilest criminals. The
crowd were accustomed to pelt the helpless victims with
rotten eggs, and even with stones, sometimes causing death.
But when the people saw Mr. Keach in the pillory, they
treated him with great respect, knowing him to be a good
man. His wife and many of his friends gathered around
him, encouraging him with their kind words of sympathy
and love. He spoke to those who were about him, saying;
'' Good people, I am not ashamed to stand here this day, with
this paper on my head. My Lord Jesus was not ashamed to
suffer on the cross for me, and it is for his cause that I am
made a gazing stock. Take notice that it is not for any
wickedness that I stand here, but for writing and publishing
his truths, which the spirit of the Lord hath revealed in the
Holy Scriptures.'' He was interrupted by a drunken priest,
and then by the jailer, and forced to stop. Finally he
managed to slip his hand loose and taking his Bible from his
pocket he said: '' Take notice that the things that I have
written and published, and for which I stand here this day a
spectacle to men and angels are all contained in this book.''
The jailer took the book from him and fastened up his hand

K

again in the hole. It was impossible, however, to silence him, and he said : "Good people the concernment for souls is very great, so that Christ died for them, and truly a concernment for souls was that which made me to write and publish those things for which I now suffer, and for which I could suffer far greater things than these."* The officers interfered and compelled him to be silent for a time, but after a while he ventured to speak again ; " O, did you but experience the great love of God, and the excellencies that are in him, it would make you willing to go through any sufferings for his sake, and I do account this the greatest honor that ever the Lord was pleased to confer upon me!" The two hours expired and he was released from the pillory. He was subjected to the same penalty at Winslow where he lived.

Mr. Keach was a man of weak constitution, and in 1689, was thought to be near his end. His physician and friends, gave him up. Hanserd Knollys, another eminent Baptist minister, knelt by his bedside, and offered a very earnest prayer, entreating that God would spare his life, and add to his days the time granted to Hezekiah. Mr. Knollys then hastily left, saying, with emphasis ; " Brother Keach, I shall be in heaven before you." It is a remarkable fact that Mr. Keach not only recovered, but lived just fifteen years according to the prayer offered in his behalf.

Hanserd Knollys was also one of those Baptist ministers who suffered from imprisonments and other persecutions, but lived to see the dawn of liberty in England. He was a native of Chalkwell, Lincolnshire, and was a man of extensive learning and of great eloquence, as a preacher. He wrote several books, among them a Latin, Greek and Hebrew Grammar, written in Latin; and received his educa-

* Ivimey's History Baptists, I , 353.

tion at the University of Cambridge, where he was convertted while a student.   After his graduation he was ordained, and entered the ministry of the Episcopal Church, where he labored faithfully for several years.   In studying the Scriptures he found that many things in the Episcopal Church were not in accordance with the word of God.   He gave up his ordination and resolved not to preach again until he could feel assured that he had a call and commission from Christ himself, but was led out of his darkness and doubt by a Puritan minister, and began again to preach with great acceptance.   In 1633, he was driven from home by persecution, and came to New England when he probably became founder of a Baptist church at Dover, New Hampshire, from 1635 to 1639.   But even here he did not escape persecution; so he returned to England in 1641, upon the solicitation of his father.   Cotton Mather, one of the greatest New England ministers of the time, does him justice and speaks of him in very high terms, saying, that "his name ought to live in their books, for his piety."*

Mr. Knollys served at one time as chaplain in the Parliamentary army.   He established a school in London, and continued to teach until near the close of his life.   His school was so successful, that he was enabled to accumulate a considerable amount of property from its proceeds.   He also preached and collected a large congregation in London, which was formed into a church of which he was ordained pastor in 1645, and in which position he remained until his death, in 1691.   He was several times compelled to leave the country for a while, in order to escape persecution; yet he lived to the advanced age of 91 years, and spent upwards of 70 years in the ministry.   His life was one of very great

*Ivimey's History Baptists, II. 349.

usefulness, and he exerted wide spread influence which lived long after him.

The "Hanserd Knollys Society" formed in 1845 for the republication of the works of early Baptist authors, was named after him. "He being dead yet speaketh."

FIRST BAPTIST CHURCH, CAMDEN N. J.

See page 257.

CHAPTER XV.

STRUGGLES AND TRIUMPHS.

HERE are some remarkable accounts of the difficulties the Broadmead church, Bristol, experienced in its early history, from the opposition of church and state, which will be interesting to relate. They are found in the published "Broadmead Records" for which we are indebted to Mr. Terrill. It is kept in the form of a diary of the church, and was published by the "Hanserd Knollys Society."

The church was founded in 1640. They met regularly for worship, and when they had no preacher the brethren prayed and exhorted. Besides the Sabbath services, they had a week-night prayer meeting held in private houses. Mr. Ewins, formerly an Episcopal minister, became the pastor of the Broadmead church in 1651. His work prospered to such an extent as to bring persecution upon him and his flock. In July, 1661, he was arrested while preaching, and imprisoned. He was released in September. but as he returned to preaching, he was again imprisoned, but soon released. In 1663, he was again arrested, and fined, and cast into prison, till the fine should be paid, where he remained several months. His people often came to him, however, and he preached to them from the window of his jail while they stood outside.* The fine demanded was £50,† and they were poor and not able to raise so much money. They would have been willing to sacrifice almost everything they had for the sake of their beloved pastor. And indeed they did, after a time, pay a part of the fine, and he was set at liberty. But the church, as well as their pastor, suffered great trouble from their enemies. Some of the members were often fined and imprisoned. The constables frequently broke up their meetings. Sometimes on hearing that the officers were coming, they would run to the garret, or into the cellar for refuge. Yet, notwithstanding these trials, the Lord prospered them, and they were enabled to keep up their meetings, even though they were compelled to forsake their chapel, and assemble in private houses. But they did not even then escape persecution. One of their expedients to evade the officers, was to have the minister preach to them from the adjoining house through a hole in the wall, made for that purpose. In the year 1667, they obtained an upper room in a warehouse, in which they met for a time ; but they were soon compelled to nail up the doors, and for several months could only meet in the lanes and highways. The plague visited Bristol in 1666, and this fearful scourge was the only thing that could stop the violence of persecution, and for a little while the church had rest.

Mr. Ewins, their pastor, died, and was succeeded by Mr. Hardcastle, in 1671. For three years they enjoyed his preaching in an old Quaker meeting-house which was secured for their use. But in 1675, their pastor was sent to jail by the bishop of Bristol, Guy Carleton, who had resolved to destroy all meetings, and make all come to the established church. The bishop was aided by a lawyer, who acted as

* Ivimey, II. 530 ; IV. 262. † $250.

spy and informer, for the sake of the fine. But the brethren
were not to be outdone.   As the chief object of their persecution was to arrest the preacher, the people all sat together
in the room with the minister in their midst.   To prevent
surprise, some "women and maids" were stationed on the
stair-case. When the lawyer and officers arrived, the alarm
was given, and the minister stopped preaching, and all
joined in singing a psalm, which was no violation of law.
Some of them, however, were generally dragged to prison.
On one occasion, the bishop himself came to the meeting to
have them arrested.   But their faith and endurance were
equal to the emergency.

Mr. Hardcastle died in 1678, and for a few years the
church, comparatively, enjoyed peace. But it was not long
before their worship was again interrupted.   Their pastor,
Mr. Fownes, was sent to prison in 1681, but he preached to
the people from the jail window.

Here are a few passages from the records of the church :

January 29, 1682. The church met at four different
places.   Many of them went in the afternoon on Durdham
Down and got into a cave of a rock toward Clifton, where
brother Thomas Whinnell preached to them.

March 12. Met in the fields by Barton Hundred, and
Mr. Samuel Buttall, of Plymouth, preached in the forenoon,
and brother Whinnell in the evening.   It was thought there
were near a thousand persons in the morning.

July 2. Our pastor preached in another place in the
wood.   Our friends took much pains in the rain, because
many informers were ordered out to search ; and we were in
peace, though there were near twenty men and boys in
search.

BAPTIST CHAPEL, PARIS, FRANCE.   See page 353.

July 16. Brother Frowns, first, and brother Whinnell, after, preached under a tree, it being very rainy.

January 21, 1683. We met at eight in the morning and though there were seven on horse back, and twenty on foot, to seek after us, we escaped, having broken up at ten.

March. This week about one hundred and fifty dissenters were convicted by our recorder, on the statutes of 23rd Elizabeth, for £20 a month,* for not coming to church.

March 25th. Mr. Fownes, though very ill, went to the meetings in the woods ; but after three-quarters of an hour, we were surrounded by horse and foot, the former in ambush.

Mr. Fownes was arrested and sent to Gloucester jail for six months.

November 14th. A day of prayer, having some hours together in the wood between London and Sodbury Road ; the enemy came upon us unaware and seized about eight persons ; but the brethren escaped to admiration. The bushes were of great service to us. A number of·the sisters were taken, and were closely questioned, but refused to tell who their preacher was, so they were let go.

December 30. Being a hard frost and snow on the ground, we met in the wood, and though we stood in the snow, the sun shone upon us, and we were in peace.

October 10, 1684. New mayor and sheriff being chosen, James Twyford, sheriff, threatens to find out our little meetings, and he would be like death, spare none.

On the 29th of November, 1685, our pastor, brother Fownes, died in Gloucester jail, having been kept there for two years and about nine months a prisoner, unjustly and maliciously, for the testimony of Jesus and preaching the gospel.†

* One hundred dollars.
† Dr. Cramp.

He was originally committed for six months, but they would not release him unless he would give bond for his good behavior, which meant that he would not preach again. This, of course, he would not do, and consequently he remained in prison.

George Fownes was not, as we may judge, the only Baptist who either suffered or died in prison in England. Ministers, especially, were very cruelly dealt with, and many endured imprisonments, some of whom have been mentioned. Francis Bamfield suffered for eight years in Dorchester jail, and ended his life in Newgate. Thomas Delaune also died in Newgate. John Miller was ten years in Newgate. Henry Forty was twelve years in prison at Exeter. John Bunyan, also, suffered twelve years in Bedford jail, and Joseph Wright, a man of great piety and learning, .pastor at Maidstone, was imprisoned in the common jail of that place for twenty years. It is not generally known that so many Baptists suffered such long imprisonments. The many are lost sight of in the greatness of the few, whose names are familiar.

A word, at least, must be said of the justly celebrated John Canne, the founder of the Broadmead church. He was born about 1590, became eminent for his learning and piety, was well versed in the Scriptures, and zealous in the work of reformation. In his early life he was a member of the Church of England. He united with the Baptists, and became pastor of a church in Southwark, London, in 1621. This church had but recently been founded and held its meetings secretly, in private houses, for fear of persecution. Mr. Canne preached for them only a short time, when he was compelled to flee. In 1641 he returned for a short time to England when he founded the Broadmead church, at Bristol, of which the illustrious Robert Hall was, in after years, pastor. The name of John Canne has been immortalized by his being the first to prepare and publish the English Bible with marginal references. He proceeded on the principle, that Scripture is itself the best interpreter of Scripture. His days were ended in Amsterdam in 1667, where English tyranny had forced him to publish his first Bible with references in 1644. It was afterwards published repeatedly, in England.

Some of the ministers of this period were not without learning. Jeremiah Ives was a man of great natural abilities and considerable learning. He was thirty years pastor of a church in the Old Jewry, London ; and was so celebrated for his tact and power in numerous disputations, that Charles II., invited him to court, to hold a discussion with a Roman Catholic priest, who was told that his opponent was a clergyman of the Church of England. Mr. Ives assumed the robes of an Episcopal minister at the king's request, without knowing the deceit intended. He pressed the priest very closely and argued that notwithstanding the antiquity of the doctrines and practices of Rome, that they were not apostolic because unknown in any writing of the apostolic age. "That argument," the priest replied, "would be of as much force against infant baptism, which was also unknown in the apostolic age." Mr. Ives readily granted it, intimating that he rejected infant baptism on the same ground ; whereupon the priest abruptly closed the discussion, saying, "that he had been cheated ; he had come to dispute with a Church of England clergyman, but it was evident that this was an Anabaptist preacher." This behavior of the priest afforded great amusement for the king and his court.*

In the early part of his ministry, Nehemiah Coxe, D. D., lived at Cranfield, Bedfordshire. He was committed to prison

*Ivimey, II. 604.

for preaching the pospel. When brought to his trial, at Bedford, he pleaded in Greek, and on examination answered in Hebrew. The judge called for the indictment, and found him therein described as "Nehemiah Coxe, Cordwainer;" at which he expressed his astonishment. Mr. Coxe insisted on his right to plead in what language he chose, and as none of the lawyers could talk Greek or Hebrew, the case was necessarily dismissed. "Well," said the judge, afterward to the learned counsel, "the cordwainer has wound you all up, gentlemen."

In these troublesome and dangerous times, preachers were often obliged to disguise themselves that they might not be recognized by the informers. " It is said that Bunyan, to avoid discovery, went from a friend's house, disguised as a carter, with his white frock, wide-awake cap, and whip in hand, to attend a private meeting in a sheltered field or barn." Andrew Gifford, of Bristol, adopted similar expedients, at one time appearing as an officer, at another as a gentleman. "Did you not meet me last night," he said one day to a friend, " going through Lawford's gate ? Why did you not speak to me?" " I did not see you, sir." " Did you not meet a tinker?" "Yes, sir." " That was I," said Mr. Gifford. George Hammond (the author of several books,) pastor of the church at Canterbury, was a very eminent and remarkable man ; and that he was also a very zealous man will appear from the following anecdotes. While going to preach at a distant place, he was overtaken by a storm of rain. While stopping under a tree for shelter, another person, from a house opposite, called to him and told him, that he was an informer, and that he had heard there was to be preaching in the neighborhood, and that he was going to give information of those present. This was the very place where Mr. Hammond was to preach, so he said : "I am a

P 159.

FRANKLIN COLLEGE, INDIANA.

See page 376.

man-taker also.'' ''Are you so?'' replied the informer ; ''then
we will go together. '' They reached the house and sat
some time among the people. '' Here are the people,'' said
Mr. Hammond to the informer, '' but where is the minister ?
Unless there is a minister, we cannot make a conventicle of
it, and, therefore, I propose that you or I should preach.''
The informer declined, of course, and Mr. Hammond saying :
'' Then I must ; '' preached, much to the man's astonishment,
and with energy and honor. The sermon was blessed to him,
for he dropped his calling and became an altered man.

'' It happened, '' says Crosby, '' that the magistrates of
Seven Oakes sent some officers to the congregation meeting at
Brabourn, who took all the men from thence and carried
them to the town, where by an order, they were kept
prisoners, all night. On the morrow, when the justices met
together, the prisoners were had before them, and examined,
and after some little discourse with them, were dismissed.
They all, with one heart, full of wonder and joy, returned to
the place from whence they were taken, to return thanks
to God for this so unexpected deliverance. When they
came to the place, to their great surprise and inex-
pressible joy, *they found the women there, who had not
departed from the house, but had spent that evening, the night
and morning, in prayer to God* on their behalf.''

Among the men of note who embraced Baptist sentiments in these times, was Dr. DuVeil, both M. D. and D. D.
He was a Jew, born at Metz, and educated in the Jewish
religion. In the course of his studies he was led to compare the Old and New Testament, and was led thereby to
espouse Christianity. His enraged father sought his life,
but he escaped. Having joined the Catholic Church he was
advanced to positions of great honor. Being called upon to

write against the Huguenots he studied their principles and history, which led him to become a Protestant. About 1677 he came to England where he enjoyed the friendship and respect of bishops Conton, Tillotson, and Lloyd, and others of the greatest dignity and worth, on account of his eminence, piety and learning. Having free access to the library of the bishop of London, he there met with some Baptist books, and afterwards sought out Hanserd Knollys, and the learned John Gosnold, into the fellowship of whose church he was soon baptized. Of course many turned their backs upon him at once, but Dr. Tillotson who respected a man for what he was, and not merely for his opinions, continued his friendship. After becoming a Baptist, DuVeil wrote a commentary on the Acts, proving therein, Baptist principles. Previously he had published a learned exposition on other portions of God's word.

There were at this time many families of prominence among the Baptists. One of the most distinguished was that of the Giffords, who, for three generations, adorned the ministry. Andrew Gifford, the head of the family, was born in Bristol in 1641, baptized in 1659, and began his ministry at Pithay in 1661. On one occasion he was invited to preach in a state church, in Somersetshire, at the funeral of the wife of a wealthy and highly respected citizen, but his enemies kept the organ playing to prevent his preaching. Seeing their intention he went into the church-yard, and mounting a tombstone, addressed his large audience without further disturbance. After this, the rector let him have his church whenever he wanted it, and both Mr. Gifford and his son frequently preached there. His popularity was very great among the colliers, who flocked to hear him in great numbers in the fields. If interrupted by officers of the law they would throw a great coat over him to disguise him, and put a pitchfork in his hand with a bundle of hay on the top of it on his shoulders, and thus secure his retreat. *   He took an active part in the rebellion of the Duke of Monmouth, but escaped the misfortune of Hastings.   " He collected a considerable sum and provided ammunition, and when the duke came near the city, he sent his son, Emanuel, to Knowl Castle, a mile out of the city, to invite the duke and his friends in; assuring him, that there were many friends and supplies provided, and that a part of the city (Bristol) walls, was undermined to let them in with ease and safety.   But the Lord Lieutenant having sent the duke word that he would burn the city if he attempted to enter it, the latter desisted.   Mr. Gifford rode out for the purpose of urging the duke to take the city, when a friend met him and told him that his plot was discovered, and that a troop of horse was in search of him, and to flee for his life.   Turning his horse loose after removing saddle and bridle, he hid himself in a bush, and soon after the troop passed, declaring that if they could catch the dog, they would cut him to pieces as small as herbs for the pot.   They soon returned from their vain pursuit and re-passed the bush in which he was hid, when Mr. Gifford remounted his horse and returned home, where he secreted himself until the danger was over.   He was a melancholy witness of the sufferings of five or six, executed without Radcliff-Gate, on account of it, but lived to share in the joy of the Prince of Orange's arrival.   The first news of the embarkation of the prince was brought to Bristol by his brother Samuel who sailed the very night before the prince, who intreated him to be his pilot.   But there was a noble Baptist woman, who did less for the Duke of Monmouth and who was not so fortunate as to escape, as Mr. Gifford."†

The story of Elizabeth Gaunt, as related by Bishop Burnet is one of sadness :—"There was in London one Gaunt,

*Ivimey II. 542.   † Ivimey I. 431.

BURNING OF ELIZABETH GAUNT, ENGLAND.

See page 162

L

a woman that was an Anabaptist, who spent a great part of her life in acts of charity, visiting jails, looking after the poor of what persuasion so ever they were. One of the rebels found her out and she harbored him in her house, and was looking for an occasion of sending him out of the kingdom. He went about in the night and came to hear what the king had said, so he, by an unheard of baseness, went and delivered himself and accused her that had harbored him. She was seized and tried. There was no witness to prove that she knew the person she harbored was a rebel except himself. Her maid witnessed, only, that he was entertained at her house: but though her crime was that of harboring a traitor, and was proved only by this infamous witness, yet the judge charged the jury to bring her in guilty; pretending that the maid was a second witness, though she knew nothing of that which was the criminal part. She was condemned and burnt, as the law directs in the case of women convicted of treason. She died with a constancy even to cheerfulness, that struck all who saw it. She said; 'Charity was a part of her religion as well as faith; this, at worst, was feeding an ememy, so she hoped that she had reward with him for whose sake she did this service, how unworthy soever the person was who had honored her to be the first that suffered by fire in this reign, and that her suffering was a martyrdom for that religion which was all love.' Penn, the Quaker, told me that he saw her die. She laid the straw about her for burning her speedily, and behaved herself in such a manner that all the spectators melted into tears."*

Passing over any further reference to the sad fate of this good and innocent victim of tyranny, let us consider the origin of the Baptist College founded at Bristol in 1770. It is the oldest Baptist theological seminary in the world.

*Burnet, History of Times etc. II. 649.

The following incident led to the origination of this useful institution, which still exists and flourishes.

Edward Terril was baptized and joined the church at Broadmead, 1658, where he was a most useful member for thirty years, during which period he suffered imprisonment several times for conscience' sake. He was a respectable school teacher and valued an education in ministers. Hence he left, by will, a sum of money, $500. a year, to the pastor of the Broadmead church, "provided he be an holy man, well skilled in the Greek and Hebrew tongues, in which the Scriptures were originally written; and devote three afternoons in the week to the instruction of any number of young students, not exceeding twelve, who may be recommended by the church, in the knowledge of the original languages and other literature." Special provision was made by him for students in destitute circumstances. These were noble gifts and led to the establishment of a theological school at Bristol for the education of students for the Baptist ministry. The church record tells us that he "was a great benefactor to the church." Bristol College is now one of the flourishing institutions of the land.

MRS BUNYAN PLEADING WITH THE JUDGES.

See page 168

CHAPTER XVI.

BUNYAN.

THE immortal dreamer, Bunyan, deserves special notice. Bunyan's " Pilgrim's Progress " is one of the most wonderful productions of the human mind. With the exception of the Bible, this work has been more widely circulated and read than any other book that has ever been written. It has been translated into many different languages. The Chinese have it in their native tongue with a picture of Christian as a Chinaman with his long pig-tail. Bunyan wrote this work during his long imprisonment of twelve years in Bedford jail. It is one of the most celebrated books in the English language, and adapted to interest and instruct both young and old.

John Bunyan was born at Elstow, near Bedford, in 1628. His father was a poor but pious tinker. The son was brought up to the same occupation, and was taught to read and write. From his youth he was addicted to vice and impiety. Though often alarmed by the warnings of conscience and the conviction of the Holy Spirit, he continued in a life of sin for many years.

During this period, his life was several times remarkably preserved. Twice he was rescued from drowning, and once he narrowly escaped being shot. While a soldier in the parliamentary army, at the siege of Leicester, in 1645, he was selected as a sentinel. One of his comrades voluntarily took his place, and was shot through the head while standing at his post.

He married a poor but pious woman, whose earthly portion consisted of two religious books. Through his wife's conversation, and the reading of these books, he was induced to go regularly to church, and was deeply convicted of sin. For a time, he thought he was too great a sinner ever to be saved, and was on the border of despair. But in 1653, he was brought out of the darkness of sin into the light and joy of faith in Christ. Mr. Gifford, a Baptist minister, baptized him, and soon after by request of the church he began to preach.

After the restoration of Charles II., he was one of the first to suffer persecution. Because he refused to obey the iniquitous laws which required all dissenters to conform to the Church of England, he was arrested in 1660, and cast into Bedford jail. He was tried on the charge of abstaining from coming to church, "and as an upholder of meetings contrary to the laws of the king," and with "teaching men to worship contrary to law." On these grounds he was condemned and sentenced to be imprisoned for twelve years in Bedford jail, a martyr for religious liberty. His courageous wife pleaded in vain with his judges for his release. While in prison, he worked industriously making laces to support himself and his family. His little blind daughter,

Mary, comforted him by her presence. He was not allowed to have any books in the jail, except a Bible and Fox's " Book of Martyrs." With no helps to study but these, he wrote the "Pilgrim's Progress," besides other works. Release from prison could have been procured for him at any time by promising not to preach, but he refused to accept liberty at any such a price. He believed that God had given him the right to preach the gospel, and rather than surrender that right to any man, he was willing to endure imprisonment and even death. In the last year of his confinement, and while still in jail, he was chosen pastor by the church at Bedford. He was released in 1672. When he visited London it is said that great crowds of people flocked to hear him preach. Even when the hour for meeting was at 7 o'clock in the morning, as many as 3000 people assembled.

Soon after he was set at liberty, he built a meeting house at Bedford, where he preached to large congregations. Often he visited his brethren in various parts of England, to sympathize with them in their persecutions, and encourage them to bear their trials with patience. Particularly attentive to the temporal wants of those who suffered for conscience' sake, he did much for their relief. The sick and afflicted were also the objects of his care. Besides, he exerted his influence very earnestly as a peacemaker. It was while on a journey, in rough weather, to effect a reconciliation between a father and son, that he contracted his last sickness. His labor of love was successful, but it cost him his life. He bore his sufferings patiently, and died triumphantly on the 31st of August, 1688, the year of the great English Revolution, in the 60th year of his age, and was buried at Bunhill Fields.

Here are lines written by Cowper upon Bunyan :

" Ingenious dreamer, in whose well-told tale
" Sweet fiction and sweet truth alike prevail;
" Whose humorous vein, strong sense and simple style
" May teach the gayest, make the gravest smile :
" Witty and well employed, and, like the Lord,
" Speaking in parables his slighted word :
" I name thee not, lest so despised a name
" Shonld move a sneer at thy deserved fame :
" Yet e'en in transitory life's late day,
" That mingles all my brown with sober gray
' Revere the name whose *Pilgrim* marks the road,
'And guides the *Progress* of the soul to God.

It was the persecuting spirit of sectarian prejudice that caused Bunyan to be despised, not only while living but long after his death. But his talents and worth were so great, that his name could not long remain in obscurity. Men of all nations and all denominations now delight to do him honor, and no one now dares to " sneer" at his illustrious fame.

A recent event shows how Bunyan's name is now regarded in England. A few years ago the present Duke of Bedford succeded to his estates and titles. It had been customary for the dukes of Bedford to give a silver cup as a prize to be won at the races. As he disapproved of horse-racing, he refused to comply with this objectionable custom. Unwilling, however, that his refusal should be attributed to a lack of generosity, rather than to moral principle, he determined to spend a larger amount in some nobler gift. His mother had loved the " Pilgrim's Progress," and had taught him to read it in his childhood. It occured to him that a statue of the immortal dreamer, erected at Bedford where he had lived, and preached, and suffered, and where he had his earthly home, would be the most suitable investment of his money. So he ordered a bronze statue to be made at a cost of $15,000, about three times the value of a race cup. It is

p. 171   JOHN BUNYAN.

a beautiful work of art, representing Bunyan standing erect ; at his feet lies the broken chain, that has been struck from his legs ; on the panel underneath, is Bunyan's autograph ; medallions in relief representing scenes from the " Pilgrim's Progress " ornament the sides of the pedestal, which, with the statue, is about nine feet high.

The unvailing of this noble statue took place on the 10th of June, 1874, and was attended with imposing ceremonies which were witnessed by a vast multitude of people, including many of the nobility, members of Parliament, and ministers of all denominations. The vail was removed from the statue by Lady Stanley, wife of the Dean of Westminster, when the band played the national anthem, and the multitudes rent the air with their enthusiastic cheers. Dean Stanley delivered a long and eloquent address, and speeches were made by other distinguished men who seemed to vie with one another in doing honor to the memory of Bunyan.

The Church of England that despised and persecuted this poor Baptist minister while living, now bestows upon him the highest honors. What a pity that some of this appreciation was not shown toward him when in Bedford jail. Times greatly change in the course of 200 years, a fact which must have deeply impressed all thoughtful minds who witnessed the unvailing of this statue in sight of the old prison where Bunyan was confined, and heard his name eulogized by men whose ecclesiastical ancestors had treated him with cruel indignity.

Dean Stanley referred to this great change, and to the triumph of religious liberty, in his address, and said ;— " Giant Intolerance, who in Bunyan's time was stout and hearty, is now deprived of his terrors." When the vast audience greeted this sentiment with loud cheers, the dean continued : " Ah, don't be too jubilant. The old giant is still alive ; he may be seen on all sides ; the spirit of burning and of judgment has not altogether departed from mankind, either from Churchmen or Nonconformists, but the giants joints are very stiff and crazy.''

The " Pilgrim's Progress" itself is a monument of such enduring splendor as to challenge the admiration of ages. Before Bunyan's fame, that of princes, nobles, judges, authors, pale, as the stars grow dim before the brighter light of the rising sun ! Indeed, it is scarcely possible to exaggerate the merits of this book, which, by common consent, is ranked among the noblest productions of human genius. Macauley says that " the 17th century produced only two men of original genius, John Milton and John Bunyan ;'' thus ranking the illustrious dreamer with the immortal poet, a companionship of which he is eminently worthy.

Bunyan was an open-communionist. It was the great mistake of his life. If a man undertakes to build a fine house and uses in its erection certain materials which in after years will give way, causing the house to fall ; or if he write his will in a way that the property which he intends shall be the inheritance of his own children will come into the possession of strangers, you would say that he makes a serious error. It was just such a mistake that Bunyan made by maintaining open communion in the church of which he was pastor. This church carried out the principle of open communion to its logical results, and received Pedobaptists into membership, as well as to the Lord's table. The consequence was, that in the course of time, the Pedobaptist party became the stronger, and elected a Pedobaptist minister as pastor. For the last thirty years, or longer, Bunyan's pulpit has been occupied by ministers who preach and practice infant baptism ! Sometimes the church has had two pastors at the

same time, and both of them Pedobaptists. So this illustrious church which Bunyan labored to establish in the
gospel faith, has been virtually handed over to the Pedobaptists, through the logical operation of open communion. *

Other churches have shared the same fate by adopting
the same suicidal policy. A few miles from Bedford, in a
small village, is an old Baptist church founded many years
ago. Its present pastor, a Congregationalist, has been there
more than forty years, and during that time he has trained a
large number of young men for the Congregational ministry.
What must be the character of Baptists who are willing to
submit to such a state of things, we may well imagine.
Such unions are always to the advantage of Pedobaptists,
never to that of Baptists. Pedobaptists are very willing for
Baptists to unite with them, but they are not willing to unite
with us. At present, Mr. Spurgeon guards against this
danger by refusing to admit Pedobaptists into membership,
though he invites them to occasional communion. If his
church should ever become more logical, and consistent, and
receive to membership all whom they invite to the Lord's
table, then the way will be opened for the Pedobaptists to
come in and take possession, just as they have done in other
cases. Spurgeon is wise enough to see the danger, and
avoids it by a logical inconsistency ; but no one can tell how
soon his church, when deprived of his leadership, may come
to regard immersion as no more a pre-requisite to membership
than to communion, and then will begin the process of
transformation, which may in a few years end in a Pedobaptist majority in Spurgeon's church with a Pedobaptist
minister preaching in Spurgeon's pulpit, and sprinkling
infants by the side of Spurgeon's baptistery. The same
cause which has produced such results, may be expected to
produce them again.

* Ivimey II., p. 35, note.

p. 175 BEDFORD JAIL. See page 158.

Hence it is a matter of deep regret that such men as Bunyan, Robert Hall, and Spurgeon, should have fallen into such a serious error, because it tends to destroy the results of their labors, and, besides, leads many others to adopt the same self-destructive policy. It is not safe to take any man , however wise and good, as our guide in all things, for the best of men are not infallible. One of the principles which we hold as Baptists, is to "call no man master!" While we delight to honor our great and good men, we refuse to follow them except in so far as they follow Christ, who, alone, is our example and pattern. The great body of the Baptists, insisting upon the right of private judgment, and taking God's word for their guide, are not easily led aside from the principles of the New Testament. Hence men who err on the subject of the communion, and rely upon their popularity to lead their church, like willing flocks into new pastures, are generally surprised and disappointed on looking back at the small number of their followers. The Baptists of this country believe with great unanimity that strict communion is simply strict baptism, and that it is scriptural; and to move them from that conviction will require something more potent than the authority of great names.

BUNYAN'S NEW TOMB

p 177

See page 169.

CHAPTER XVII.

MEN OF MIGHT.

BUNYAN died in 1688; and in the same year William of Orange came to England to rule over her people, and give them civil and religious liberty. It was not complete freedom that the new king brought, for the bigotry of the age prevented him; but the liberty granted was large compared with that of preceding reigns. King William wished the "Test" and the "Corporation Acts" repealed so far as they related to Protestant dissenters, but failed to secure this reform. With great difficulty he secured the passage of the "Act of Toleration," by which the operation of many persecuting acts was restrained, and meetings permitted to Baptists.

The Episcopal Church was still oppressive, and the Baptists deprived of many rights, but the king protected them as far as he could.

In 1689 the Baptists "put forth" a Confession of Faith which formed the basis of the Philadelphia Confession of Faith. It is called the "London," and also the the "Century" Confession, because it was adopted in London "by the ministers and messengers of upwards of *one hundred baptized* congregations."

Among the Baptists of this and the succeeding reigns, were many men of eminence. One of these eminent persons was Mordecai Abbott, Esquire, who was Receiver-General of the Customs, after passing through other offices with reputation to himself. "He continued in them all a strict nonconformist." Many dissenters qualified for office, as the Test Act required, by receiving the Lord's Supper in the Church of England. He refused to do it, and was upheld in his refusal by the king, William III., who esteemed him highly. He was not ashamed of his "baptized brethren," and was faithful in the discharge of his public and private duties as a Christian. Mr. Abbott was not alone in refusing to submit to the requirements of the Test Act.

Ivimey, speaking of the period between 1688 and 1708, says; "The sentiment expressed, that the Baptists in general opposed the absurd and wicked practice of taking the Lord's Supper as a qualifying test to civil officers, rests upon the fact that Mr. Joseph Stennett, who was at that time their most eminent minister, and who may fairly be presumed to speak their sentiments, opposed most strongly such conduct."*

Some, it may be. yielded to the temptation, but the prevailing sentiment among the Baptists was against it, and about 1742, Mr. Baskerville, a member of one of the London Baptist churches, was expelled for communing, occasionally, in the state churches for the sake of office, and what is more, this action of the church was sustained by all the London churches.

In this period of history the celebrated Rev. Abraham Booth, author of "The Reign of Grace," lived and wrote He was born in 1734, and became pastor in London in 1758. He was converted early and died in 1806.

* Vol. III., p. 380.

M

It is a matter worthy of remark that at this time there were many families of note, both in and out of the ministry, who were Baptists from generation to generation. Among them the Hollis and Stennett families, the former, laymen, and the latter, ministers. There were many notable families among the Baptists throughout all their history, but persecution singled them out as shining marks, and, prior to this, families who adhered to the Baptists awhile were forced to yield, to flee, or to suffer extermination.

We have mentioned as one of the distinguished Baptist families, that of the Giffords. We have already spoken of Andrew Gifford, of Bristol, where he and his son succeeded each other in long pastorates of the Pithay church. His grandson, Dr. Andrew Gifford, was the most distinguished member of the family. He was born in Bristol, August 17, 1700, was the subject of divine grace at an early age, was baptized when 15 years old, and removed to London in 1729. He formed the Eagle Street church, London, and was its pastor for fifty years. His was a most successful ministry.

The ministry of Dr. Gifford was eminently useful in the conversion of sinners, and in building up the church of God under his pastoral care. He was a pathetic and yet powerful preacher, and his sermons were highly evangelical. He was a Calvinist of the old school, his system having been formed upon the confession of faith of the Baptist churches, published by the assembly in 1689. The main topics of his discourses were: The fall of man,—Redemption by Christ,—The divinity of our Lord,—The work of the Spirit,—The sweetness of the promises,—The perseverance of the saints in holiness to heaven. After he had briefly explained his text, with these and similar doctrines, he made a direct appeal to the

FURMAN UNIVERSITY, GREENVILLE, S. C

See page 376.

heart, interested all the passions of the soul,and summoned conscience before a solemn tribunal. Dr. Rippon says of him, " His heart was in the work, and upon some occasions, particularly, it might have been said of him as of one of the reformers : his contenance was alive, his eyes were alive, his hands were alive, in short, all were alive. When he was above eighty years of age he was more active and zealous in his Master's work, than many young men of twenty five."*

He enjoyed the esteem of many of the nobility, who attended his ministry and cultivated his friendship.   Notwithstanding his position and success, he was humble and attentive to pastoral duties, and always accessible to his flock, whom he loved tenderly, and by whom he was loved in return.   Mr. Gifford was a zealous Baptist, but a man of catholic spirit.   He was a great admirer of Rev. George Whitefie'd, with whom he was intimate, and for whom he preached.   Once, on his way to hear the eloquent divine preach, he was asked if he were going to hear Whitefield, when he replied: "I am going to light my farthing rush-light at his flaming torch."

In the year 1757, he was appointed to the distinguished station of Assistant Librarian of the British Museum, for which he was eminently qualified.   He excelled in perfect acquaintance with ancient coins and manuscripts, and his collection of coins, which was one of the most curious in the kingdom, was purchased by George III. His duties here were not suffered to interfere with his pulpit and pastoral work, but rather enlarged his opportunities and usefulness.   He continued in this honorable position until his death in 1784, aged eighty-four. His last words were : " What should I do now were it not for an interest in Jesus Christ." Dr. Gifford's

*Ivimey, III. 601.

intimate friend, Rev. John Ryland, Baptist pastor at North-ampton, delivered a remarkable oration at his grave, which has been compared, by no incompetent judge,"to the thundering eloquence of Demosthenes."

Mr. Gifford left several charitable legacies, among them was one to the Baptist Academy at Bristol, of his books, pictures, and manuscripts, with a vast variety of curiosities. He caused an elegant room to be fitted up especially for their reception, which is called the "Gifford Museum."

An interesting anecdote is told of him while Assistant Librarian of the British Museum. It is given by Dr. Rippon: "Some gentlemen were inspecting the museum, under the doctor's guidance, amongst whom was a profane youth, who hardly uttered a sentence without taking the name of the Lord in vain. The doctor, who had kept his eye upon him, was at length asked by him whether they had not a certain very ancient manuscript there. On coming to it, the doctor, presenting it, asked the youth if he could read it. Being answered in the affirmative, the doctor wished him to read a paragraph, which was; ' *Thou shalt not take the name of the Lord thy God in vain.*' The irreverent youth read and blushed ; the countenances of his companions seemed to acknowledge the justness of the reproof, and the polite and Christian manner in which it was administered."

The Stennett family contained no less than four ministers in as many successive generations, all distinguished for piety and learning, and whose united service in the Baptist denomination extended over more than a century. Rev. Edward Stennett was the head of the historic part of the family. His church was at Wallingford, and occasionally he preached at Pinner's Hall, London. He espoused the cause of the parliamentary army during the civil wars, and suffered

much for the gospel's sake.   For a long time he resided and
held his meetings in Wallingford Castle, and where he was
safe from all enemies of the church, because none dare enter.
Once he and his little band were, by a number of remarkable providences, preserved from prosecution.   When he
appeared for trial for holding meetings in the castle, none of
the prosecution appeared, some accident had happened to
each, which prevented his attendance, and Mr. Stennett
was released.*

Rev. Joseph Stennett, his son, was born at Abington in
1663, and was converted in early life.   In 1690 he became
pastor of the Sabbatarian Baptist church meeting in Pinner's Hall, but preached on Sunday for other Baptist churches.
Here he remained pastor until his death, July 11, 1713.   He
was well trained in the modern and ancient languages as well
as in philosophy and science.   He was a faithful pastor and
a good preacher, and had extensive influence, not only among
Baptists, but among all who respected learning and character.

He was generally chosen by his brethren, when they approached the government, to address the throne.   The
address of the Baptists, written by him, to William III., on
the defeat of the "Assassination Plot," was widely commended ; and a copy of his sermon upon the victory at
Blenheim, in 1704, was presented by some noble person,
without his knowledge, to Queen Anne, who sent him a gift
as a token of her appreciation.

He wrote many hymns which, with his "Songs of Solomon," obtained for him a high reputation as a poet, and
secured him the commendation of poet laureate, Mr. Tate.
One of the last acts of his life was to preach the funeral
sermon of his intimate friend, the Rev. John Piggott, one of

* Ivimey, II. 71.

the leading ministers of London, and of his denomination. Mr. Stennett died, July 11th, 1713, aged 49. There were other Baptist hymn-writers of note—Miss Anne Steele, and Dr. Beddome, author of "Did Christ o'er sinners weep," were among the number.

Rev. Dr. Joseph Stennett was born in London, March 6, 1692. His early education was carefully bestowed. He was converted and baptized at the age of fifteen, and at twenty-two commenced his ministry His father died when he was twenty-one, and he labored with churches out of London until his forty-fifth year, when he became pastor of Little Wild Street Regular Baptist church. He was a man of fine powers of mind and graces of heart, and was one of the most eloquent preachers of London. He was author of several works and was made doctor of divinity by the University of Edinburgh on the recommendation of His Royal Highness, the Duke of Cumberland. His latter days were passed away in great suffering, during which he continued cheerful and serene, scarcely without an interruption. He died, February 7, 1758, aged 66. Two of his sons were ministers, Joseph and Samuel; the latter succeeded his father in the pastoral office, after having first assisted him, having served in all, forty-seven years.

Rev. Dr. Samuel Stennett was, probably, the most illustrious member of this noble family. He, too, was converted and baptized when young. He was born at Exeter, in 1727. He was one of the brightest ornaments of the Baptist denomination, a faithful shepherd of the flock of Christ, and a man whose public and private life was exemplary in every respect. His extensive learning secured for him the doctorate from "King's College and University of Aberdeen," in 1763. The celebrated philanthropist, John Howard, was a member

NINGPO, CHINA, BAPTIST PREACHERS.

See page 367.

of his church, and corresponded with him. Many of our best hymns were composed by him. He died, August 24th, 1795, 68 years of age. A uniform edition of Dr. Samuel Stennett's works has been published in London, *with all his writings on baptism omitted.* This is not the only instance of the kind, where the truth held by Baptists has been suppressed. It shows the need—now supplied—of a Baptist publication society. Our principles are important because scriptural, and needed by the world.

Thomas Hollis was one of a remarkable family of Baptists. John Hollis, his brother, and their father were men of great liberality towards educational, religious, and benevolent objects, being among the largest givers of their day. He was an eminently successful merchant of London, charitable and benevolent. He presented Harvard University, Cambridge, Massachusetts, with a valuble set of mathematical and philosophical apparatus, and made at various times valuable presents of books to the library. Besides, he endowed two professorships, one of divinity, and the other of mathematics; and ten scholarships, four of them to be Baptists. Up to 1727, his benefactions to the college amounted to about $30,000, which was the largest sum received by the college from any one person up to that time. One of the buildings is named "Hollis Hall." As he was a Calvinist he required the professor of divinity to be "of sound or orthodox principles," but he did not restrict it to Baptists. Yet for years, no Baptist, nor any other "orthodox" Christian, either had the chair, or was even a trustee to control it. On the board of trustees the orthodox or evangelical members were allowed to die out, and Unitarians were elected by the rest to fill their places. Harvard has not altogether forgotten its noble benefactor. In the beautiful dining-room of Memorial Hall are two portraits of Thomas Hollis, one of life-size placed in a conspicuous place. He is thus honored among the great, but his denominational descendants have long since been denied any management in the affairs of the College.

Thomas Hollis, the father, was a member of Pinner's Hall, London, for 60 years. He lived in a frugal manner in order to be able to give more to the Lord's cause. The father died, September, 1718 ; and the son was baptized at 20, in 1680, and died, January, 1730, aged 72, greatly lamented both in England and America. There were other members of this rich and liberal family, but these are most prominent.

With the Revolution of 1688 the storm of persecution, for the most part, passed away. The clouds had parted and broken, and the sun was at length permitted to shine upon our Baptist fathers. The sea was calm and the way plain before them. Exhaustion, however, followed the excitement of oppression. Persecution, that had permitted the life and religious enterprise of the churches only at the expense of great exertion, and ceaseless vigilance, now ceased. Its heavy hand, that had been a sort of stimulus to Christian activity, withdrawn, left the churches to relapse. Much of the marvelous courage that had been displayed, disappeared, and the strength that had enabled them to endure, was suddenly lost when liberty was granted them to labor.* While the ministers engaged in endless and dry theological controversies from the pulpit, the people sat sleeping in the pews. All was inactivity. Rev. John Ryland estimated the number of members in the Baptist churches of England and Wales, in 1753, at nearly 5000. They were far more numerous sixty-five years before. The years of prosperity were not improved for the extension of the Redeemer's kingdom.

* Semple says that it was the same in Virginia.

Dr. Cramp, following other historians, ascribes this decline, in part, to the preaching and writing of Rev. John Brine and Dr. Gill, who, for nearly half a century, were the chief men in the denomination. They gave, it is said, undue prominence to the doctrines of the Scriptures concerning the divine purposes, which led to the neglect of practical godliness, on the part of others. "It is certain," says Dr. Cramp, "that these eminent men and all their followers went far astray from the course marked out by Christ and his apostles. They were satisfied with stating men's danger, and assuring them that they were on the high road to perdition. But they did not call upon them 'to repent and believe the gospel.' They did not entreat them 'to be reconciled unto God.' They did not warn 'every man and teach every man in all wisdom.' The churches could not, and did not, under their instruction engage in efforts for the conversion of souls. They were so afraid of intruding on God's work that they neglected to do what he had commanded them. They seemed to have supposed that *preservation* was all they should aim at; they had not heart enough to seek for extension. No wonder that the cause declined."*

But Spurgeon bears a very different testimony concerning John Gill. He says: "The system of theology with which many identify his name has chilled many churches to their very soul, for it has led them to omit the free invitations of the gospel, and to deny that it is the duty of sinners to believe in Jesus: but for this Dr. Gill must not be altogether responsible, for a candid reader of his commentary will soon perceive in it expressions altogether out of accord with such a narrow system; and it is well known that when he was dealing with practical godliness he was so

* Cramp's Baptist History, p. 499.

bold in his utterances that the devotees of Hyper-Calvinism could not endure him. 'Well, Sir,' said one of these 'if I had not been told that it was the great Dr. Gill who preached, I should have said I had heard an Arminian.' " †

John Skepp was a self-taught man, and pastor of a Baptist church in London. He died in 1721. In 1730 he was followed in the pastorate by John Brine, who continued in that relation for thirty-five years. The church was in Paul's Alley, Cripplegate. Though, like his predecessor, he refused to address the invitation of the gospel to the unconverted, "because that would be interfering with God's work;" yet his last hours testify to his true piety. It was then that he ordered these, his dying sentiments to be put upon his tombstone in Bunhill Fields where they are to-day: " I think I am of sinners the chief, of saints the least: I know that I am nothing; but, by the grace of God, I am what I am."

John Gill, D. D. was the great contemporary and fellow-laborer of John Brine, and may be ranked as "the most learned man, in some respects, that has appeared in our denomination." He was born, November 23, 1697, at Kettering, Northamptonshire, where Andrew Fuller afterwards became pastor. Before he was 11 years old, he made rapid advance in Latin and Greek, at school. He was taken from school, however, on account of the bigotry of the teacher, who insisted upon the attendance of the scholars upon prayers at the parish church on week days. He then tried to get admission into a seminary for the ministry, but was refused because too young. But, brave and determined as he was, though young he spent part of his time with his father in his business—the woolen trade, and part in study. Even before this he resorted so frequently to the booksellers for the purpose of reading, that it became proverbial to say

† The Metropolitan Tabernacle, &c., page 47.

VASSAR COLLEGE, POUGHKEEPSIE, N. Y.   See page 376.

that a thing was as certain as that John Gill was in the bookseller's shop. John, however, was not to be laughed out of anything. He pursued his studies with such ardor, that, before he was nineteen, he had read the principal Greek and Latin classics ; had gone through a course of logic, rhetoric, natural and moral philosophy, and acquired a considerable knowledge of the Hebrew tongue. Religion was dearer to him, however, than learning. "His learning and his labors were exceeded only by the invariable sanctity of his life and conversation."

It was in 1716 that he joined the Baptist church of his native place, upon the profession of his faith in Christ, and by baptism. The church called him at once to the ministry, and, after studying with a minister, he in 1720, became pastor of the church near London, of which Mr. Keach had been pastor, and whose son-in-law, Mr. Benjamin Stinton, his successor, had just died. Here he was very successful in gathering a congregation, and in saving many souls.

He was only 23 years of age, but "he now applied himself with intense ardor to Oriental literature, and, having formed the acquaintance of a very learned Jewish Rabbi, he read the Targums, the Talmud, and every book of rabbinical lore which he could procure." "In this line he has none to excel him in the annals of literature. His great learning induced the Ministry of Aberdeen, unsolicited, to make him doctor of divinity. His commentary on the Bible in nine large folio volumes, which was originally given to his people in expository sermons from the pulpit, is a very valuable and learned work. At the close of this Herculean labor, he was not satisfied to rest, but wrote his 'Body of Divinity,' which contained his thoughts upon practical and doctrinal divinity. This he also first preached. He was the author of several other learned works." Great student as he was, he labored in his study to within two weeks of his death, which took place, Oct. 14, 1771, in the 73rd year of his age, and the 51st of his pastorate.

There are two of his valuable utterances which are especially worthy of mention as showing his good principle and piety. In 1730 he was to deliver one of nine lectures, delivered once a week, meant to correct certain infidel and erroneous sentiments then beginning to prevail. Dr. Taylor, one of the lecturers, spoke in severe terms of Calvinistic doctrines. Dr. Gill began a controversy with him, when some of Dr. Taylor's friends told Dr. Gill that he would lose the esteem and subscriptions of some wealthy persons if he did not desist. Dr. Gill replied ; " Don't tell me of losing; I value nothing in comparison with gospel truths. I am not afraid to be poor.' "

A short time before he died, he said ; " I depend wholly and alone upon the free, sovereign, eternal, unchangeable love of God, the firm and everlasting covenant of grace, and my interest in the Persons of the Trinity for my whole salvation, and not upon any righteousness of my own, nor on anything in me, nor done by me under the influence of the Holy Spirit. Not upon any services of mine, which I have assisted to perform for the good of the church, do I depend, but upon my interests in the Persons of the Trinity, the free grace of God, and the blessings of grace streaming to me through the blood and righteousness of Christ, as the ground of my hope. These are no new things to me, but what I have been long acquainted with,—*what I can live and die by.*"*

It is asserted, as we have seen, that during the more than fifty years that these good men swayed the Baptist denomina-

* Ivimey, III. p. 438.

tion, that there was a great decline, which all the influence of their learning and piety could not arrest; and that " it remained for other men to arouse the denomination from slumber, and to lead them to victory." " It was mainly," it is said, " by the influence and preaching of Whitefield, that the condition of affairs was changed, and that men were raised up to lead the churches in work for Christ." Of some of these men, to whom this honor is accorded, we propose to speak. Among them were the Halls—father and son.

Rev. Robert Hall, the father, is best known through his illustrious son—Rev. Robert Hall, A. M. The son was the most remarkable man of his age for learning, eloquence, and piety. He was one of those who, with his father, took part in reviving the slumbering missionary spirit among the Baptists of England. He was born May 2, 1764. His mother was distinguished for great common sense and piety. While an infant he was very delicate and feeble, and was not expected to reach maturity. He could neither walk nor talk till he was two years old. "His nurse taught him his alphabet from the gravestones in a burial ground." Afterwards he resorted, after school hours, to this same graveyard with his book, where for hours he reclined upon the grass. It is thought that he here contracted the dreadful disease and pain in the back from which he suffered so intensely during his whole life. None endured more than he of physical suffering, and "he was a fine example of the triumph of the higher powers of mind, exalted by religion, over the infirmities of the body."

He is said to have combined "the eloquence of an orator, the fancy of a poet, the acuteness of a schoolman, the profoundness of a philosopher, and the piety of a saint." Dugal Stewart says of him: "Whosoever wished to see the English language in its purity must read the writings of Robert Hall. He combines the beauties of Johnson, Addison, and Burke, without their imperfections." His intellect early developed its extraordinary vigor. When only nine years of age, he read and re-read with great interest Butler's Analogy, and Edwards on the Will, two books that are seldom found in the hands of one so young. At eleven, his teacher confessed that his pupil had gone beyond him; and his piety, even at this early age, was so manifest, that his delighted father thought of him for the sacred office of the ministry.

In 1778, he entered Bristol College to study theology, and in two years finished his course, and was ordained to the gospel ministry, at 16 years of age. At King's College, which he next entered, he formed his life-long acquaintance and friendship with Sir James Mackintosh, who said that he became "fascinated with his brilliancy and acumen, in love with his cordiality and ardor, and awe-struck by the transparency of his conduct and the purity of his principles. He became assistant pastor at Broadmead and tutor in Bristol Academy in 1785, and pastor at Cambridge in 1790. "His labors were not only greatly admired, but blessed to the revival of evangelical piety, and a large increase of the church and congregation." He became pastor at Leicester, in 1807. Wherever he went vast congregations attended upon his words, and of all classes of society and of mind.

He succeeded Dr. Ryland at Broadmead in 1826, and died with the flock, with which he spent the first year of his ministry, in 1831. His death was truly sublime and triumphant. He said : "I am in God's hands, and I rejoice that I am. I have not one anxious thought, either for life or death. I think I would rather go than stay ; for I have seen enough of the world and have an humble hope. My sufferings are great, but what are my sufferings to the sufferings of Christ. God has been very merciful to me. Come, Lord Jesus, come" —he could utter no more.   His daughter supplied the rest —"Quickly," and he gave her an assenting smile and died.

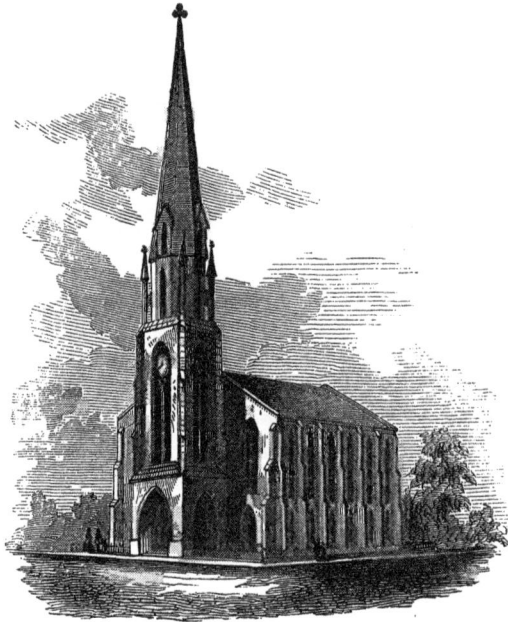

COLISEUM PLACE BAPTIST CHURCH, NEW ORLEANS, LA.

See page 266.

COLBY UNIVERSITY, WATERVILLE, MAINE.

See page 373.

CHAPTER XVIII

THE NEW WORLD.

E will now leave England, and crossing the Atlantic, follow the trail of Baptist history in the new world. Among those who left their homes in the old world and became the first settlers of America, there were Baptists. Others sprang up, as they have ever done, where Baptists were unknown before, led by the pure word of God and the teaching of the Holy Spirit to embrace the simple doctrines of the gospel. Thus it was that Roger Williams and a number of his friends became Baptists.

There is some uncertainty as to which was the first Baptist church established in America. There are two churches in the little state of Rhode Island each of which claims that honor, the first church of Providence and the first church of Newport. As near as can be ascertained the former was constituted in 1639, and the latter in 1644. Others however state that the Baptist church at Tiverton is the oldest, dating back to the year 1607. The first in Massachusetts was the little Welsh Baptist church at Swansea formed in 1663.

In the year 1602 a company of dissenters, persecuted by the Church of England, fled from their homes and sought refuge in Amsterdam, and afterward in Leyden. Having ob-

tained permission to emigrate to the new world they set
sail in the Mayflower from Plymonth, England, and after a
tedious and dangerous voyage, these Pilgrim Fathers landed,
December, 1620, at Plymouth, Massachusetts.

The Baptists were probably among the early settlers of
New England.   Cotton Mather, an early writer, calls them
" Godly Anabaptists," and says,—" Some few of these people have been among the planters of New England from the
beginning and have been welcome to the communion of our
churches which they enjoyed, reserving their particular
opinions unto themselves.

Dr. David Weston says : "Baptist principles are dis-
coverable in New England from the very earliest colonial
settlements.   The Puritans of Plymouth had mingled with
the Dutch Baptists during the ten years of their sojourn in
Holland, and some of them seem to have brought over
Baptist tendencies even in the Mayflower.   Dutch Baptists
had emigrated to England and extended their principles
there ; and from time to time a persecuted Baptist in
England sought refuge in America, and planted here
brought forth fruit after his kind.   But as every off-shoot of
these principles here, was so speedily and vigorously beaten
down by persecution, and especially as, after the banishment
of Roger Williams, there was an asylum a few miles distant,
just over Narraganset bay, where every persecuted man
could find liberty of conscience.   Baptist principles made
little progress in New England colonies, except in Rhode
Island for the first one hundred and twenty years."

It is strange that those who crossed the ocean to find
liberty of conscience for themselves, should deny it to others.
From the very first all dissent or heresy was forbidden.   It
was unlawful and punishable as a crime to neglect or oppose

the existing, or standing church ; or to set up worship in
opposition to it; to refuse to be taxed for the support of its
ministry ; to oppose its faith ; or, to build houses of worship
for dissenting churches. Especially were Baptists the
objects of persecution because they opposed infant baptism,
an unregenerate church membership, and the union of
church and state. Fines imprisonment and banishment
were the penalties imposed there for holding Baptist sentiments.

A law was passed by the General Court, November 13,
1644 banishing those who "refused to countenance infant
baptism and the use of secular force in religious things."* "A
like method of treating the Baptists in courts, from pulpits
and from the press has been handed down by tradition ever
since," writes Isaac Backus in 1777.† Nevertheless Winthrop says, "Anabaptists increased and spread."‡ Many
such laws were passed and much suffering was endured by
the Baptists under them.

Roger Williams was driven from the colony of Massachusetts because of his Baptist principles, and became the
founder of the state of Rhode Island. He was born in 1599,
in Wales. The Baptists of America are indebted to Welsh-
men for laying the foundation of their denomination, to a
large extent, in North and South Carolina, New York, and
Virginia, and they were the first to found a Baptist church
in Rhode Island, New Jersey, Pennsylvania, Massachusetts,
and Delaware ; and Wales has continued to this day to furnish new material for our churches, while some of our
ablest and most prominent ministers are from that country.

In early life Mr. Williams enjoyed the patronage of Sir
Edward Coke, the celebrated English lawyer. Educated at

*Backus History of the Baptists, Newton, I. 127.
† Vol. I. page 127.
‡ Backus I. page 126.

Oxford, he became a minister of the Church of England, preferring the ministry to the law. He left England because he could not conscientiously conform to some parts of the doctrine and worship of the established church. He came to America about the year 1630, and was soon afterward called to preach at Salem where he became assistant pastor. While in Boston he had refused communion with the church there, and had declined to take the oath of a free-man. These facts awakened opposition and he was obliged to leave Salem. He went to Plymouth, where he was pastor for two years, when he was re-called to Salem. But ere long, he was accused of preaching against the assumption of power in religious affairs by the civil magistrate, and besides, was charged with holding other views tending to anabaptism. He was tried by the court and sentenced to be banished. By order of the court he was to depart out of the colony within six days, because he had " broached and divulged divers new and dangerous opinions against the authority of the magistrates, as also, writ letters of defamation, both of the magistrates and churches here."

Mr. Williams did not go as he was ordered, so the Boston authorities sent for him. When he sent an excuse, an officer was ordered to arrest him and put him on board of a ship bound for England. But when the officer reached Salem, Mr. Williams had left the place three days before, and had gone, no one knew where. He had fled from the cruelties of his Christian brethren, to find refuge and hospitality among the savages of the forest. It was in the midst of a New England winter, January, 1635, when this apostle of liberty left his home and plunged into the depths of the gloomy forest. For fourteen weeks he wandered " in winter snow," which, says he, "I feel yet; * * not knowing what bread or bed did mean." He went first to Rehoboth,

fifty miles south of Salem.   Here he was joined by his family
and some friends.   His sufferings during those fourteen
weeks of exile in the wilds of the forest, had been very great.
But he had not yet found a resting place.   The authorities
advised him to cross the river and go beyond the bounds of
the colony.   So, leaving the huts which they had built, he
and his little company embarked in a little boat and started
on a voyage of discovery, to seek a new home and a place
where they might plant the standard of soul-liberty.   On
their way they were hailed by a company of Indians on the
shore, with the friendly interrogation, "What cheer?" a common English phrase, which the Indians had learned from the
colonists.   Tradition reports that Roger Williams landed
near a spring which is pointed out at this day.   Here the
settlement of Rhode Island began.

> "Oh, call it holy ground.
> "The soil where first they trod!
> "They have left unstained what there they found—
> "Freedom to worship God"

In grateful acknowledgment of the divine hand that had
guided and preserved him, Mr. Williams gave to the new settlement the name of Providence.   The government which
he established was based upon the principle of perfect
religious liberty.   It required obedience to the civil magistrate
only in civil things.   A man's religion was held to be a matter for which he is responsible only to God, and with which
civil governments have no right to interfere.   All such
interference is an infringement of the most sacred rights of
men.   Freedom in matters of religion is not simply a privilege,
but a right belonging to all men alike, whatever their forms
of religion may be, whether Christian, Mahometan, Jew or
Pagan.   These were the views held by Mr. Williams, and
incorporated into the government of Rhode Island.   Hence
the religious freedom which he established was not toleration,
but liberty in its largest, fullest, freest sense.

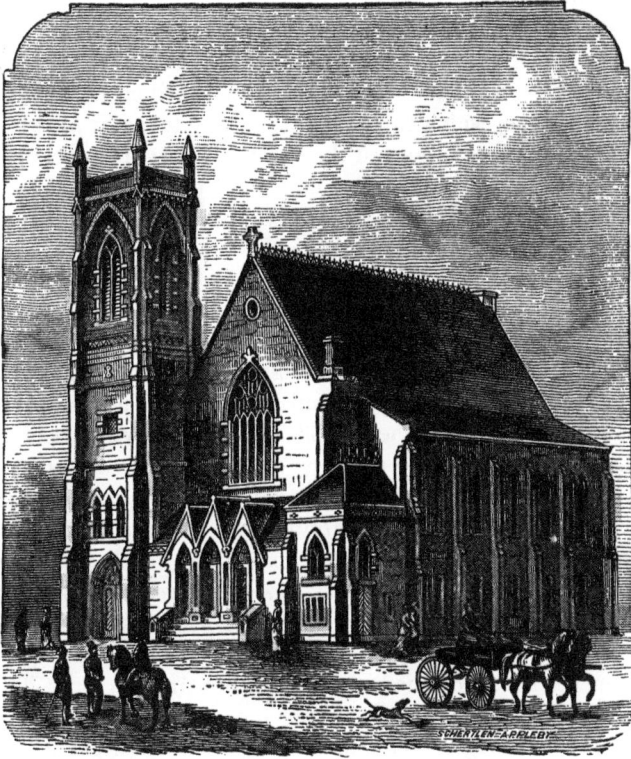

FIRST BAPTIST CHURCH, BALTIMORE, MD.

See page 258.

The religious freedom of Rhode Island, differs as widely from the liberty allowed in Maryland by Lord Baltimore, as right differs from privilege. The one was freedom, the other was toleration. Rhode Island gave to all men freedom of worship as a right, with which the state has no business to interfere. Maryland gave her citizens freedom of worship as a privilege, which the state had a right to grant or withhold, and actually reserved the right to interfere in certain cases, as for instance, if a man denied the doctrine of the Trinity, or spoke against the Virgin Mary he was subject to the penalty of the law.

Dr. David Weston says; "When colonists settled America, they brought with them across the Atlantic, the system of legislation for consciences. Massachusetts and Connecticut fined, imprisoned, whipped, banished or even put to death those who opposed the established orthodoxy. Catholic Maryland, fined, whipped or banished all who uttered reproachful words against the Virgin Mary and put to death a denier of the Trinity. Virginia had her nine pound tobacco tax for the support of Episcopacy. When Roger Williams, banished from Massachusetts because he was a Baptist, founded a settlement in Rhode Island, then for the first time in the history of the world, there was a civil government which claimed no jurisdiction in religion. The great principle of religious freedom was first practically applied by Roger Williams." Bancroft, in speaking of Roger Williams, says; " He was the first person in modern Christendom to assert the doctrine of liberty of conscience in religion. When Germany was the battle-field for all Europe, of implacable wars of religion, it became his glory to found a State and to stamp himself upon its rising institutions, in characters so deep, that their impress has remained to the present day and can never be erased without the total destruction of his work."

Although Mr. Williams had embraced Baptist sentiments pretty fully before his banishment, yet he was not baptized until after his settlement in Rhode Island. Along with him there were twelve persons who became Baptists, with no guide but the New Testament. They knew of no Baptist minister whose services they could procure, and hence they selected one of their number, Ezekiel Holliman, to baptize Mr Williams who then administered the ordinance to the others.

It was strange and somewhat irregular, but, no doubt, justifiable under the circumstances. And yet no one would think it right to resort to such an expedient, when the ordinance could be received from an ordained minister who had himself been baptized. These twelve persons formed themselves, in March 1639, into a church with Roger Williams as their pastor. This was the First Baptist church of Providence and the first in America. Mr. Williams afterwards left the society, but the church then organized continues to this day.

Roger Williams once saved the colonies from being destroyed by the Indians. Mr. Backus says: "As God overruled the cruel selling of Joseph to the heathen, as a means of saving the lives of many people ; so the banishing of Roger Williams made him the chief instrument of saving all the English in New England from destruction." He had gained, by his kindness and wisdom, the friendship of the Indians and when a plot was formed among several tribes for the destruction of the colonies, Mr. Williams discovered it and gave the warning to the English, and at the same time used his influence with the Indians to turn them from their purpose. It is said that on one occasion he went out with his staff in hand, to meet the Indians in order to plead with them.

"Brother Williams," said an Indian chief to him; "you are a good man, and you have been kind to us many years. Not a hair of your head shall be touched."

The colony of Massachusetts continued to persecute the Baptists with greater severity, and large numbers suffered from fines, imprisonment, whipping or banishment. One of the most remarkable cases was that of Obadiah Holmes, who went with two other Baptists from Rhode Island to visit, in 1651, an aged brother at Lynn, who had been whipped for being a Baptist. While holding religious services at this brother's house on the Sabbath, they were arrested and fined and imprisoned. The others were in a short time released, but Mr. Holmes was retained to be more severely punished as a public example. He was sentenced to be whipped in Boston in September 1651, and so barbarously was the sentence executed that for days and weeks he "could take no rest but as he lay upon his knees and elbows, not being able to suffer any part of his body to touch the bed whereon he lay." The sentence pronounced upon him, contains these words ;—"You did take upon you to preach and baptize; that you did baptize such as were baptized before, and thereby did necessarily deny the baptism before administered to be baptism; and did also deny the lawfulness of baptizing infants."

As he was led to the place of punishment he said to the crowds of people who were assembled to witness the scene; "That which I am to suffer for, is the word of God and the testimony of Jesus Christ." In his own account of the affair, he says; "As the man began to lay the strokes upon my

SOUTH JERSEY INSTITUTE, BRIDGETON, N. J.

See page 377.

back, I said to the people, 'Though my flesh should fail, and
my spirit should fail, yet God would not fail.' So it pleased
the Lord to come in and to fill my heart and tongue as a vessel
full, and with audible voice I spoke forth, praying the Lord
not to lay this sin to their charge ; and telling the people that
now I found he did not fail me and therefore, now I should
trust him forever, who failed me not. For in truth, as the
strokes fell upon me, I had such a spiritual manifestation of
God's presence, as I never had before, and the outward pain
was so removed from me that I could well bear it, yea, and
in a manner, felt it not, although it was grievous, as the
spectators said, the man striking with all his strength, spitting upon his hand three times, with a three-corded whip,
giving me there with thirty strokes. When he had loosed me
from the post, having joyousness in my countenance as the
spectators observed, I told the magistrates ; you have struck
me with roses, and said, moreover, although the Lord hath
made it easy to me, yet I pray God it may not be laid to your
charge.''

Many were touched with sympathy for the noble sufferer,
and the Baptist cause was greatly strengthened by the very
means that were used to crush it. As Mr. Holmes says ;
'' My bonds and imprisonment have been no hindrance to
the gospel ; for before my return some submitted to the Lord
and were baptized, and divers were put upon the way of inquiry.''

Mr. Holmes was again about to be arrested when, making
his escape by night he returned to his home in Rhode Island.
The next day after his departure, a constable came to search
the house where he had lodged. Thus, probably, he was saved
the pain, and Boston the disgrace, of a second whipping.

One of the most shameful cases of persecution for conscience' sake was that of Henry Dunster, patron and presi-

dent of Harvard University and one of the greatest masters of the Oriental languages. Quincy says: "Dunster's usefulness, however, was deemed to be at an end and his service no longer desirable in consequence of his falling, in 1653, as Cotton Mather expressed it, 'into the briers of anti-pedobaptism', and of his having borne 'public testimony in the church at Cambridge against the administration of baptism to any infant whatsoever.' * * Indicted by the grand jury for disturbing the ordinance of infant baptism in the Cambridge church, sentenced to a public admonition and laid under bands for good behavior, Dunster's martyrdom was consummated, being compelled, in October, 1664, to resign his office of president. * * He found the seminary a school, it rose under his auspices to a college. No man ever questioned his talents, learning, exemplary fidelity and useful ness.''

The evil fruits of the union of state and church, and of infant baptism soon began to appear in New England. Inasmuch as church membership was a condition of citizenship, unconverted men soon filled the churches. As early as 1657, conversion ceased to be demanded as a pre-requisite to church membership. An effort was made to shield the table of the Lord, by the adoption of the Half Way Covenant, which admitted those who had been baptized and whose lives were not scandalous to all the privileges of church membership, except coming to the Lord's Supper. But there were those who could not see why those baptized in infancy should be kept from the Lord's table, since they were recognized as members af the church. In 1696, a church was formed in Hartford, and in 1699, another in Boston, "upon the express principle that baptism, alone, without evidence of conversion

† History of Harvard; Vol. 1 p. 15-18, as quoted by Dr. Weston in Backus, 1. p. 22.

should admit to full communion.'' Other churches followed and soon few were left to advocate a regenerate membership, except the Baptists. Hence the pulpits, recruited from the pews, came to be filled with unconverted ministers, and "the New England churches presented the sad anomaly of a company of *dead* men, listening to a *dead* gospel, preached by a *dead* minister."

There were some few exceptions to the rule. The illustrious Jonathan Edwards was one who contended for a change of heart in pulpit and in pew. For this, however, his church at Northampton by the advice of an ecclesiastical council, dismissed him from the pastorate. Owing to the seeming hopeless degeneracy of the times many withdrew and formed churches called Separate churches. Such a condition of things could not continue long. God poured out his Spirit and a great revival spread throughout the country under the preaching of Jonathan Edwards and George Whitefield, and many ministers and people were converted. More "New-Light" or "Separate" churches were formed, composed of those who professed a change of heart, and with these union churches many holding Baptist sentiments united. It was not, long however, before these found out that a Pedobaptist church was no home for Baptists, and they withdrew and formed Baptist churches. This movement "began about the year 1750, and by 1760 was rapidly working. For the next twenty years, an average of two Baptist churches a year was formed, largely by this process, in Massachusetts alone." But what became of the churches that had departed from the faith?

The following statement is made by Dr. Weston: "Infant baptism among Congregationalists, with its Half-Way Covenant, paved the way for Unitarianism of to-day. 'The

Congregational churches of Massachusetts', says Uhden, 'awoke from their stupor, and lo ! Harvard College and their strongholds had become Unitarian.' But one church in Boston remained Orthodox, and its pastor was a Semi-Arian, and its evangelical element was too small to sustain a prayer-meeting. Some of its members were quickened at a Baptist revival ; they set up again their neglected prayer-meeting, and invited Baptists to come in and aid them, and they came. Thus 'a renovating movement commenced, that has been the origin of all the Orthodox Congregational churches with which the city of the Pilgrims is now blessed. When infant baptism had put out the fires on its own altars with the exception of one solitary shrine, and had caused it even to burn dim and low, the flame was kindled again from altars which its unscriptural rite had never been suffered to profane.' "

Baptist principles have preserved the churches of this country, from the lifeless formalism which prevails generally wherever infant baptism has been allowed to work out its legitimate results, without the restraint of Baptist teaching and example. The difference between the Baptist and Pedobaptist practice in this matter is clearly stated by the learned and pious Pascal, who says ; " In the infancy of the Christian church, we see no Christians but those who were thoroughly instructed in all matters necessary to salvation. Then, no one was admitted into the church but after a most rigid examination ; now, every one is admitted before he is capable of being examined. Formerly, it was necessary *to come out from the world, in order to be received into the church;* whilst in these days, we enter the church almost at the same time that we enter the world. The distinction is almost entirely lost ; the church of the saints is all defiled with the intermingling of the wicked, and her children are they who carry into her very heart, her deadliest foes."

Speaking of the great awakening, Dr. D. Weston says :

o

RICHARD FURMAN, D. D.

See page 255.

"Trace back the record of church history to the early
centuries, and it will be invariably found that every time of
quickening and reformation, has produced Baptists. Brought
out of dead formality and actuated by living piety, men
have naturally cast off the mere form of infant baptism, and
have substituted for it the original rite of believer's baptism,
by which the regenerate and loving heart expresses its
loyalty to Christ. The Donatists, reformers of the fourth
century, when infant baptism was a recent innovation not
yet universally accepted, were Baptists. The Albigenses,
reformers of the seventh century, so far as history enables us
to decide, were Baptists; and so were the Waldenses and
Petrobrussians, reformers of the eleventh and twelfth
centuries, who kept the light of pure Christianity burning
when everywhere else in the world it was quenched in the
slough of Romish corruption. The Arnoldists and Hussites,
reformers before Luther, and who prepared the way for him,
were Baptists. Wickliffe of England whom historians have
agreed to call 'the morning star of the Reformation,' was
a Baptist. The views of these reformers were not always
definitely stated, or perhaps definitely settled in their own
minds; but they all held substantially the doctrines which
are now the peculiar tenets of Baptists. The Great Reformation of the sixteenth century could never have occured if
it had not been heralded by Baptists. It was the same in
the Great Awakening."*

* Baptists and the National Centenary, p. 13.

CHAPTER XIX.

THE VIRGINIA BAPTISTS.

HE Baptists of the Old Dominion deserve special mention. During the first century of the colony, which was settled in 1607, the Baptists are not mentioned by name, but Morgan Edwards speaks of Baptists in North Carolina as early as 1695, who had gone there from Virginia to escape intolerant laws. Prof. J. C. Long, D. D., LL. D., of Crozer Theological Seminary, an eminent authority, says, that it is almost certain that there were no Baptist organizations in Virginia, as early as 1695 ; though there may have been individual Baptists ; and that the laws were so stringently enforced in reference to conventicles, that had there been Baptist churches, we would have heard something about them.

Virginia was settled by cavaliers from England, who were loyalists devoted to their king ; and churchmen wedded to the Episcopal Church. By their charter the Episcopal was the established religion of the colony. Departure from the church was treason against the state. Hence a struggle for liberty, civil and religious, was to be expected.

In 1611, Governor Dale ordered every man to come to the minister to be questioned as to his religious belief. The penalty for the first refusal was whipping ; for the second, a double flogging, and a confession of the the fault on Sabbath day before the congregation ; and for the third offense, whipping daily until pardon was asked and the law complied with.

As early as 1643, a law was enacted, " to preserve purity of doctrine," forbidding any one to teach, or preach publicly or privately, who was not a minister of the Episcopal Church, and did not conform to its mode of worship. It was first banishment, and in 1661, imprisonment for nonconformity.

In 1673, a house of worship was commanded to be erected on every plantation, and the service to be Episcopal. Every body was required to attend church, or be heavily fined, and no one could sell his tobacco till his tax for the support of the Episcopal minister was paid.

Geo. B. Taylor, D. D., says ; "Such laws prevailed from the settlement of Virginia, 1607, to the Revolution, 1775, except during the Protectorate. For this entire period, as Hening says ; 'The religion of the Church was the religion of the ruling party in the State, and none other was tolerated.' These laws were vigorously enforced."*

Dr. Taylor also says : " Specially the severe laws against those refusing to practice infant baptism, prove the existence of some who rejected that rite. The Quakers have been referred to ; but they were never numerous in Virginia. The preamble to one of the acts, punishing those rejecting infant baptism, declared there were *many*, not merely *neglecting* (as careless persons might have done,) but *refusing* to have their children baptized. Moreover, such persons are further described as acting out of their averseness to the established religion, etc."†

* †Virginia Baptists.

J. B. JETER, D. D. See page 380.

Rev. R. B. Semple says that there were three sources from which the Baptists of Virginia came; from England, Maryland, and New England. "The first were emigrants from England, who about the year 1714, settled in the southeast parts of the state," and formed, at that time, the first church organized in the state at Burleigh, Isle of Wight county.†
The church still exists under the name of Mill Swamp. They were Arminian in doctrine, but finally became Regular Baptists. They appealed for a minister to their brethren in England, who ordained and sent them Robert Nordin, who remained their pastor till his death in 1725. Dr. J. C. Long remarks, that the inference to be drawn from the action of the Burleigh church in sending to England for a pastor is, that there were no ordained Baptist ministers in Virginia, or even in North Carolina at that time.

The Kehukee Association was formed in 1765, and the Portsmouth in May, 1791. The second company of Baptists of whom Semple speaks came into Virginia from Maryland, and from them arose what were then known as the Regular Baptists, .in contradistinction to the Separates. These were not so numerous as the Separates, but were a large and respectable body of people. Edward Hays and Thomas Yates, members of Sater's Baptist church in Maryland, came with a company and settled in Berkley county in 1743. They were soon followed by their minister Henry Loveall who preached to the people and baptized fifteen persons. The church was re-organized in 1751, by some ministers of the Philadelphia Association, with which body the church then united. Samuel Heton and John Garrard were successively pastors of the church.

While their brethren in other parts of the state were contending with hostile whites, they were defending themselves against savages. The country was then thinly inhabited

† History Virginia Baptists, p. 344.

and subject to the inroads of Indians, nevertheless the church grew in zeal and numbers. The Ketocton church was formed probably, in 1756, and the association known by that name in 1766. About 1760 Rev. David Thomas, a " learned" Baptist minister, came from Pennsylvaina first to Berkley, and then to Fauquier county, and formed and became pastor of the Broad Run church. Among those whom he baptized were Daniel and William Fristoe, and Jeremiah Moore, so well known as able preachers of the word. Lewis Lunsford, "who in point of talents as a preacher, was never excelled," was born in Stafford county of indigent parents, and baptized by William Fristoe. Lunsford carried the standard of the cross far and wide, and planted it below Fredricksburg in the counties of the Northern Neck.

The most important company from which the Baptists of Virginia arose was, according to Semple, the " third party" and came from New England. They were called the "New Lights," and were under Shubael Stearns, their pastor. They first came to Opekon, Berkeley county, in 1754, where there was already a Baptist church with John Garrard as pastor. Here Stearns met his brother-in-law, Daniel Marshall, a missionary to the Indians, who had just become a Baptist. They joined companies and went to Hampshire county, where hearing that the people of North Carolina were thirsting for the preaching of the gospel, to hear which some had been known to ride forty miles ; they went a journey of two hundred miles to Sandy Creek, Guilford county, North Carolina, and there, November 22, 1755, constituted a church with sixteen members, of which Stearns became pastor.

" Thus organized," says Semple, " they began their work, kindling a fire which soon began to burn brightly indeed, spreading in a few years over Virginia, North and South Carolina and Georgia."* "Into parts of Virginia, adjacent to the residence of this religious colony, the gospel had been quickly carried by Mr. Marshall. He had baptised several in some of his first visits. Among them was Dutton Lane, who shortly after his baptism, began to preach. A revival succeeded, and Mr. Marshall at one time baptized forty-two persons. In August, 1760, a church was constituted under the pastoral care of the Rev. Dutton Lane. This was the first Separate Baptist church in Virginia, and thus, in some sense, the mother of all the rest. This church prospered under the ministry of Mr. Lane, aided by the occasional visits of Mr. Marshall and Mr. Stearns. They endured much persecution, but God prospered them, and delivered them out of the hands of all their enemies."†

"In 1770," says Dr. J. C. Long, "there were but six Separate Baptist churches in all Virginia. In 1774, there were fifty-four, so mightily grew the word of God."‡

The Separates or New Lights, and the Regular Baptists became, finally, one body, and were henceforth known in history as the Baptists of Virginia.

Speaking of their common sufferings for conscience' sake Dr. George B. Taylor, says: "Time would fail to tell of the persecutions they suffered legally, and under color of law, and at the hands of ruffians instigated, in some cases, by the gentry and parson. Dr. Hawks, the Episcopal historian, says: 'Cruelty taxed its ingenuity to devise new modes, of punishment and annoyance.' Our ministers were fined, pelted, beaten, imprisoned, poisoned and hunted with dogs; their congregations were assaulted and dispersed; the solemn ordinance of baptism was rudely interrupted, both adminis-

---

* History Virginia Baptists, p. 3.
† Semple's History, p. 5.
‡ Address in MS.

trators and candidates being plunged and held beneath the
water till nearly dead ; they suffered mock trials, and even
in courts of justice were subjected to indignities not unlike
those inflicted by the infamous Jefferys ; nor were these cases
few and confined to restricted localities, as some have seemed
to think.   *   *   *   But these things could not prevent the
progress of the truth.   Those men of God were full of
courage, and zeal, and love for the truth and for Jesus, and
pity for perishing souls ; and they went everywhere preaching the word, rejoicing that they were counted worthy to
suffer for the name of Jesus, and gladly encountering, in the
glades and mountains of what is now West Virginia, fatigue,
cold and hunger."*

Among the noble sufferers, was Samuel Harriss, styled
" the apostle of Virginia "; and born in that state in 1724.
He was a member of the legislature, colonel of militia,
captain of Mayo Fort, commissary for the fort and army,
judge of the court, sheriff, and church warden.† He was a
remarkable man, and became serious and melancholy without
knowing why.   By reading and conversation, he discovered
that he was a hopeless sinner, and that a sense of his guilt
was the cause of his gloom of mind.   He ventured to attend
Baptist preaching," and obtained relief by faith in the
Saviour.   Semple thus graphically describes his conversion:
" On one of his routes to visit the forts in his official character, he called at a small house, where he understood there
was to be Baptist preaching.   The preachers were Joseph
and William Murphy.   * *   Being rigged in his military
dress he was not willing to appear in a conspicuous place.
He seated himself behind a loom.   God, nevertheless, found
him out by his Spirit.   His convictions now sunk so deep,

* Virginia Baptists.
† Semple's History, page 377.

that he could no longer conceal them. He left his sword and other parts of his rigging, some in one place, and some in another. The arrows of the Almighty stuck fast in him, nor could he shake them off, until some time after. At a meeting when the congregation rose from prayer, Colonel Harris was observed still on his knees, with his head and hands hanging over the bench. Some of the people went to his relief; and found him senseless. When he came to himself, he smiled, and in all ecstacy of joy, exclaimed, 'Glory! Glory! Glory!' " Daniel Marshall baptized him in 1758. From that time his life was one act of devotedness and zeal. Practising rigid economy in his house, he employed his whole surplus income in advancing the cause of religion. At the time of his conversion, he was engaged in erecting a large mansion for the accommodation of his family, in a style suited to his rank and station ; it was turned into a meeting-house, and he continued to reside in the old building. * * * He began at once, like Paul, to preach. " There was scarcely any place in Virginia, where he did not sow the gospel seed. * * His excellency lay chiefly in his addressing the heart, and perhaps even Whitefield did not surpass him in this. When animated, himself, he seldom failed to animate his auditory. Some have described him as pouring forth streams of celestial light, shining from his eyes, which whithersoever he turned his face would strike down hundreds at once. He was often called ' Boanerges'."* He died in 1794. "Shubael Stearns, Daniel Marshall, and Samuel Harriss were the principal founders of the Baptist interests in the South. They were the first three, and their names should be held in everlasting remembrance".†

Col. Harris' standing did not save him from persecution.

* History Virginia Baptists, page 317.
† Cramp's History of the Baptists.

HOLLINS INSTITUTE, BOTETOURT SPRINGS, VA.

See page 377.

Once he was arrested and carried into court, as a disturber of the peace. A Captain Williams, vehemently accused him as a vagabond, a heretic, and a mover of sedition everywhere. The court ordered that he should not preach in the country again for the space of twelve months; or be committed to prison. He told them that he lived two hundred miles away, and was not likely to disturb them again for a year, and was dismissed. On his way home, having gone farther, he came again into Culpepper, where this happened, and attended a meeting. He presently rose and said; " I partly promised the devil, a few days past, at the court-house, that I would not preach in this country again in the term of a year. But the devil is a perfidious wretch, and covenants with him are not to be kept; and therefore I will preach. He preached and was not molested. On another occasion, he was pulled down, while preaching, and dragged about sometimes by the hair of the head, and sometimes by the legs. At another time he was knocked down by a brutal fellow, while preaching. Having gone once to Hillsborough to preach to prisoners, he was locked in himself and kept for some time.†

John Waller was born in Virginia in 1714. He was of an honorable family, "manifested a great talent for satirical wit," and was educated for the law, but gave way to his unbridled inclinations to vice, and became a gambler. His wickedness and profanity, obtained for him "the infamous appellation of "Swearing Jack Waller." It was frequently remarked, that there could be no deviltry among the people, unless he was at the head of it. Once he had three warrants served on him, at one time. Sometimes he was called the devil's adjutant to muster his troops. To these failings may be added his fury against Baptists. He was one of the grand

† Semple's History Virginia Baptists, p 382.

jury that presented Louis Craig for preaching. Craig addressed the jury thus; "I thank you gentlemen of the grand jury, for the honor you have done me. While I was wicked and injurious you took no notice of me, but since I have altered my course of life and endeavor to reform my neighbors, you concern yourselves much about me." * When Mr. Waller heard him speak in this manner, and observed the meekness of his spirit, he was convinced that Craig was possessed of something he had never seen in man before. He thought within himself, that he would be happy if he could be of the same religion as Mr. Craig. From that time he began to attend their meetings, and feeling himself to be a sinner, to call upon the name of the Lord. His convictions were so deep and pungent that he abstained for several months from all but necessary food, and was almost driven to despair. But on his knees in prayer he, at last, found peace. He was baptized in 1767, began to preach at once, and was greatly blessed in his ministry. His death in 1802 was truly glorious, and while his pains appeared to be excruciating, yet no murmur was heard from his lips.

June 4, 1768, Waller, Louis Craig, and James Childs, were seized by the sheriff and brought before three magistrates, who stood in the meeting-house yard, and bound over to appear before court. To the court the prosecuting attorney said :—"May it please your courtships, these men are great disturbers of the peace, they can not meet a man upon the road, but they must ram a passage of Scripture down his throat."† The authorities offered to release them upon condition that they would not preach. This they refused and were sent to jail. As they went through the street of Fredricksburg to prison they sang :—

" Broad is the road that leads to death," etc.

*Semple's History Virginia Baptists, p. 404.
4Semple p. 15.

Hon. John Blair, deputy-governor, became interested in their case and wrote of them to the attorney :—"Their petition was a matter of right, you may not molest these conscientious people, so long as they have themselves as becometh pious Christians. * * I am told they administer the sacrament of the Lord's Supper near the manner we do, and differ in nothing from our churches, but in that of Baptism, and their renewing the ancient discipline, by which they have reformed some sinners and brought them to be truly penitent. Nay, if a man of them is idle and neglects to labor and provide for his family as he ought, he incurs their censures, which have had good effect. If this be their behavior, it were to be wished we had some of it among us.."*

The attorney paid no attention to the letter. They remained in jail forty-three days, and preached through the grated windows ; the mob without trying in vain to keep the people from hearing.

William Webber and John Waller were once on a preaching tour, when a magistrate drew back his club to knock Webber down as he was preaching, but some one behind caught the club, and saved him. But as two sheriffs, the parson and a posse were at hand to aid him, he arrested Webber, Waller, James Greenwood and Robert Ware, and cast them into prison, because they refused to cease preaching. " The prison swarmed with fleas. They borrowed a candle of the jailer, and, having sung the praises of that Redeemer whose cross they bore, and from whose hands they expected a crown in the end ; having returned thanks that it was a prison, and not hell, that they were in ; praying for

* Semple, p. 15.

themselves, their friends, their enemies, and their persecuters, they laid down to sleep."* Next Sunday they preached to their friends who came to them in the prison and announced preaching for every Wednesday and Sunday. While preaching, their enemies often beat drums that they might not be heard. "It was not until after thirty days' close confinement and sixteen days in bonds, that they were set at liberty."

Sometimes the leading men of the state church would attend Baptist meetings to argue, with the preachers, as men of a a baser sort used force, and would call them false prophets in sheep's clothing. " Waller and the other preachers boldly and readily replied, that if they were wolves in sheep's clothing and their opponents were the true sheep, it was quite unaccountable that they were persecuted and cast into prison : it was well known that wolves would destroy sheep, but never till then that sheep would prey upon wolves."†

The Baptist General Association of Virginia, after existing in other forms and under other names from 1771, was organized as at present, June 9, 1823. At its grand jubilee meeting held in Richmond, May, 1873, Dr. J. L. M. Curry, during his masterly speech, showed a spoon used by Waller, while a prisoner for conscience' sake, and a brick from the foundation of the old jail at Urbana, Middlesex County, in which were imprisoned several Baptist preachers. He asked that the brick might go into the foundation of the monument to be erected to the memory of these noble sufferers for Christ. He also held up the lock and key of the old Culpeper jail, where James Ireland, Elijah Craig, John Corbeley and Thomas Ammon, preachers, and Adam Banks and

* Semple's History, p. 15.
† Semple, p. 21.

Thomas Maxfield, laymen, and John Delaney, were imprisoned. The latter, though not a member of the church, was arrested for allowing a prayer meeting to be held in his house, and the others for conducting it.

The Baptist church at Culpepper now stands on the site of the old jail. Preaching began there long before the meeting-house was erected. James Ireland, a godly and eminent man while in prison, though greatly enfeebled by cruelties, preached through the grated windows, to the people, who had gathered outside to hear him. This noble man dated his letters while in prison: "From my palace in Culpepper." This reminds us of these lines:

" And prisons would palaces prove,
"If Jesus would dwell with me there."

He had much to endure during his confinement. Several attempts were made to murder him. They first put powder under the floor of his room to blow him up, then tried to suffocate him by filling his cell with the fumes of burning brimstone, and finally with the aid of a physician poisoned him ; but his life was spared.

Persecution made Baptists shun publicity. "Still," says Dr. David Weston, " though overborne and suppressed for a hundred years, Baptist principles were secure in their own immortality, and were, even in Virginia, silently, unobtrusively, but effectively laying a foundation for subsequent glorious triumphs."* When release from persecution finally came, then, as Dr. Howell beautifully says ; " Church after church noiselessly arose like the shining out of the stars of evening, and sparkled like gems in the American firmament, which they were destined ere long to fill with radiance and beauty."

* Baptists and the National Centenary.

P

And now there are 215,604 Baptists in the State. Only two other States, Georgia and North Carolina, can boast a larger number. In Richmond, where the First ehurch was formed in 1780, the Baptists out-number all other denominations combined.

2d BAPT. CH., ATLANTA, GA.

See page 262.

CHAPTER XX.

THE NORTH AND INDEPENDENCE.

HE Baptists have ever been ardent lovers of liberty, civil and religous. This characteristic has ever brought upon them persecution from tyrants and bigots. The Baptists of America were true to their principles, and the beginning of the conflict between England and her colonies, for independence, found the Baptists on the side of their oppressed countrymen, and there they stood until America was free. They are said to have been among ardent advocates of, and leaders in, the American Revolution. This is true of the Baptists North as well as South, where they sowed the seed of freedom that was to produce such wonderful results in all the land.

Rev. Isaac Backus, says of their attitude during the Revolution : " No denomination in America have acted with more prudence and vigor than the Baptists. In the fall of 1778, our Legislature [Mass.] passed an act to debar inimical persons [Royalists] from returning into this State, wherein three hundred and eleven men were named as such ; and our enemies are welcome to point out one Baptist among them if they can."* It was principle that arrayed the Baptists on

* Backus' History of the Baptists, Newton, II. 247.

the side of the colonists, for England had, more than once, shielded them from their persecuting neighbors. This is said in general of Massachusetts, but there are not wanting, noble instances of patriotic devotion throughout the northern states.

"The leaders, as well as the mass of Baptists, were engaged in the war on the side of the colonists. Their ministers went into the army, some as chaplains, others as officers, and others still as privates, and inspired greatly by their patriotism their fellow soldiers. Among these may be mentioned Rev. Charles Thompson and Rev. Hezekiah Smith, D. D., of Massachusetts; Rev. Dr. Rogers of Philadelphia and Rev. David Jones of New Jersey. The descendants of the latter are now distinguished Baptists of Philadelphia. [The Hon. H. G. Jones, D. C. L., is a grandson.] He was a bold and invaluable man, and was as often in the front of the battle as among the wounded in the hospital. Others entered the army west and south. Rev. John Gano, first pastor of the First Baptist Church, New York City, was granted leave of absence to enter the army as a chaplain. * * * Washington says: 'Baptist chaplains were among the most prominent and useful in tne army.' and Howe: 'The Baptists were among the most strenuous supporters of liberty.' "*

Dr. Cathcart gives interesting sketches of two well known Baptist laymen of Revolutionary times, Colonel Joab Houghton and John Brown, which we reproduce. "Colonel Houghton was one of the first to advocate the calling of the New Jersey Provincial Congress that overthrew English rule there. One Sunday morning while he was worshiping in the Baptist meeting-house at Hopewell, New Jersey, of

---

* Wm Cathcart, D. D., in Centennial Offering.

which he was a member, a messenger, all breathless, came
in and whispered something in his ear. The information
was respecting the battles of Concord and Lexington. Dr.
S. H. Cone, grandson of Colonel Houghton, thus describes
the scene :[*]

"Stilling the breathless messenger, he sat quietly
through the services, and when they were ended, he passed
out, and mounting the great stone block in front of the
meeting-house, he beckoned to the people to stop, men and
women paused to hear, curious to know what so unusual a
sequel to the service of the day could mean. At the first
words, a silence, still as death, fell over all. The Sabbath
quiet of the hour and of the place, was deepened into a
terrible solemnity. He told them all, the story of the
cowardly murder at Lexington by the royal troops ; the
heroic vengeance following hard upon it ; the retreat of Percy;
the gathering of the children of the Pilgrims around the
beleaguered hills of Boston : then pausing and looking over
the silent throng he said slowly, 'Men of New Jersey, the
red-coats are murdering our brethren of New England !
Who follows me to Boston ?' and every man of that audience
stepped out into line and answered : 'I !' There was not a
coward or a traitor in old Hopewell Baptist meeting-house
that day."

Says Dr. Cathcart, commenting upon this scene : "The
annals of the American Revolution cannot furnish in its long
list of fearless deeds and glorious sacrifices, a grander spectacle than this Sunday scene in front of the Baptist church
of Hopewell. Joab Houghton's integrity, honesty of purpose, and military capacity, must have been of an unusual
order to have secured for his appeal, such a noble response.

[*] Wm. Cathcart D. D., in Centennial Offering.

And the men who gave it must have been nurtured in the lap of liberty in childhood, and taught enthusiastic love for her principles in all subsequent years. But this was the spirit of American Baptists in the Revolution."

The account of John Brown is equally interesting. He was of Providence R. I., and Brown University was named after his father, Nicholas. He was also appointed a committee of one to build the present church edifice of the First Baptist church which he did at a cost of $25,000 in 1774. It excited the admiration and surprise of the English Baptists, and was the best the Baptists had in America. It was he who struck the first blow in the war of Independence. It was as early as June, 1772. A British war vessel, the " Gaspee", ran ashore below Pawtuxet. Mr. Brown who had a large fleet of merchant vessels, when he heard of it, ordered eight large boats to be placed in charge of Captain Abraham Whipple, who, with 64 armed men rowed for the " Gaspee". When they drew near the vessel, shots were exchanged and Lieut. Buddington of the " Gaspee" was wounded. " This was the first British blood spilt in the war for Independence." The crew of the " Gaspee" fled, and Captain Whipple blew her up.

" While the defence of the civil rights of America appeared a matter of great importance, our religious liberties were by no means to be neglected ; and the contest concerning each kept a pretty even pace through the war." *
In this double contest, no man was more prominent than Isaac Backus himself, who was a sufferer, as well as his noble mother, from oppressive laws. The town of Ashfield, Mass. was settled by Baptists. In 1770, a few Congregationalists built a meeting house, called a minister, and taxed the Baptists for his support. The greater part of his salary of

* Backus, II. 199.

David Jones

See page 230.

$1,000. came from Baptists. Because they refused to pay this burdensome tax, 398 acres of their land were seized, together with their homes, cattle, crops, and graveyards—constituting everything of many families, and sold to pay the tax. Thus they were despoiled and made homeless, and told to leave if they did not like it. The property was sold far below its value, and the Orthodox minister was one of the purchasers.

In 1774 the law of 1573, was renewed, Massachusetts requiring that certificates should be recorded in each parish where Baptists lived, in order to exempt them from tax for the state church support, for a copy of which certificate, a charge of four pence was made. This afforded no relief. It was additional injustice. That is, they must buy a copy of the law giving them protection from unjust taxes. Backus says "this was equal to three pence sterling, the same which was laid on a pound of tea, which brought on the American Revolution."

The Baptists feeling that they needed protection against unjust laws imposed upon them by the colonists, as the colonists needed protection against England's tyranny, took measures to secure their rights. On the 14th of September 1774, the Warren Association of Baptist churches, which first met in 1767, convened at Medfield, and sent the Rev. Isaac Backus to present a petition from them to the First Continental Congress, then assembled in Philadelphia. In that address, they proclaimed the Baptist loyalty to the cause of the colonists, and set forth their sufferings, reciting the Ashfield outrage. While they were willing to unite in defence of the common rights with the colonists, they demanded equal civil and religious rights with them. In that address they say: "As the Baptist churches in New England are most heartily concerned for the preservation and defence of the rights and privileges of this country, and are deeply affected by the enroachments upon the same which have been lately made by the British Parliament, and are willing to unite with our dear countrymen to pursue every prudent measure for relief, so we would beg leave to say, that as a distinct denomination of Protestants, we conceive that we have an equal claim to charter rights with the rest of our fellow subjects, and yet we have long been denied the full and free enjoyment of those rights, as to the support of religious worship.   "Therefore we * * * have * * sent unto you the reverend and beloved Mr. Isaac Backus * * to lay our case * * before you * * for our relief."*

Mr. Backus was to seek the co operation of the Philadelphia Association then in session. A large delegation was appointed by the association to aid this cause. Mr. Backus and the committee together with some influential members of the Society of Friends, in Philadelphia, who joined in the petition, met the Massachusetts delegates and some members of Congress from other states, and had a four hours conference with them, in Carpenter's Hall, October 14, 1774.

John Adams, delegate from Massachusetts, and afterwards president of the United States, said, "They might as well expect a change in the Solar system, as to expect that we would give up our ecclesiastical establishment:" by which he meant the support of the Congregational churches by taxation. Paine, another delegate said : "There was nothing of conscience in the matter ; it was only a contending about a little money." Mr. Backus replied : "It is absolutely a point of conscience with me, for I cannot give in the certificates they require, without implicitly acknowledging that power in man which I believe belongs only to God."† The

* Backus, I, 200, note.
† Backus, II. 202 p.

delegates then promised to do what they could for the relief of the Baptists. John Adams returned home and reported, that Mr. Backus had been to Philadelphia to try to break up the union of the colonies. It is well for us as a nation, that all the country's leaders had not the same contracted views of liberty.

The first blood spilt in the war for freedom by the American people was shed at Lexington and Concord, Massachusetts, April 19, 1775. On the 4th of July, 1776, the Declaration of Independence of the American colonies was pronounced in Philadelphia, and sent over the land. The old bell in Independence Hall, which was then rung has the inscription upon it, "Proclaim liberty throughout the land to all the inhabitants thereof." But there was no liberty in that sound for Baptists, except in prophecy. Liberty came not then, either to the country or to the Baptists. The spirit of John Adams was not yet dead. The Baptists had to contend with the colonists for a long time before liberty was a reality.

John Hart, of Hopewell, New Jersey, was a Baptist and a signer of the Declaration of Independence. He was a man of integrity and worth. He gave the grounds and built upon it, the meeting-house for the Baptists of this town, which still stands to-day. He represented New Jersey in the First Continental Congress, in 1774. He risked and lost everything—home and property, by putting his name to that instrument. English troops hunted him, and he had to flee for his life. One night he slept in a dog-house with the dog. At an other time he was forced to leave the bed side of his dying wife. His native state has honored him and has erected a granite monument to his memory, over his grave at Hopewell, with this inscription upon it : "Honor the Patriot's Grave." He was in 1776, elected speaker of the New Jersey

WELSH TRACT CHURCH, DELAWARE.

See page 257.

House of Assembly, to which position he was elected for the third time.

While our Baptist brethren were fighting for the colonists, Massachusetts was making unjust laws against them. "In 1778, upon the organization of the independent government, laws against Baptists were incorporated with the State Bill of Rights, and in 1780, were adopted with the State Constitution. The People who had risen in their majesty and power, and hurled from their necks the yoke of British oppression, immediately turned to fasten a still more galling yoke upon the necks of their brethren."*

In 1789, when the people of Massachusetts assembled to consider the propriety of adopting the Federal Constitution, it was in danger of not being adopted. If Massachusetts rejected it, probably it would fail of adoption in the other states. They turned towards Massachusetts to see what her action would be. Dr. Wm. Cathcart points out, that it was mainly through the instrumentality of Baptists, and especially owing to the efforts of those eminent Baptist ministers, Drs. James Manning and Stillman that it was adopted and that glorious instrument saved. Isaac Backus voted for it.† In the midst of profound silence, at the request of John Hancock, president, Dr. James Manning led the Convention in an eloquent, appropriate, closing prayer.

Rev. Isaac Backus says, that ten years before this Convention, a noted Congregational minister had said to the rulers of Massachusetts: "Let the restraints of religion once be broken down as they infallibly would be by leaving the subject of public worship to the humors of the multitude, and we might well defy all human wisdom to support and preserve order and government in the state. * * * Yet

*Dr. D. Weston, in Baptist Centenial, p. 22.   † History, II. 335.

this same man, in the convention of 1788 (9) wherein much
was said against adopting a constitution of government which
had no religious test in it, was then in favor of the constitution, and to promote the adoption of it he said; 'God
alone is the God of conscience, and consequently attempts
to erect human tribunals for the consciences of men are im-
pious encoachments upon the perogatives of God.' "*

"Though," continues Mr. Backus, "many have imagined
that such liberty favors infidelity, yet Christianity is in full
favor of it; and the power of the gospel against all the
powers of Rome, prevailed as far and farther than the Roman
Empire extended, for two hundred years, and Christianity
has never appeared in the world in its primitive purity and
glory since infant baptism was brought in, and after it the
sword of the magistrates to support religious teachers."†

Even after our national independence was secured, and
the Constitution. and its amendment were ratified by the
independent states, the persecution of Baptists in New
England continued contrary to law.

The church at Barnstable, founded in 1771, was in the
years 1788-90, taxed for $150. for the support of the Con-
gregational minister whom they did not have, and when they
had their own pastor to maintain. The Warren Association
protested in January, 1799-80 strongly, that the oppression
was stopped, but the money was not returned.

At Harwick, where Baptists had worshiped forty years in
their own meeting-house, there was no Congregational minister. But in 1792 when the Baptist church was without a
pastor, a Congregational minister was sent to the place. The
Baptists treated him kindly, but still maintained their own

*† History, II. 336.

worship. In 1794, however, the handful of Congrega·
tionalists taxed the Baptists for their minister, and in 1795,
six men were seized, and five of them imprisoned for refusing
to submit to their imposition. The Baptists sued for redress
in the local court, which was granted, but their oppressors
took it to the higher court, which decided unjustly against
the Baptists, who were compelled to lose $500.

In 1779, a pious deacon of the same church wrote:
" The collector of Harwick seized four or five bushels of my
rye, and sold it for one dollar, and made me pay two dollars
for costs. Again, he seized three tons of my hay and sold it
for forty-nine shillings, and returned me five shillings and six
pence. For all this I was taxed to their ministers but seven
shillings and a penny.

In 1804, Isaac Backus wrote respecting the liberty
the law allowed: " Yet Massachusetts and Connecticut act
contrary to it to this day." And it was not till 1833, that
Massachusetts erased from the statutes her obnoxious and
oppressive law. Let Baptists be called bigots no more.
Who can cast a stone at them?

REV. ABEL MORGAN, A. M.

See page 457

CHAPTER XXI.

THE SOUTH AND LIBERTY.

HE Baptists in New England, and in other states north, fought long and well to secure liberty, civil and religious; but in Virginia, one of the grandest conflicts the world ever beheld, was begun, carried on and successfully ended, mainly through the heroic efforts of the Baptists The Old Dominion was the battle field, on which, was waged the war for the civil and religious liberties of this country and of the world,—not with English soldiers, but with misguided and intolerant churchmen.

The growth of the Virginia Baptists was so rapid and great that their strength encouraged them "to entertain serious hopes, not only of obtaining liberty of conscience, but of actually overturning the church establishment, from whence all their oppressions had arisen.*

. In May 1774, several Baptist ministers, in prison, among them David Tinsley, wrote letters to the General Association then in session. The association set apart two days for public fast and prayer, for their " poor blind persecutors,". and for

* Semple's History, p 25.

the release of their brethren.*   In 1775, the whole denomination in Virginia, united in general association, to strive
together for the overthrow of the state church, they determined
to petition the political convention, and to circulate petitions
all over the state for signatures, asking for the abolition of
the established church, and equality before the law of all denominations in their rights and privileges.   They also advised
resistence to, and war for independence from Great Britain.

   " Baptists, were to a man favorable to any revolution .by
which they could obtain freedom of religion."† At one time
they would have been satisfied with liberty of conscience,
and cheerfully have paid their tithes for the support of the
state church.   But now, nothing less than the overthrow of
all ecclesiastical distinctions would satisfy them.   After great
efforts they had obtained licenses to preach in certain places,
but they wanted to be unmolested to preach the gospel to
every creature.

   Their meekness in suffering persecutions, and their faithfulness to Christ and truth, created the sentiment that helped
them in the struggle for freedom.   Their petition was
presented to the Virginia political convention in May, 1776.
" The address of the Baptists, was received and produced,
specially that part relating to civil freedom, a profound
impression.   This Convention framed the famous bill of
rights, the 16th article of which secures religious freedom.
The same body instructed the Virginia delegates in Congress
to vote for a declaration of independence.   *   *   *   It has
generally been held, that the action of the Virginia Convention was not only among the earliest movements in that
direction, but exercised a potential influence in the action of

* Semple, p. 56.
† Semple, p. 62.

Q

Congress. But let it be remembered, to the honor of the Virginia Baptists of that day, that their action was a year prior to that of the Convention, and undoubtedly, exercised a potential influence in moving the Convention, and through the Convention the Congress. Thus did the Virginia Baptists effect a mighty achievement for both civil and religious freedom."*

The first republican legislature of Virginia met in October, 1776, and an act was passed exempting the different societies of dissenters from contributing to the support of the established church and its ministers, and removing the restraints of worship. The salaries of the Episcopal clergy were only suspended, however, and the question of the general assessment for the support of religion, was only postponed. One step forward was gained, at least, and the Baptists continued to petition.†

In 1779, the salaries of the clergy of the establishment were taken away ; the general assessment bill was defeated and the famous act for establishing religious freedom prepared by Thomas Jefferson was presented. Efforts were made in 1784, to restore in a measure the dis-established church. The general assessment bill permitting the taxation of the people for the support of religion, the tax collected to be distributed among the different denominations, was revived and postponed. All other denominations as a whole, favored, advocated and petitioned for it, except the Baptists. They were the only ones who plainly remonstrated, says Semple. They stood alone in opposition to it. The General Committee remonstrated. To defeat the bill they resorted to petitions. Papers protesting against the bill were

* Dr G. B. Taylor, Virginia Baptists.
† Semple, p. 32.

circulated everywhere by them, for signatures for presentation to the assembly. " When the assembly met, the table of the House of Delegates almost sunk under the weight of the accumulated copies of the memorial sent forward from the different counties, each with its long and dense column of subscribers. The fate of the assessment was sealed." Besides, Jefferson's act for the establishment of religious freedom, was at once passed.

The memorial and remonstrance against the assessment bill was drawn up by James Madison, afterwards president of the United States, at the instance, probably of the Baptists, whose friend he was, and presented to the general assembly. Semple says :—"For elegance of style, strength of reasoning, purity of principle, it has perhaps, seldom been equalled."*
"The defeat of the general assessment bill was due considerably," says the same author, " to the active opposition of the Baptists."

The establishment after a long, and desperate struggle, was finally overthrown and all denominations and ministers stood equal before the law. Baptist ministers could now perform the ceremony of marriage, and Baptist people were no longer compelled to support Episcopal clergymen. Dr. Hawks, the Episcopal church historian of Virginia says :—"The establishment was finally put down. The Baptists were the principal promoters in this work, and in truth, aided more than any other denomination, in its accomplishment."

Dr. Wm. Cathcart points out the fact, that the Baptists in Virginia took an important part in securing the adoption of the Federal Constitution by their own state. They have the honor through their own influence, more than any others, of having saved it to the state and country at large. Through

* The memorial prepared by Madison is in the Appendix of Semples' History.

MERCER UNIVERSITY, MACON, GA.

See page 376.

the exertion and self sacrifice of a Baptist, John Leland, Virginia was led in her Convention to ratify the Federal Constitution. During the absence of James Madison from Virginia on public business, John Leland was chosen a candidate for the place that Madison would have filled, if he had been at home, in the Convention that met in 1788 to ratify or reject the Federal Constitution. Madison upon his return, spent half a day with Leland which resulted in the withdrawal of the latter in favor of the former. Leland threw all his influence which was great, in favor of Madison, who was sent to the Convention. Patrick Henry was opposed to the new Constitution, because he thought it "squinted towards monarchy." He carried the people with him and could have defeated it in the Convention, but for the presence and powerful influence of Madison. The Honorable J. S. Barbour, of Virginia declares ; " That the credit of adopting the Constitution of the United States, properly belongs to a Baptist clergyman, formerly of Virginia, named Leland : ' If,' said he, 'Madison had not been in the Virginia Convention, the Constitution would not have been ratified, and as the approval of nine States was necessary to give effect to this instrument, and as Virginia was the ninth State, if it had been rejected by her, the Constitution would have failed, (the remaining States following her example,) and it was through Elder Leland's influence that Mr. Madison was elected to that Convention. It is unquestionable that Mr. Madison was elected through the efforts and resignation of John Leland and it is all but certain. that, that act gave our county its famous Constitution.' "*

The sufferings of the Baptists and their struggles for liberty, helped to unify them. Henceforth, from 1787, we hear no more about " Separate" or " Regular" Baptists, simply the Baptists of Virginia.

* Dr. Cathcart, Centennial Off   pp. 93, 96.

The work of the Baptists in Virginia, was not, however, done. They had still another battle to fight in Congress for the overthrow of ecclesiastical establishments, and for securing constitutional liberty throughout the land. The danger was not past. Dr. Cathcart quotes Thomas Jefferson, who says:—"There was a hope confidently cherished about A. D., 1780, that there might be a State Church throughout the United States, and this expectation was specially cherished by Episcopalians and Congregationalists." John Adams believed in leaving the matter to the states, each state having its own establishment. This design, it was the work of Baptists to frustrate. They did not want the Constitution of the United States, nor of any state, to be made a religious creed, but they were determined to have religious liberty for themselves and all the world.

In 1787 the Federal Constitution was ratified by the requisite number of states, and became the law of the land. The next year the question arose among the Baptists of Virginia, whether it made sufficient provisions for religious liberty. It prohibited any religious test for a qualification for office, but it was their unanimous opinion that religious liberty was not sufficiently provided for. Acting upon the advice of Mr. Madison, an address from the Baptists of the whole state was presented by them to President Washington, in August, 1789. It was written by John Leland, and set forth, that the religious rights of the Baptists were not secured by the Federal Constitution.*

Washington replied, that he never would have signed that instrument, had he supposed it endangered the liberties of any religious society, and that he would at once, move for

* Isaac Backus seems to have shared this same feeling. Hist. II. 335 note.

its amendment, since by it, religious freedom was rendered insecure. Washington in his address at this time, pays this tribute to the patriotism of the Baptists : "While I recollect with satisfaction, that the religious society of which you are members, have been, throughout America, uniformly and almost unanimously, the fast friends of civil liberty, and the persevering promoters of our glorious Revolution, I cannot hesitate to believe that they will be the faithful supporters of a free, yet efficient general government."* As the result of this address, the next month, James Madison proposed in the House of Representatives, the first amendment to the Constitution of the United States. It met with violent opposition, at first, but was finally passed. It was also approved by two-thirds of the states, and became the law of the country.

"But suppose," says the distinguished author above quoted, "it had not been adopted; Massachusets might have had a State Church to-day, and her citizens rotting in prison, because they could not conscientiously pay a church tax, and any State might have established the Episcopal Church, and then committed Baptists or other ministers to prison as they did in Virginia, down to the Revolution. And Congress might have decreed that the Catholic Church was the religious fold of the nation, and might have levied taxes to support her clergy, and made laws to give secular power to her cardinals, archbishops, bishops, and priests over her schools, religious opinions, and personal freedom.* * Without it, sacerdotal tyranny might have destroyed all our liberties. The grandest feature of our Constitution is the first clause of the first amendment. The Baptists have always claimed that the credit of this amendment belongs, chiefly, to them. * * * The Baptists asked it through Washington ; the request commended itself to his judgment, and to the

* Backus' Hist. Baptists, Newton, II., 340.

generous soul of Madison, and to the Baptists, beyond a doubt, belong the glory of engrafting its best article, on the noblest Constitution ever framed for the government of mankind."*

Here is the amendment as it reads in "Story, on the Contitution:" "Congress shall make no law respecting an establishment of religion, or prohibiting the free exercise thereof; or abridging the freedom of speech, or of the press; or the right of the people peacefully to assemble, and to petition to the government for a redress of grievances."

This ought to have ended the struggle, but it was not till 1798, that all dissenters were practically put upon "perfect equality" with Episcopalians.

James Madison was one of the most enlightened statesmen of his day, and that he fully understood what the Baptists were contending for, the following from an unpublished address of Dr. J. C. Long, shows full well:

"James Madison was not a member of a Baptist church himself, though his brother, General Madison, was; but he took great interest in the Baptists, on account of their sufferings. When George Mason, in the Virginia political convention, of 1776, wrote, in the celebrated Bill of Rights, that all men should enjoy the fullest *toleration* in the exercise of religion, Madison said; 'No, write instead, all men are entitled to the free exercise of their religion, according to the dictates of their consciences.' And so it was written. What prompted one of the youngest members of that assembly to insist upon the change of a word? Where did he get his views? He did not find them in his books. His friends, the Baptists, taught them. Was it from them that he learned the true principles of religious freedom?"

*Centennial Offering, p. 98, 111,

The question has sometimes been asked ; " Would the Baptists become a State church, if the opportunity offered ?" We answer ; No, judging by their principles and their past actions. They have ever refused for themselves, what they have declared a wrong for others to receive. For instance, in Virginia in 1792, "the Baptists had members of great weight in civil society ; their congregations had become more numerous than any other Christain sect." They doubtless controlled the government of Virginia, and yet they secured equal liberty there for all. In Wales, the Baptist churches and ministers declined state support by taxation of the people, such as others received, which was offered them, though they were as poor as any. For one hundred and fifty years, the Baptists had the sole power and rule in Rhode Island, and the evil example of others around them, but, unmoved in their principles, they used their power for the good of all alike. The utter failure of Baptist principles has been again and again foretold, but Baptists have stood the test of centuries, and they have, more than any others, given civil and religious freedom to the world. With the origin and perpetuity of American liberty they have had much to do. How appropriate, then, that a Baptist, S. F. Smith, D. D., should give to our country its national hymn :—

" My country, 'tis of thee, etc.

DELAWARE AVENUE BAPTIST CHURCH,
WILMINGTON, DEL.

See page 257.

CHAPTER XXII.

BEGINNINGS.

THE origin of the Baptists in other parts of the United States, and Canadas, next claims attention.*

The Swansea, Massachusetts, church was organized in 1663; and one at Charlestown, which became the First of Boston in 1665. The doors of the first meeting-house in Boston, were nailed up, and the Baptists forbidden to worship in it at their peril. Now, Baptists are the most numerous there, and the edifice of the First church is the handsomest and costliest Baptist house of worship in the world. C. B. Crane, D. D., has just resigned as pastor. This is the church of which Dr. Neal was, for so many years, pastor, with Rev. J. T. Beckley associate. Tremont Temple, the home of the Union Temple church, is central in location, and seats 3300 people. Boston city mission work, aiming at the resuscitation of old churches, as well as the planting of new, is vigorously prosecuted. Dr. Seymour's Ruggle Street church, is an example of what consecrated talent and wealth can do for the people.

---

* The invaluable Baptist Encyclopædia, by Dr. Wm. Cathcart, has been of great service in securing accuracy, and fullness, in this chapter.

At Kittery, Maine, a Baptist church was formed in 1682, but was scattered by persecution within a year. In 1768, another was organized at Berwick; Joshua Emery, pastor. Membership in the state, 20,039.*

The first church established in Connecticut, was at Groton, in 1705, through Valentine Wightman. Despite persecution, Baptist principles, introduced from Rhode Island, in 1674, spread. The first baptism was administered in 1674, to several persons, and created intense excitement. Communicants, 20,843.

Mrs. Scammon, a noble Christian, came from Rehoboth, in 1720, to New Hampshire. She led many to Christ, and spread Baptist views by the circulation of Baptist literature. In 1755, after her death, a church was formed at Newton. It is claimed that the first church was formed at Dover, in 1638, by Hanserd Knollys. It is said by Winthrop, that "he gathered some of the best minded into a church body, and became their pastor." And Backus, that he "was minister there, from the spring of 1638, to the fall of 1645." Membership, 8,775.

A number of Congregationalists in Vermont, having embraced Baptist sentiments, and being reinforced by Baptist ministers from other states, the Baptists secured a foothold. A church was formed in 1768, at Shaftsbury, and another in 1773, at Pownal. Total in the state, 9,410.

Next in order of time, a church was formed in 1682, at Charleston, South Carolina. William Screven, a Baptist minister, and deacon Humphrey Churchwood, and eight other brethren, fleeing from persecution in Maine, took refuge in Charleston. Here they either found a church, formed one, or brought with them their own organization from

*Baptist membership in the various states, according to Year Book, 1884.

Kittery. William Screven became pastor. Isaac Chandler, and Oliver Hart, were afterwards pastors. The second church was the Ashley river, formed in 1736, and the third, the Pee Dee, came from Delaware, in 1738, led by James James, whose son, Philip, was the pastor. Membership in the state, 160,925.

Among the distinguished men the Baptists of this state have produced, may be named Richard Furman, D. D., and Richard Fuller, D. D., the latter properly compared to England's great preacher, Robert Hall, in regard to the matter and structure·of his sermons, as well as to their delivery.

In 1682 the state of Pennsylvania was settled by Friends, under Penn. Religion was here left somewhat untrammeled by law, as it had been wholly so in Rhode Island since 1836, or for nearly fifty years. Thomas Dungan, a Baptist of Newport, preached Christ to the settlers with great success, and a church was formed at Cold Spring, near Bristol, Bucks County. A few scattered stones near the spring mark the spot Lower Dublin church, the mother of the Philadelphia churches, was formed in 1688, at Pennepek. The first meeting-house was of logs. "The first minister they had was the Rev. Elias Keach. He was the son of the famous Benj. Keach, of London. He arrived in this country, a wild youth, about the year 1686. On his landing he dressed in black and wore bands, in order to pass as a minister. The project succeeded to his wishes and many people resorted to hear the young London divine. He performed well enough till he had advanced pretty far in the sermon ; then stopping short, he looked like a man astonished. The audience concluded that he had been seized with a sudden disorder ; but, on asking what the matter was, received from him a confession of the

*Backus' Hist. Newton, I. 325.

imposture, with tears in his eyes, and much trembling. Great was his distress, though it ended happily : for from that time he dated his conversion. He heard of Mr. Dungan, of Cold Spring. To him he repaired to seek counsel and comfort, and by him he was baptized and ordained. From Cold Spring Mr. Keach came to Pennepek and settled a church there, * * and thence traveled through Pennsylvania and the Jerseys, preaching the gospel in the wilderness with great success, in so much that he may be considered as the chief apostle of the Baptists in these parts of America."* The cut of the Lower Dublin church, and that of Hopewell Academy, are from Dr. David Spencer's " Early Baptists of of Philadelphia."

Among the prominent churches of Philadelphia are the First, G. D. Boardman, D. D. pastor, and the Memorial, Wayland Hoyt, D. D., pastor.

In 1707, the Philadelphia Association was formed. The Association consisted "of but five churches, viz.: Lower Dublin, Piscataway, Middletown, Cohansey and Welsh Tract." It has now 83 churches, with 23,588 members, whose contributions for the year were over $346,500. In the state, 65,879 members.

The Philapelphia City Mission, of which Col. C. H. Banes is president, Rev. James French, superintendent, and Rev. P. L. Jones, secretary, is doing a good work in planting such chapels as that at Tacony, Rev. W. W. Ferris, pastor.

Baptists at first were afraid of the assumption of power by associations, and this hindered their formation. It was not till 60 years after the birth of the Philadelphia organization, that the Warren Association, of Rhode Island, was formed,

* Morgan Edward's History of Baptists of Pennsylvania.

and there were only three others formed before it—one, each, in South Carolina, in 1751 ; in North Carolina, in 1758 ; in Virginia in 1766.

New Jersey has become an important state for Baptist interests, but we can only briefly refer to the origin of Baptist churches there. As early as 1667 there were eighteen Baptists among the original settlers of Middletown, where a church was formed in 1688. Abel Morgan, A. M., one of the ablest men of his day, was ordained in 1734, and spent the whole of his long life in the pastorate of this church. The Piscataway church was formed in 1689, and the Cohansey in 1690. "These four, with that at Charleston, were all the Baptist churches that were formed south of New England before the year 1700. * * Many of those who constituted the church at Cohansey came from Ireland ; though one of them was Obadiah Holmes Esq., a son of the sufferer at Boston in 1651."* In 1712 the Cape May church was formed. The state convention was organized in 1830, and Daniel Dodge, D. D., was its first president. Baptists in the state 33,616. Rev. I. C. Wynn, D. D., is pastor of the First church Camden.

Sixteen Baptists organized as a church, with Thomas Griffith, pastor, came from Wales in 1701, to Penncpek, and, in 1703, to Welsh Tract, Delaware. The Baptists of Delaware were once numerous and flourishing, but became reduced in strength, because all the churches embraced anti-mission views. The first of the present missionary churches, the Second of Wilmington, was formed in 1835. Missionary Baptists, in the state, 1,928. "The Delaware Union" is presided over by Washington Jones, the leading layman in the state. Rev. Geo. C. Needham is pastor of the Delaware Avenue church, Wilmington.

* Backus.

An English Baptist, Henry Sater, was the first to introduce Baptist usages into Maryland, in 1709. He maintained
public worship in his own house, inviting Baptist ministers
to preach there. Through his influence a Baptist church was
formed at Chestnut Ridge, in 1742. The First church,
Baltimore, known as the "Round-top," was organized in
1785. J. W. M. Williams, D. D., has been pastor for over
33 years. Their present house of worship was erected in
1878. F. M. Ellis, D. D., is pastor of Eutaw Place church,
Baltimore. Baptists in State, 9,807.

It is not known precisely when the Baptists appeared in
New York, but some who fled from persecution, elsewhere,
found refuge there in the 17th century. They were not,
however, to find rest long. William Wickenden, of Providence, was imprisoned there by the English, four months for
preaching the Gospel.

In 1712, Valentine Wightman of Connecticut, preached
for a short time and baptized about a dozen persons. One of
them, Nicholas Eyers, became their pastor. A church was
organized in 1724, and a house of worship built on Golden
Hill, in 1728. The church disbanded after 1732. What is
now the First church was established, June 19, 1762, with 27
members, under the ministry of John Gano. They first
worshiped in the house of Jeremiah Dodge, 1745, and then
in a sail-loft on Williams street. They have a fine house
now. The church edifice and lot of the Calvary Baptist
church, R. S. McArthur, D. D., pastor, dedicated in 1884,
cost $460,000. will seat 1300, and is one of the finest in the
city. During Dr. McArthur's pastorate of over 13 years,
the church has contributed, for all benevolent purposes, nearly
one million dollars, and in March, 1882, $71,000 was sub-
scribed for missions, at one morning service. Its membership,

is 1300. The picture of the Strong Place church, Brooklyn, F. H. Kerfoot, D. D., pastor, is given, as well as that of the Calvary, New York. Members in the State, 113, 886.

North Carolina was a great centre of Baptist influence in the South, at an early day. Baptist ministers from New England, New Jersey, Delaware, and Pennsylvania, labored there. According to Morgan Edwards, there were many Baptists in the state in 1695. It was not until 1727, that a church was formed, the Shiloh, by Paul Palmer, from Welsh Tract, Delaware. To Shubael Stearns, of Boston, must be attributed, under God, the extensive spread of Baptist views and practices, and the remarkable revival of religion by which the 18th century was distinguished. Many of the New Lights seeing the inconsistency and evil of infant baptism, became Baptists, and Stearns was of that number. He became a Baptist in 1751, and was ordained. Deeply impressed with the idea that he was called of God to do a great work in a distant land, he accordingly set out with some friends and settled first in Virginia, but finally in North Carolina, in 1755. A Baptist church was formed at once of sixteen persons at Sandy Creek, of which he became pastor. Semple says; "The church soon swelled from 16 to 606 members." Morgan Edwards, says ; "Sandy Creek is the mother of all the Separate Baptists. * * This church, in 17 years, has spread her branches westward as far as the great Mississippi, southward as far as Georgia, eastward to the sea, and Chesapeake Bay ; grand-mother and great-grand-mother, of 42 churches, from which sprang 125 ministers."

Mr. Stearns died with his church in 1771. Among the original sixteen of the Sandy Creek church, was Daniel Marshall. He played a very important part in the early history of the Baptists South. He was born of pious parents

R

WASHINGTON JONES.

See page 257.

at Windsor, Connecticut, in 1706, and was a brother-in-law of Shubael Stearns. It is said of his wife : " Without the shadow of an usurped authority over the other sex, Mrs. Marshall, being a lady of good sense, singular piety and surpassing eloquence, has, in countless instances melted a whole concourse to tears by her prayers and exhortations." Mr. Marshall was converted and joined the Presbyterian church in his 20th year. Aroused by the fire of Whitefield, he left all and went to labor among the Mohawk Indians as a missionary, till the Indian war broke out, when he went first to Pennsylvania and thence to Virginia. " Here," says his son, " he became acquainted with a Baptist church belonging to the Philadelphia Association, and as the result of a close, impartial examination of their faith and order, he and my dear mother (his first wife) were baptized by immersion," and here he was licensed as a preacher.

The church at Abbott's Creek, North Carolina, of which he was ordained pastor by Shubael Stearns and Henry Ledbetter, was planted by him. He traveled extensively in Virginia where he baptized Samuel Harris, who traveled and preached with him, planting the gospel in many places. Often he went into Georgia, also to preach, and once, while on his knees leading his audience in prayer, he was seized for preaching the gospel and ordered to leave the state. He did not obey, but formed a church at Kiokee. He died November 2, 1784. Among his last words were these ; " This night I shall probably expire. But I have nothing to fear. * * An eternal weight of glory is mine. * * I have been praying that I may go home to-night." The Baptists in North Carolina number 226,757.

Baptists were among the first people to settle Georgia, having come in the same ship with Oglethrope, who settled the State in 1733. Nicholas Bedgewood came over with

Whitefield, about 1751, and took charge of the Orphan House, below Savannah. He became a Baptist in 1757, was ordained, and in 1763 baptised several officers and inmates of the Orphan House. A church was probably formed there. Above Savannah, Rev. Benj. Stirk preached in his own house at Tuckasuking in 1761, where a church was constituted. These churches were branches of South Carolina churches, the members holding membership in that state. Daniel Marshall settled north on Kiokee Creek, in 1771, which became a centre of Baptist influence and growth. The church formed there in 1772, was the first in the state. Daniel Marshall, his son and grandson, were pastors successively. In 1773, Edmund Botsford, from England, baptized 148 persons and organized the Botsford church. The first association of Georgia was organized in 1784 with six or eight churches. Georgia has the largest Baptist population of any state ; 249,626. H. McDonald, D. D., is pastor of the Second church, Atlanta, the picture of which appears.

Mississippi is one of the great Baptist states, having 149,953 Baptists. A company of Baptists from South Carolina and Georgia settled near Natchez, in 1780, and formed the Salem church with Richard Curtis, Jr., as pastor. The Spanish authorities were incensed at the baptism of a Spanish Roman Catholic, and threatened, and even arrested, some of the Baptists, who were forbidden to preach under penalty of transportation to the mines of Mexico. Mr. Curtis and others were forced to escape in 1795, but returned in 1797, and under the the protection of the United States, that had now obtained possession, the Baptists flourished.

The history of West Virginia and Virginia was identical until a very recent date, and both included in the Old Dominion. The oldest church, in what is now West Virginia, is Simpson's Creek, formed in 1774. Greenbrier church was formed in 1781, through the efforts of Rev. John Alderson, from New Jersey, who also organized the Greenbrier Association, in 1807. Total Baptists in West Virginia, 29,149.

Two churches were established in East Tennessee, in 1765. They were scattered in 1774 during the Indian war. The first permanent church was formed in 1780, at Buffalo Ridge. In Middle Tennessee, Baptists were among the early settlers. A church was formed on Red River, by Joseph Grammer, in 1791, and another in 1791 by missionaries from Kentucky. There are 106,016 Baptists in Tennessee.

The first church organized in Kentucky was at Elizabethtown, near Louisville, in 1781, by Joseph Bennett and John Garard. Many others followed in quick succession. Three associations existed in 1785. The first Protestant church formed in "the West" was established here. The early settlers in 1775 were Baptists. Daniel Boone's brother, Squire, was a Baptist preacher. In 1776, Thomas Tinsley and William Hickman, both Baptist ministers, came to Harrodsburg. Kentucky has become, in every respect, a Baptist stronghold, which shows the importance of early beginnings. The Walnut Street church, Louisville, has T. T. Eaton, D. D., as pastor. Total in State, 166,676.

It is claimed by some that the first Protestant church organized in what was then termed the North West Territory, was a Baptist church at Columbia, Ohio, in 1790, whose first pastor was John Smith, afterwards, during Jefferson's administration, United States Senator. Forty-five settlers from Pennsylvania and New Jersey located at the mouth of the Little Miami river in the summer of 1789. Six of them were Baptists, who immediately commenced holding religious meetings, each taking his turn as he was able, in carrying on

TACONY BAPTIST CHURCH, PHILADELPHIA, PA,

See page 256.

the service. The number increased to nine when the **Rev.** S. Gano, of Providence, R. I., visited them in 1790, and formed the Miami church. This meeting-house built in 1793, was the first Protestant place of worship in Ohio. Baptists in the state, 50,583.

J. M. Peck, D. D., says, that the Baptists were the first Protestants to enter the state of Illinois. They held meetings until the Rev. James Smith of Kentucky labored among them. He was captured by the Indians and ransomed by the brethren for $175.00, a large sum then and to them. The first church was formed at New Design in 1796. The Baptists of Chicago have an interesting history. Dr. Temple residing there appealed to the Home Mission Society through Dr. Going for a missionary. Dr. Going sent Allen B. Freeman, an educated, "talented and pious" young preacher. Dr. Temple paid $200. of his salary. October 19th 1833, the First church was organized with fifteen members. The picture of the Immanuel church, Chicago, G. C. Lorimer, D. D., pastor is given. In the state, there are 70,263 Baptists.

In 1798 the Baptists formed a church in Indiana, now known as the Charlestown church. It was organized by Isaac Edwards from New Jersey. Membership, 44,113.

It is not known when the Baptists first appeared in Arkansas, but it seems that Rev. David Orr planted there a considerable number of churches. The first church organized was at Fouche A'Thomas, towards the close of the last century. The Spring River Association was formed in 1829. Number in the state, 59,516.

The First Baptist church in the District of Columbia was formed in Washington City, March 7th 1802, with six members. Rev. William Parkinson, chaplain to Congress, preached to them. The Rev. O. B. Brown was their first pastor, in 1807. Baptists in the District, now, 8,297.

The Baptists were the first Protestants to enter Missouri with the gospel, which they did in 1796. The first baptism there and indeed west of the Mississippi was administered by Rev. Thomas Johnson of Georgia, in 1799. The Tywappity church, was the first organized in 1805, by Rev. David Green and revived again in 1809. Bethel church was formed in 1806. These Baptist settlers were allowed to exercise their religious sentiments, but their children were claimed for the Catholic Church. The St. Louis Association was organized in 1817. J. M. Peck, D. D., came to St. Louis in 1817, and with Rev. James E. Welsh, organized the first church there in 1818. In the state, 93,748 members.

In Alabama, the Flint River church was the first organized, October 2nd 1808, in the house of James Deaton and composed of twelve persons. The Bassett's Creek church formed in 1810, by Elder J. Courtney was the second. Members, 168,103.

Baptist ministers came into Louisiana from Mississippi, in 1798, and preached. Bailey E. Chaney, one of them, was imprisoned by the Spanish authorities for preaching, and only was released on condition that he would desist. Joseph Willis, a mulatto, and a Baptist preacher, organized a church in 1812, on Bayou Chico. He became first moderator of the Louisiana Association, in 1818, and labored very successfully west of the Mississippi. Hebzibah church, was formed in 1814, and a church in New Orleans, in 1818, with Benjaman Davis, pastor. S. Landrum, D. D., is pastor of the Coliseum Place church. Members in the state, 66,026.

Orison Allen and wife, came to the present site of Pontiac, Michigan, in 1818. Elon Galusha, visited the spot in 1822, and preached and organized the first Baptist church in the state. Lemuel Taylor, a lay preacher, and Elkanah Comstock, a minister, did much service. Membership in the state, 27,452.

The Danville was the first Baptist church in Iowa. Mr. and Mrs. Mauley, from Kentucky, and some Baptists from Illinois, organized the church. Rev. John Logan, of Illinois, preached October 19, 1834, by invitation, and the next day the church was constituted. Members in the state, 23,477.

In Wisconsin, the first Baptist church was organized in Milwaukee, in 1837, by Rev. James Griffin, who became pastor. Members in the state, 11,651.

Texas is a marvel of rapid growth, and real progress, and the Baptists there are in the front rank. It is startling to learn that there are 128,034 Baptists there, with a thousand ministers, and twice as many churches. Yet only in 1840, was the Texas Union Association formed, with three churches. They have now three organizations covering their great territory, engaged in cultivating the field for Christ; viz : "The State Convention," formed in 1848; "The General Association," in 1867 ; and "The Eastern Convention," in 1877.

Kansas, in 1860, had 40 churches, which were then organized in a state convention, and now reports 17,513 members, in 428 churches.

The work of the Baptists among the American Indians, has been truly marvelous. There were reported in 1878, in the Indian Territory, 100 Baptist churches, 5000 members, 30 Sabbath-schools, and 75 native pastors. The number now is, 6,419. There were also 3 associations—active missionary bodies, contributing according to their means for the support, and propagation of the gospel, some of them sustaining the gospel in their own tribes, and sending it to others. Among the Creeks, baptisms, for months, occurred daily. The Levering Manual Labor School, named after a well known family of generosity, in Baltimore, and lately established, promises to be of great service in the training of Indian youth. Indian University is another Baptist school

The first church formed in Oregon, was the West Union, in 1844; in California, the First San Francisco, in 1849 ; in Minnesota, the First St. Paul, in 1849 ; in Nebraska, the First Nebraska City, in 1855 ; besides. there are Baptists in Florida, New Mexico, Utah, Idaho, Dacota, Montana, Washington, Colorado, and Wyoming. In Florida, there are 23,812 communicants.

The Baptists in British America are closely allied with their American cousins, and deserve more than a passing notice.

In 1760 Shubael Dimmock and family fleeing for con- science' sake from Connecticut, and John Sutton and some companions from New Jersey, settled at Newport, Nova Scotia. Here Sutton remained about a year, and preached, and baptized several, among them Dimmock's son, Daniel. No church was formed, though the Dimmocks and Sutton who were all ministers, preached and baptized. Ebenezer Moulton came from Massachusetts to Yarmouth, N. S., in 1791, with the first settlers, and preached and baptized a number, among them a Mrs. Burgess. No church was formed, and Moulton returned. He preached at Horton, Nova Scotia, with great success.

In 1763, some Baptists came to Sackville, New Bruns- wick, from South Swansea, Massachusetts, and among them was Nathan Mason. They had formed themselves into a church before leaving home, with Mason as pastor. They soon returned to Massachusetts. While in Sackville their number increased to sixty, but the church died upon the departure of their brethren. Another church was formed there in 1799.

The first Baptist church formed in Nova Scotia, was at Norton, October 29, 1778, of ten members, with Nicholas Pierson, as pastor, through whose labors 55 persons were added to the church in 1779, and 1780 Congregationalists were admitted to this church as members, and the other early churches organized, adopted the open communion practice. Dr. Cramp says that the Halifax church was strict communion. The Halifax church was formed in 1795; Newport, in 1799; and Sackville, in 1799. The pastors of the churches were all Baptists, and the converts were all baptized, and soon it was found both inconvenient and inconsistent to have a mixed membership and open communion, so, in 1809, strict communion became the practice of all the churches.

The first association—"The Nova Scotia and New Brunswick," was formed at Lower Granville, Nova Scotia, June 23, 1800, and comprised ten churches. The ministers instrumental in its formation were great men in their day, and labored well for Christ. The names of T. H. Chipman, James Manning, Enoch Towner, Harris Harding, Edward Manning, T. S. Harding, Joseph Dimmock and Joseph Crandel, will live while the Baptist name survives.

From these humble beginnings the Baptists of the Dominion have come to be a strong and influential body, aggregating in 1884, 744 churches, 506 ministers, and 63,044 members. They are missionary in spirit and in practice, and the friends of humanity and education as well as of religion.

In the Lower Provinces is Arcadia College, Prof. Rand, D.D., president. The Jarvis Street church, Toronto, B. D. Thomas, D. D., pastor, will compare favorably for architectural beauty with any edifice in America. At Toronto is McMaster Hall, J. H. Castle, D. D., president, a theological seminary worthy the name of its founder. The classical department is Wookstock College, W. N. Wolverton, A. M.. president.

The Standard Publishing Company of Toronto, is the Baptist Publication Society of Canada. Hon. Wm. McMaster has given $60,000. to this company, the profit of which is to go for missions.

We have spoken, in this chapter, of some results, as well as of beginnings, but these are all only beginnings. As the people of the North American Continent are only in the infancy of their progress, so there is a great future for the Baptists of America.

HOPEWELL ACADEMY, N. J.

See page 372

CHAPTER XXIII.

THE SUPPER.

HE ordinances of Baptism and the Lord's Supper, teach in symbolic language the fundamental doctrines of the gospel. When rightly understood they tell the whole story of the cross, and point out the way of salvation through the sacrifice of Christ. They are silent, but effective witnesses to the truth, and their impressive testimony often carries the word with power to the heart. In their scriptural form as symbols and illustrations of Bible truth, both these ordinances are full of precious meaning. In baptism the burial of the believer in the watery grave, and his rising therefrom, beautifully symbolizes the great facts of the Saviour's burial and resurrection, while it also represents the believer's death to sin and resurrection to the new life of faith, and at the same time points forward to the final resurrection from the grave, to a life of immortality. In the communion, in like manner, we have a visible pictorial representation of the Saviour's death, and of our participation in the benefits of his atonement. The broken loaf and the wine poured out, significantly and tenderly remind us that the body of our Saviour was broken on the cross, and his blood shed, in order to secure for us the blessings of salvation. The frequent observance of this ordinance reminds us that our spiritual life is sustained by constant feeding upon Chiist and repeated supplies of divine grace, while on the other hand the one act of baptism shows that the new life has but one beginning, since the new birth takes place but once. We need only to consider the vast importance of the doctrines which these ordinances symbolize in order to see the necessity of observing them as they were instituted by our Saviour. We cannot change their outward form without changing their spiritual meaning, and thus destroying their value as symbols of gospel truth.

The remarks of Conybeare and Howson, in reference to baptism, may be applied with equal force to both of these ordinances. They say : "It must be a subject of regret that the general discontinuance of this original form of baptism, (though perhaps necessary in our northern climates,) has rendered obscure to popular apprehension, some very important passages of Scripture."

As Baptists, we have always held that neither the coldness of the climate nor any other reason can justify any change in the ordinances of the gospel, which sacrifices their spiritual meaning, and at the same time sets aside the authority of Christ's commands.

The almost uniform practice of the American Baptist churches has been " close " or restricted communion, and, here, directly after the account of their origin in the various states, it would be well to consider the grounds upon which the practice rests. If rightly understood, our practice needs no defense. All that is necessary to silence every objection, and satisfy every candid objector, is an explanation. A mere statement of the case ought to make it clear to every unprejudiced mind, that we are no more close or restricted in our communion, than other denominations, for they, and we, administer the supper on precisely the same principles. In order to make the matter perfectly plain, let us first consider what principles are held in reference to the supper by all evangelical denominations.

FIRST—All believe that conversion or regeneration is a prerequisite to the supper. That only true believers who have been born of the spirit have any right to sit down at the Lord's table.

SECONDLY—All believe (with few exceptions) that baptism is a prerequisite to the communion, and that only baptized Christians should participate in the Lord's Supper.

THIRD—All believe that an "orderly walk," or a consistent Christian life, is a prerequisite to the communion, and that even baptized believers who embraced any hurtful error, or act inconsistently with their profession forfeit their right to this ordinance.

All evangelical denominations require this much at least, and make what they deem scriptural terms or restrictions. Pedobaptist churches administer the communion on these principles and Baptists do the same, so that, in reference to this ordinance, all occupy the same ground.

As prerequisites to communion—

Pedobaptists ⎫
Baptists ⎬ Require ⎰ 1. Conversion.
　　　　⎭ 　　　　⎱ 2. Baptism.
　　　　　　　　　　 3. A consistent life.

Here any one can see at a glance that so far as relates to the principles on which communion is administered, there is really no difference between Baptists and Pedobaptists. All would agree that conversion and a consistent life are prerequisite to communion, but there are many who take a different view in reference to the necessity of baptism before the Lord's Supper.

As this is the only point in the above statement that is
likely to be called in question, we will give some quotations
from standard authorities. If we would know what a
denomination holds and teaches, we must go to their
standard writers. That Pedobaptist churches hold baptism
to be a prerequisite to communion, is shown by what follows.

Dr. Griffin says : " I agree with the advocates of close
communion, that we ought not to commune with those who
are not baptized and, of course, are not church members, even
if we regard them as Christians. Should a pious Quaker so
far depart from his principles as to wish to commune with
me at the Lord's table, while yet he refused to be baptized I
could not receive him, because there is such a relationship
established between the two ordinances that I have no right
to separate them ; in other words, I have no right to send the
sacred elements out of the church."*

This is the language of an eminent Presbyterian, and
expresses the view held in common by both Presbyterians
and Baptists.

Dr. Hibbard, an eminent Methodist writer whose book
is accepted as good authority, says : " It is but just to remark
that, in one principle, the Baptist and the Pedobaptist
churches agree. They both agree in rejecting from communion at the table of the Lord, and in denying the rights
of church fellowship, to all who have not been baptized.
Valid baptism they consider essential to constitute visible
church membership. This also we hold. The only question
then that here divides us is, what is essential to valid baptism ?
It is evident that, according to our views, we can admit them
to our communion ; but with their views of baptism, they
can never reciprocate the courtesy ; and the charge of close
communion is no more applicable to the Baptists then to us,

* As quoted by J. W. T. Boothe, D. D., in a published sermon on, Gospel
Order, page 20

LOWER DUBLIN BAPTIST CHURCH, PHILADELPHIA, PENN.

See page 25.

s

inasmuch as the question of church membership is determined by as liberal principles as it is with any other Protestant churches ; so far, I mean, as the present subject is concerned, *i. e.*, it is determined by valid baptism."*

Bishop Simpson in his " Cyclopœdia of Methodism," says ; " It is the order of the church that persons shall be baptized before they shall be admitted to the Lord's Supper or to full membership in the church.

Dr. Wall, of the Church of England, says: " No church ever gave the communion to any persons before they were baptized. Among all the absurdities that ever were held, none ever maintained that any persons should partake of the communion before they were baptized."†

Dr. Cathcart truthfully remarks that, " The creeds of all denominations, with the exception of a small body of open communion Baptists, are agreed in describing communicants as ' those in the fellowship of churches.' Baptized persons are the only proper communicants, as they only ought to be church members. The communicants in the first churches were all baptized."

But better still, the universal practice of the Christian church, in placing baptism before the communion, has been based upon the plain and obvious interpretation of what the Scriptures require. Let us look at a few facts which have a bearing on this point.

1. The great commission contains the direction given by our Saviour to his apostles, Matt. 28 : 19-20 ; " Go ye therefore and teach all nations, baptizing them in the name of the Father, and of the Son, and of the Holy Ghost ; teaching them to observe all things whatsoever I have commanded you."

* Dr. Boothe p. 21 of sermon.
† Dr. Boothe's Sermon p. 20.

Here three things are enjoined : 1. Teaching or preaching the gospel ; 2. Baptizing those who believe ; 3. Instructing them to observe the commands of Christ, including the observance of the Lord's Supper. No one ought to presume to change this *order* by placing the communion before baptism any more than he would change it by placing baptism before preaching the gospel or before repentance and faith. These directions are the church's '' marching orders'' which ought to be obeyed without alteration or diminution by those to whom they are given.

2. If we examine the history of the apostles as they went forth to execute their commission, we shall expect to find them acting according to their interpretation of its meaning. They evidently understood it as requiring that baptism should precede the communion, for so far as the record goes, they never administered the communion to any persons who were not previously baptized. The example of the apostles in such a case ought to be regarded as having all the weight of an infallible interpretation of the Saviour's words. The two together ought to be accepted as sufficient authority for that *order* of the ordinances which has been observed in the Christian church almost universally.

3. The symbolism of the two ordinances requires that baptism should precede the communion. We have considered this point at length. It is only sufficient to remark, that baptism symbolizes the new birth or the beginning of the Christian life, and hence this ordinance is administered but once, since the new life has but one beginning. The communion on the other hand is administered repeatedly, because it symbolizes the nourishment of the spiritual life by constant feeding upon Christ by faith. Now it is evident that the fitness of things requires that the ordinance which represents the beginning of the new life should precede the

ordinance that represents its continued nourishment and support. Hence it must be clear that believers should be first baptized before partaking of the communion, since to reverse this order would be to confuse the symbolism, and so to destroy the significance of the ordinances. Here then is the *order* again : baptism before communion, as it is life before growth.

Here is what Dr. Hodge says upon the subject of gospel *order;* "The facts of science arrange themselves. His (the man of science) business is simply to ascertain what the arrangement given in the nature of the fact is. If he mistake, his system is false, and, to a greater or less degree, is valueless. The same is obviously true in regard to the facts or truths of the Bible. They cannot be held in isolation, nor will they admit of any and every arrangement the theologian may choose to assign them. They bear a natural relation to each other, which cannot be overlooked, or perverted, without the facts themselves being perverted."*

This is a true principle laid down by Dr. Hodge. Apply it to baptism and the Lord's Supper. There is a scriptural order which we are bound to follow in belief and practice ; baptism precedes communion, and hence, only the baptized believers should be invited to the Lord's Supper. Do otherwise, and the "natural relation" of the two ordinances is "overlooked or perverted," and "the facts themselves" are "perverted " As we find the ordinance so we are compelled to keep it, simply because it is not our own, but the Lord's, table.

Baptists and Pedobaptists, then, differ not in reference to the communion but in regard to baptism. Our communion is no more "close" or restricted than theirs, but our baptism

* Theology I, 18.

is more restricted. We believe in one and only "one baptism" that is immersion. They admit several forms of
baptism—sprinkling or pouring, and immersion.   If they
believed that sprinkling is the only scriptural mode of baptism
then they could not invite Baptists to their communion (or
membership) because they would regard us as unbaptized,
just as we cannot invite them because we regard them as
unbaptized.   Their invitation to the communion seems more
open than ours because we hold to one form of baptism while
they admit several.   It would seem more to the point if they
should call us *close Baptists* instead of *close communionists.*
An Episcopalian minister once said : "You Baptists are strong
upon the question of immersion, but weak in your views of
strict communion."   He admitted the whole question.   Our
restricted communion stands upon our views of baptism, and
we are therefore just as strong on the communion question
as we are on the question of baptism—no more, no less.   If,
on our views, regarding immersion, we are right, then we are
right in our strict communion, and right is right for ourselves and others too ; and to do the contrary is sin ; and
others should come to us and not we go to them.

It is gratifying to know that some of our Pedobaptist
brethren understand our position and give us credit for consistency.   The *Interior,* the church organ of the Western
Presbyterians, as quoted by Rev. W. H. H. Marsh says ;
" The difference between our Baptist brethren and ourselves
is an important difference.   We agree with them, however
in saying that unbaptized persons should not partake of the
Lord's Supper.   Their views compel them to think that we
are not baptized, and shut them up to close communion.
Close communion, in our view, is a more defensible position
than open communion, which is justified on the ground that

baptism is not a prerequisite to the Lord's Supper. To chide Baptists with bigotry, because they abide by the logical consequences of their system, is absurd."

A Presbyterian minister said ; "You regular Baptists are fighting the battle for us all. Open communionism rests upon only a sickly sentimentalism, and if that sentimentalism carries the day in your denomination, it will soon be making trouble in other churches. May God help you regular Baptist, to stand firm."

Rev. Thos. K. Beecher is reported to have said ; that he admired the regular Baptist, though not agreeing with them, and that if he believed as they do in reference to baptism, he would refuse to commune with any not immersed believers, under any pretence.

Said Rev. Dr. John Hall, of New York ; "If I believed with the Baptists, that none are baptized but those who are immersed on profession of faith, then I should, with them, refuse to commune with any others."

We heard a distinguished Methodist minister make the same statement in the presence of leading ministers of other denominations, and not one said a word.

Says Rev. Dr. R. Fuller ; "Dr. Sprague, that most venerable of all Presbyterian ministers, said to us when we were preaching for him in Albany, some years ago, ' I cannot see how a Baptist can admit to the Lord's Supper one whom he cannot regard as baptized ;' and every sincere man in any denomination agrees with him. In the matter before us, what is termed charity, is not only perfidiousness to Jesus, but to our Pedobaptist brethren, since it confirms them in error ; error which they hold in sincerity, but which is not less error on that account ; error which is most pernicious to the great doctrine of a spiritual church membership, and against which our fidelity to the gospel order, as to the two ordinances, is a kind, but constant and faithful remonstrance."*

In reference to union in Christian work, spiritual worship, and fraternal fellowship, Baptists are just as ready as any to join their brethren of other denominations, because here all stand on the one common platform of scriptural principle. But in reference to union in church fellowship, Baptists can join only with baptized, *i. e.,* immersed believers, since, according to their view of scriptural teaching, none but such are entitled to church membership, and to a seat at the Lord's table. In order to invite our Pedobaptist brethren to commune with us, we must either admit that they are scripturally baptized, and that sprinkling is baptism, or we must deny that baptism is prerequisite to the Lord's Supper. Our denomination is not prepared to take either of these positions, because we hold as established principles of Bible truth, that immersion, alone, is Christian baptism, and that baptism must go before communion. It is claimed, that, should Baptists adopt open communion, as it is called, a union of the different denominations would result. We answer, that those churches which profess to be open communion do not unite. Presbyterians and Methodists profess to be open communion, and yet they do not unite. We often see a church of each of these two denominations in a small village where there is room but for one church. The Presbyterians north and south, do not unite,—open communion does not bring them together ; and at the Pan-Presbyterian Council in Philadelphia, a part of that Presbyterian body refused to sit at the Lord's table with the others. When the various branches of the Presbyterian family, or the many sects of the Methodists unite among themselves, then it will be

* Religious Herald, February 4, 1875.

DANIEL DODGE, D. D.

See page 257.

time for Pedobaptists to lecture Baptists about their close
communion as a bar to Christian union. We fear that the self-
same spirit that keeps Pedobaptists apart, impels them to
unjust and bitter assaults upon the Christian denomination of
Baptists. What does it avail to sit together at the table of
the Lord, unless we have the spirit of Christ?

The Baptists cannot bring about a union at the Lord's
table by adopting sprinkling as baptism, because they do not
believe it to be scriptural; but Pedobaptists could secure
this union by adopting immersion as the common form of
baptism, without violating any command of Christ. Who
ever heard of Pedobaptists re-baptizing members received
from Baptist churches? If union is so desirable, it is more
reasonable for them to sacrifice mere convenience, than for
us to surrender principle.

It is sometimes asked, " But why refuse the Lord's Supper
to those whom we hope and expect to meet in heaven? Let
us answer this question by first quoting again from that standard authority among Pedobaptists, the eminent Presbyterian,
Dr. Hodge ; He says, " All who die in infancy are saved. * *
The scriptures nowhere exclude any class of infants, baptized
or unbaptized, born in Christian or in heathen lands, of believing or unbelieving parents, from the benefits of the
redemption of Christ."* Yet, Dr. Hodge and the Presbyterian Church refuse baptism to some infants not excluded
from heaven, simply because they are not the children of
believing parents.† Is it fair that Baptists should be cen-
sured by Presbyterians for refusing the supper to those who
shall meet us in heaven, when they themselves refuse the other

* Theology, vol. I. p. 26.
  Theology, III. p. 574- 3.

ordinance to members of the same class? And it may be added that we are consistent, and stand on scriptural ground, while the inconsistency of Dr. Hodge, and those who follow him, is apparent. "We deny to none the freedom of religious opinion, and the right to form churches on their own principles. *We only claim the same right.*"

BAPTIST PUBLICATION SOCIETY BUILDING,
PHILADELPHIA.

See page 362.

CHAPTER XXIV.

BAPTISTERIES.

E are now reading the histories of ancient nations upon exhumed and newly discovered coins, vessels, paintings, ruins, memorial monuments and inscriptions. Many things are brought to light that confirm the records of history, profane and sacred. A celebrated scientist has lately proved to the world that Homer is not a myth, but gives a poetic account of historical facts.

In the same way we read, to-day, in the baptisteries and their accompanying inscriptions and paintings, scattered all over the regions where the early Christian churches were planted, the history of the primitive church. As to-day, Old Testament history is confirmed by Babylonish records on tiles of clay, and Moabitish inscriptions on tablets of stone ; so the New Testament doctrine and practice of believers' immersion, is proved by ancient baptisteries to have been the doctrine and practice of the primitive Christians for centuries. And the story told by these Christians monuments, preserved through the ages, is a link in the chain, binding in faith and practice, as to the subject and mode of baptism, Christ and his apostolic churches, with the Baptists of to day.

At first, the sea, lakes, rivers, pools and baths, and other natural and artificial bodies of water, were used for baptism. John was baptizing in the river Jordan, and there Jesus was baptized. "And John was also baptizing in Ænon (which means "the springs") near to Salim, because there was much water there." And there, says Dean Stanley, "He plunged them under the rapid torrent."

From the very first, pools and cisterns were used, as well as rivers and springs. These were abundant about Jerusalem. Besides provision made for drinking purposes, the water supply was very plentiful. In that hot climate, where natural supplies were limited, arrangements were made for bathing, not only for health and comfort, but for religious purposes. Says Dean Stanley ; " Every synagogue, if possible, was by the side of a stream or spring." Indeed, every good sized house had a bath in the centre of it. The jailer, tradition says, was baptized in a bath in the jail yard. According to tradition, also the centurion was baptized in his own bath, which is pointed out to the traveler, to-day, at Cesarea.

The ancient pools and cisterns in and around Jerusalem were, doubtless, used by the apostles and early church for baptizing, and hence entitled to the name of baptisteries. In some of these, the 3000 converted at Pentecost were, probably, immersed.

At that early day, we could hardly expect to find baptisteries built for the purpose, for the churches had no houses to worship in of their own, but utilized private dwellings and synagogues. After awhile, however, houses for worship were constructed, and baptisteries were provided near by, or in them.

H. C. Fish, D. D., describes a baptistery in the land of Palestine, discovered among the ruins of ancient Tyre. He visited Tyre while excavations were being made "by Prof. Sepp, on the site of the famous church edifice built about the year 315 after Christ, by Paulinus, bishop of Tyre. Eusebius preached at its dedication. Here he preached the sermons in his ecclesiatical history." Prof. Sepp, not himself a Baptist, said to Dr. Fish : "Here is the old bapistery." "It is a marble structure, close to the wall, evidently as old as the church, and an original part of it. * * It is of white marble, in the shape of a cross. 'There are four steps at either end, leading down into it, and a hole is seen on the level of the floor for letting out the water. The extreme length inside is five feet six inches. The depth is three feet. The width three feet and seven inches." Prof. Sepp said ; "They immersed people here." "Did they not also baptize the children ?" asked Dr. Fish. "O no," replied the professor, "they only baptized the grown people, then."

"But," said Dr. Fish, "is it not rather small, taking out the space occupied by the steps ?" He at once went down into it, and lowered himself below the level of the top, saying, "This is the way they baptized themselves."

As Dr. Fish remarks, "Candidates often knelt in the water and projected the head and shoulders forward, doing it, perhaps, generally, three times. There is ample room for this, as one readily sees. The officiating minister stood beside the baptistery."

"There was no church in all Phoenicia to be compared with this for size and splendor. There are no other foundations of an original church edifice in any state of preservation like this, so ancient, in all the world." And the most of other ancient baptisteries are modern compared with this.

BAPTISTERY IN THE CATACOMB OF SAN PONZIANO, ROME

See page 289

"Here then," says Dr. Fish, "is a new witness for the ancient practice of immersion. If an exquisite font or basin, holding a pint or two of water, had been exhumed, evidently used for baptism, and no baptistery, it had been seized upon as a strong proof of the antiquity of sprinkling."

Dr. Cote, in his book on "Baptism and Baptisteries," gives a list of over 60 in Italy alone, as late as the year 1337, and back to the 4th century, in which that of Tyre was built.

During the persecutions of the Christians by the Roman emperors, and until the reign and conversion of Constantine, they hardly dare worship or baptize publicly, so they fled to the extensive underground tombs that honeycomb the earth beneath some parts of the city, and are called the Catacombs. Here they worshiped, baptized, and even lived, died, and were buried. In the catacomb of San Ponziano, at Rome, there is an antique baptistery. On the arch over the reservoir is a fresco painting of the baptism of Christ, which belongs, according to Boldette, to the 6th century. Bottari says ; "Upon the wall, over the arch, the Redeemer is represented up to his waist in the waters of the river Jordan, and upon his head rests the right hand of John the Baptist, standing on the shore. It is by mistake that modern artists represent Christ in the Jordan, up to his knees only, and John pouring water upon his head." John places his hand upon the head of Christ to immerse him. That John "went down into the water" with Jesus, seems probable, from the oddity of the picture.

A crystal stream of water runs through the catacomb, and flows into a reservoir made for the purpose. This is the baptistery.

A pedobaptist writer, Rev. W. H. Withrow, after measuring the pool, says: "It is obviously too small for immersion, and was evidently designed for administering the rite as shown in the fresco;" which, he says, represents John pouring water on the Saviour's head. Dr. Geo. W. Anderson, after stating the above, disproves Mr. Withrow's *opinion* by facts. He shows that the latter's measurement and suppositions, are alike erroneous.

Dr. Anderson says: "On a visit to Rome, I went to see this baptistery. My own conviction, as I stood on the platform, looking down into the pure limpid water was, that it was made expressly for immersion. Wishing to be able to speak with correctness about it, I took my tape-line from my pocket and measured its dimensions. It was, according to a note made at the time, very nearly four and a half feet long, and three and a half wide, in front. The water was within about six inches of the platform, or landing place, at the foot of the stairs. It was very clear, and the bottom was readily seen by the light of our little tapers. My first impression was that it was very shallow. Our guide, in ascending the Janiculum Hill to the entrance of the catacomb, had cut a staff, full as high as his head, and had fortunately carried it with him in our long underground walk. With it I was enabled to measure the depth of the water. It was three feet deep.

"Now is it or is it not, 'obviously too small for immersion?' It so happened that I had seen three candidates baptized, that is, immersed, the evening previous, at a little place of worship in the forum of Trajan. The baptistery which was used was not more than two feet and a half wide, the same in depth, and, probably, six feet long; about the same size as the porphyry baptistery in the Bibliotheque National at Paris, in which it is said that Clovis was baptized. I can testify that the three candidates were really immersed, yet when I compared the baptistery which was used, with this in the catacomb, I had no hesitancy in pronouncing the latter much more convenient."

"In January, 1872, Dr. Warren Randolph, of Philadelphia, in company with Rev. J. Wall and a member of one of the Waldensian churches of Northern Italy, visited the baptistery of St. Ponziano. As they stood there they read several passages from the New Testament in regard to the ordinance of baptism. The Waldensian had been led to doubt whether the rite that had been performed upon him was that which the Lord commanded. As he listened to the reading of these impressive words from the epistle to the Romans, which speaks of being buried with Christ in baptism, and looked down into the clear pool of water, he asked to be baptized then and there, confessing his faith in Jesus Christ. There was no question of the suitableness of the place on the part of Dr. Randolph or Mr. Wall, and he would then and there have been immersed had it not been deemed inexpedient to incur any possible censure from the officers of the government."

The baptisteries in the catacombs are the connecting link between the days of Christ, when fountains, rivers and pools were used, and the period of separate church edifices for Christian baptism. So that the term baptistery is applied to a building, generally separate from the church, for the purpose of baptism. They were made of various form, size, and material.

Brande, making a distinction between baptisteries and fonts, says, that the baptistery was not placed in the vestibules of the early churches, as fonts were in the churches of a later day, but was entirely separate, and even at some distance from them. And that it was not until after the 6th century that fonts were placed in the great vestibule of the church, indicating that baptism was the door of entrance into the church.

But this was not the universal rule, as we shall see. They were distinct from the church, in at least 16 cities of Italy, alone, and built as late as 1337.

The Baptistery of Constantine was built by Sixtus III., who died, A. D., 440. It stands near by the church of St. John of Latern at Rome. It is a large octagonal building of brick, 75 feet in diameter decorated with marble,. There is a connecting chapel on each side of the baptistery, one dedicated to John the Evangelist, and the other, to John the Baptist. There are ten columns of porphyry, eight inside, surrounding the baptistery, and two at the entrance. The cupola of the building rests upon eight more columns. The baptistery was at one time of porphyry, and covered entirely both within and without, with silver, the weight of which was estimated at 3008 pounds. In the middle of the basin, stood a column of porphyry, bearing on its top a golden phial, full of precious ointment. On the edge of the font were figures of seven hearts of solid silver, and a lamb in massive gold, which poured water into the basin previous to the administration of baptism. R. G. Hatfield, describing its present condition in the "Baptist Quarterly," of July, 1869, says: "At the centre of the building, within the columns, is the baptistery. It is a depression in the floor, in shape like the building itself, surrounded by heavy railings, and balustrades of marble, about 3½ feet high, and 88 feet around. The well is 28 feet in diameter, paved with marble, and its depth is 22 inches below the pavement of the building, or 32 inches below the marble coping upon which the railing stands. That the well was deeper, originally, is shown

by the marble paneling of the sides, the lower rail or band of which is now almost entirely buried. It was originally 3½ feet deep.'' There are a gate and marble steps leading to the floor of the well.

On the centre of the well is a font, or urn, of green basalt, large enough to immerse a child in. It is elevated upon a pedestal, and approached by steps. It is, evidently, of later date, and supplanted the old baptistery as infant, superceded believers' baptism. And "the small bowl-sized fonts now used, are monuments" attesting "that sprinkling has supplanted immersion." The deep baptistery would hardly have been constructed for the font. Here, then, is a silent witness of the rise of infant baptism.

This well held a large quantity of water, and there was room within the building for the congregation assembled to witness the ceremony. There are two small rooms now called chapels, which were evidently used by the candidates for changing their clothing.

There are more baptisteries at Rome, but we cannot pause here to consider them. Even connected with St. Peter's, is a baptistery in which Benedictus XIII., who was pope in 1724, restored the ancient rite of baptism by immersion, and constructed a "large basin in which adults could be immersed."

We can only mention one or two of the most remarkable of the many baptisteries of Italy. That at Florence is octagonal in form, and one hundred feet in diameter. It was built, probably, in the sixth century. It is a splendid building, with dome and marble floor. It is highly finished inside, with mosaic and ornaments. Its great bronze doors, with their beautiful bas-reliefs, surpassing those at the capitol at Washington, are said by Michael Angelo to be fit for the gates of Paradise. It is detatched from the cathedral, but stands near by. It is a splendid edifice of white and black marble. Internally, a gallery which runs nearly round the whole building, is supported by sixteen large granite columns, and the vaulted roof is decorated with mosaics. Mr. Hatfield says, that there is now no sunken basin, but at the centre, in the floor, the coping in octagonal form is seen, indicating where the old baptistery was. It is about the size of that at Rome, and an inscription bears testimony to the fact of its former existence and size. It has been filled up, and the urn placed on the pavement.

Dr. Cote says, " In the centre of this stood, originally, a very fine octangular basin of a diameter of twelve feet. This large font was destroyed by Francesco de Medici upon the occasion of the baptism of his son Philip, in 1576, greatly to the displeasure of the Florentines."

Dr. Cote says of the baptistery of Cremona; "This magnificent Baptistery is generally thought to be not much posterier to the 10th century. The building is octagonal, about sixty feet in diameter, and has sixteen columns of Veronese marble, which supports the roof and cupola. In the centre is a large octagonal marble basin of a diameter of six feet. The building is in a plain and simple Lombard style It has, what is very rare in this class of edifices, a fine projecting porch, supported by lions.

The windows, by which it is scantily lighted, might serve for a Norman castle. The walls within, are covered with ranges of Lombard arches, and fragments of fresco are seen in the gloom.

Dr. Cote gives a picture of the baptistery of Pisa, also, from which we get some idea of its external magnificence. It was begun in 1153. "This baptistery is of singular

design.   The plan is circular, with a diameter of one
hundred and sixteen feet ; the walls are eight feet thick, the
building is raised on three steps and surmounted with a
dome in the shape of a pear.   The external elevation is
divided into three stories.   * * The interior is much admired for its proportions.   * * The dome is famous for its
echo,'' and rests upon two orders of granite columns.   " In
the centre of the baptistery is a large octagonal basin, fourteen feet in diameter, and four feet deep.   It is provided
with an outlet for the escape of the water.   The basin can
be filled by means of a tube connecting with a pump outside of the building."

There is an interesting scrap of history connected with
the baptistery at Parma.   It was begun in 1106, but not
finished till 1281.   It is octagon in shape, and six stories
high, ending in a dome.   It is frescoed inside.   " In the
centre stands a very large octagonal basin, cut out from one
block of yellowish red marble.   It is about eight feet in
diameter and four feet deep, and contains another basin in
the form of a Greek cross, in which the administrator stood
during the performance of the rite.   That this font was
formally used for baptism by immersion, is clearly attested by
the following extract taken from the official report forwarded
to the Pope, November 21, 1578, in which is given a full
description of the baptistery, and its uses.   This report is still
preserved in the church records of Parma."

Dr. Cote here quotes the report, and continues : " In
one corner of the baptistery is a small font, or at least, what
is now used as such, covered with Runic foliage and strange
animals ; it stands upon a lion setting his paws upon a ram.
All the children born in Parma are now brought to this font
to be sprinkled, a practice which was introduced after the
16th century, and mentioned for the first time in 1622."

Leaving Italy, and passing over other countries, let us speak, finally, of one baptistery, each, in Germany and England.

Rev. W. H. Whitsitt, in a sketch of his visit to Lorffel-holy chapel, an alcove of the church of St. Sebald, Nuremburg, Germany, says :—"The chief object of interest in it, besides some striking pictures from old masters, was a baptismal font, cast solid from copper, said to weigh thirty-two tons. It was ornamented by various reliefs, and is considered one of the oldest works of art in Nuremberg. What particularly attracted my attention was, an arrangement by which fire could be kindled under the font for the purpose of heating the water. ' What is the meaning of this?' I inquired, pointing to the fire place. ' O,' said my attendant, 'in former times, it was the custom to heat the water before performing baptism.' 'And why has that custom been discontinued?' 'Because the church no longer immerses as formally,' was the reply. 'Look at this font, if you please. It can hold water enough to dip a child, neck and ears, and because the weather was often cold, it was sometimes found necessary to heat it. That was the custom of antiquity that has happily been abolished.' Here, I interrupted my usher with the question, 'On whose authority was this custom abolished? Does not the Bible require those who believed, to be *immersed?*' 'O yes,' was the answer, 'nobody doubts that, but the church has taken the liberty to change this ordinance, because it does not suit our climate. Only look at this font before us. As innocent as it now appears, it was once the occasion of the total destruction of the building about us. On the eleventh day of April, 1361, the Emperor Wedzel, son of Emperor Charles IV., was baptized in it, and the fire which was kindled in order to heat the water, not being watched, communicated to the floor of the church, and that night the whole of the majestic edifice became a prey to the flames—nothing was saved but this font, the cause of all the mischief.' I admitted that many inconveniences were inseparable from baptism after the Scripture mode, but insisted that these were no sufficient *excuse or occasion* for changing what was divinely ordained. About such questions my attendant insisted that there existed, of right, a difference of opinion, and that such casualties as the burning of a great church edifice justified the authorities in adopting sprinkling instead of immersion.

Dr. William Cathcart gives this account of an " Ancient English Baptistery :" "In the seventh century, Northumberland, in England, was the scene of numerous and wonderful conversions from paganism and of a grade of piety not unworthy of the best days of Christianity." Here " Organized resistance to Romanism lived longer than in any other part of Saxon England. * * Only in A. D. 664, was the papacy able to triumph. * * "About eleven miles from the Cheviot Hills, separating England from Scotland, and about the same distance from Alnwick Castle, the celebrated seat of the dukes of Northumberland, and near the village of Harbottle, there is a remarkable fountain. It rises on the top of a slight elevation, and now it is about thirty-four feet long, twenty feet in breadth, and two in depth, but it is capable of being made deeper by placing a board over an opening at one side. A stream issues from the spring, which forms a little creek. A few shade trees and benches surround it bearing the usual knife-marks of visitors. The traditions of Northumberland point out this fountain as one of the baptisteries of Paulinus, the Apostle of the North of England, where he immersed 3000, during Easter of A.D., 627.

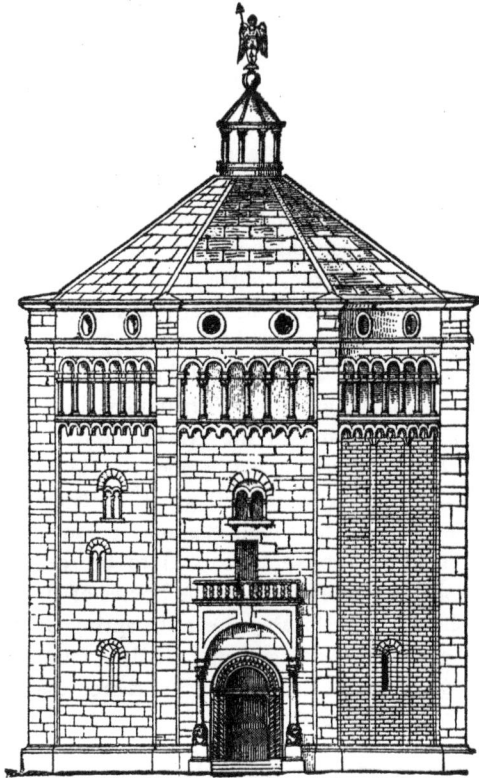

BAPTISTERY OF CREMONA, ITALY.

See page 295.

" The History of Northumberland contains and confirms the testimony of tradition. The spring is in a place of public resort for the population for many miles, and for numerous strangers, on account of its early baptismal associations. The writer saw several visitors during a half hour which he spent beside its waters. An ancient statue, as large as life, which formerly lay prostrated in the spring, now stands against a tree on its margin. The drapery of the ' bishop,' as the statue is called, shows that it was set up at a very remote period, probably only two or three centuries after Paulinus, whom it was doubtless intended to represent. A large crucifix now stands in the centre of the fountain, erected under the superintendence of the aged vicar of the parish, (a worthy clergyman who graduated at Oxford,) which bears the following inscription : ' In this fountain called the " Lady's Well,'' on the introduction of Christianity, in the Saxon reign of Edwin, and early in the 7th century, Paulinus, an English bishop, baptized about 3,000 people.' A short distance from the spring is the village of Holystones where a nunnery once stood, to which the well belonged. Some scanty remains of the convent are still to be seen, and the stones are easily to be detected in the houses of the hamlet. This establishment was located near the spring at an early day, to gain a special blessing from so holy a fountain ; and it is strong corroborative evidence of the sacred use to which Paulinus devoted its crystal waters.''*

We have now traced in the christian monuments of Asia and Europe, of Phoenicia, Italy, Germany, and England, the history of the down-fall of Bible baptism,—the immersion of the believer, and the rise of infant sprinkling.

* The cut respresenting the " Lady's Well " is from Dr. Cathcart's "Baptism of the Ages."

CHAPTER XXV.

THE GREAT COMMISSION.

MARK 16 : 15, 16, and Matthew 28 : 18, 19, contain as we have seen, Christ's great commission to his church. Baptists give proof of their apostolic origin, and, better still, their strict obedience to this command, in two respects. First; They have received it for themselves, constituted their churches upon its basis, and observed its order ; and, secondly ; They have carried the gospel to others, as it requires. Says Dr. T. G. Jones : " Here is furnished the authority under which the apostles acted in proclaiming and establishing the kingdom of Christ among the nations. Nothing is easier than to show that it called for the establishment of Baptist churches, and that the apostles and evangelists faithfully fulfilled its provisions."

The fact to be emphasized here is, that Baptists have been faithful and successful in giving the gospel to the world, in obedience to the Savior's commission, or, in other words, that they are a missionary people , and, in this respect, are like the churches and Christians of the apostolic age. Some Baptist churches, it is true, have imbibed an anti-mission spirit, and have refused to engage in the work of giving the gospel to the world. But such churches are gradually dying out, and their total extinction is only a question of time. It is a remarkable fact that churches which most actively engage in the missionary enterprise are most prosperous.

Let us now glance at the history of modern missions. This great movement had its origin among the Baptists of England, and was the means of awaking the missionary spirit among other denominations, so that what was at first a little stream, has gathered to itself other streams, until it has become a great river, which flows out to all nations, offering the water of life to the perishing, everywhere.

The first step was taken in the year 1779 by Rev. Robert Hall, father of the celebrated preacher of that name. A sermon which he preached before the Northamptonshire Association, did much to give shape to the growing tendency of the denomination. His text was Isaiah 57: 14; "Cast ye up, prepare ye the way, take up the stumbling block out of the way of my people." The sermon was enlarged and published and widely circulated. From that time we may discern religious progress. Thoughtful concern for the souls of others began to manifest itself.

But there was another cause which probably contributed to the development of the spirit of missions.

In the year 1784, at a meeting of the Northamptonshire Association, the monthly concert of prayer for missions was inaugurated. This, doubtless, has been one of the most efficient causes in the development and growth of the missionary cause.

The missionary enterprise began with prayer, and the monthly concert of prayer has become world-wide, being observed by all denominations of Christians. Of late years, however, it has not been so generally observed, though efforts are now being made to revive it. Surely an agency of such importance ought not to be allowed to fall into disuse.

Rev. Andrew Fuller, about this time, published a tract which helped the missionary movement. It was entitled "The Gospel of Christ, Worthy of all acceptation ; or, The Obligations of men fully to credit and cordially to approve whatever God makes known : wherein is considered the nature of Faith in Christ and the true Duty of those where gospel comes in this matter."

To William Carey, however, more than to any one, is due the origin of modern missions. He was the first to catch the inspiration, and his zeal and enthusiasm surpassed all others. In 1791, a friend who knew of his interest in missions, placed fifty dollars in his hands, saying, "Write about it." This enabled him to publish his "Inquiry into the obligations of Christians to use means for the conversion of the heathen ;" a treatise which had great influence. The missionary spirit began to rise among ministers and people, and the very next year, 1792, at the anniversary of the association at Nottingham, in May, Carey preached before them a sermon of overwhelming power, from Isaiah 54 : 33 ; on the obligation of the church to "EXPECT GREAT THINGS FROM GOD, AND ATTEMPT GREAT THINGS FOR GOD." His earnest words produced a profound impression. "Is it not practicable and obligatory" he asked, "to attempt the conversion of the heathen ?" And when it seemed that they were going to separate without reaching any definite result, Mr. Carey, in an agony of distress and indignation, seizing Mr. Fuller by the hand, demanded if they were going to part without doing anything in the matter. This appeal was irresistible, and the result was that a resolution was adopted to appoint a committee to prepare a plan for a

HOUSE AT KETTERING, ENGLAND, WHERE THE FIRST BAPTIST MISSIONARY SOCIETY WAS
ORGANIZED, OCT. 2, 1792.

See page 305.

Baptist missionary society. It was but little thought of at the time, but to us it is an event of vast importance, as we view it in connection with the results that have flowed from it.

On the twelfth day of the following October, this committee, consisting of twelve ministers, met at Kettering in the back parlor of Mr. Beeby Wallis. This was the birth place of one of the greatest enterprises of this or any other age,— the first modern Protestant missionary society. Here and then was formed, "The Particular Baptist Society for the propagation of the Gospel among the Heathen." This result was reached only after long and prayerful discussion and deliberation. The men who organized this society had but little of this world's-goods, but they were rich in faith, and while to carry the gospel to the heathen would require a large amount of money, they believed that God was able to supply all that would be needed. They started the financial part of the enteprise by their own personal subscriptions, which amounted to sixty-five dollars each.

This was a small beginning for a missionary society, but it was a very respectable contribution for twelve ministers, in view of the times and their very small salaries. One of the number, Rev. Samuel Pearce, had the honor of securing from his people in Birmingham, the first church collection for modern missions.

After the society was formed, other questions arose. Who are willing to go? and to what part of the heathen world shall we send? At that day these seemed very difficult questions, but they were soon providentially answered. God, in answer to prayer, furnished the men and opened for them a field of labor. Mr. Carey promptly offered his services, and Dr. John Thomas, who had been a practicing physician in India, and had also been engaged in preaching to the heathen as he had opportunity, offered himself to be sent back as a missionary to that country. He had returned to England in order to stir up the Baptists to engage in the work of foreign missions, and was glad to take part in the new enterprise. These two men, Carey and Thomas, were accepted by the society, and India was selected as the field of their labors.

The society was very weak, and had few friends and little sympathy, while there was a great deal of opposition to the movement. In order to raise money to pay the passage of these first missionaries, Mr. Fuller went from door to door begging the more wealthy Baptists of London to contribute to the cause. From most of them, he met with such a cold reception, and was so often refused, that he was compelled to turn into the lanes and alleys, that no one might see him weeping over his failure and disappointment. There were many who refused money even for this noble enterprise. But he persevered until at last enough money was secured to send these two devoted men to India, and they set sail for their chosen field of labor on the 13th of June, 1793.

Mr. Fuller did a great deal, not only in originating the work, but also in sustaining it and carrying it on. He was appointed financial secretary of the missionary society, and accomplished a great work in overcoming the prejudices of the people, and gaining their sympathies for the missionaries and their work, and in raising money for their support. In carrying on this work in the home-field, Mr. Fuller performed an amount of labor in the way of correspondence traveling, preaching, writing, and collecting, and in geernal managing the affairs of the society, which required an amount of energy and activity almost unequaled.

He not always received the co-operation even of ministers. Many of the pastors did not understand the great commission, and a great part of Mr. Fuller's work was to convert them to right views. It is said that at one time he was very anxious to obtain an introduction into some of the pulpits in the Eastern part of England, where there was a strong prejudice against him. A plan was arranged so that he might have an opportunity to preach to some of the people without their knowing by whom they were addressed. A friend of his who had been appointed to preach before the association, gave his place to Mr. Fuller. No one knew the strange preacher, but all were delighted with his sermon, and many expressed the wish that Mr. Fuller had been there to hear it, as they considered it a complete refutation of the doctrines held by him.

At length one of the ministers who was in the secret, rose and very gravely moved that the thanks of the association be given to Rev. Andrew Fuller for his excellent sermon, and that he be requested to print it. The result was that their prejudices were removed, their sympathies were gained, and their pulpits were opened for him to plead the cause of missions.

Another good story is told of Mr. Fuller. He once called on a pious and benevolent nobleman, who, though a churchman, was friendly to dissenters, and very generous in his charitable gifts. When Mr. Fuller had stated to him the nature and claims of the mission, his lordship handed him a guinea. Observing that it was given with an air of indifference, Mr. Fuller asked ; " My Lord, does this come from the heart ?" " What matter is that ?" replied the nobleman ; "suppose it does not come from the heart, it may answer your purpose as well. If you get the money, why should you care whether it comes from the heart or not ?"

U

"Take it back," said the man of God. "I cannot take it. My Lord and Master requires the heart." "Well, give it back to me," said the nobleman, "it did not come from the heart." He took the guinea, and stepping to his desk, drew a check on his banker for twenty pounds, about one hundred dollars, and handing it to Mr. Fuller, said; "This comes from the heart. I know the principles by which you are governed. I love the Lord Jesus Christ and his cause, and know that no offering is acceptable to him unless it comes from the heart."

Mr. Fuller continued to fill the office of secretary of the missionary society for twenty-three years, and by his zealous advocacy of the cause, and his wise management of the society's affairs, laid the foundations of a work that has gone on with ever-increasing efficieney and power. The mighty impulse which he gave to the missionary movement at its start, still continues to operate in carrying it forward, and the influence of his writings and his example, are among the undying forces which contribute toward the fulfillment of the great commission. Faithfully did Fuller hold the rope while Carey went down into the mines.

ANDREW FULLER, D. D.

See page 306.

CHAPTER XXVI.

THE CONSECRATED COBBLER.

WILLIAM Carey was the great pioneer of Protestant missions of modern times. He was a shoemaker by trade, and when he proposed to undertake the work of missions, people ridiculed the idea of such humble men as Carey and his associates converting the heathen, so, in derision, they were called "Consecrated Cobblers."

William Carey was born on the 17th of August, 1761. He was the son of the parish clerk and was brought up an Episcopalian. At the age of twenty-two years he was converted, and baptized by Dr. Ryland, who, speaking of the event, shortly after, said, that he had baptized a poor journeyman shoemaker, in November 1783, in the river Neu. Being a shoemaker, he worked at his bench, and at the same time applied himself to study with such diligence, that he soon became wonderfully proficient in the languages of the original Scriptures, as well as in several of the modern languages.

While working at his trade, making and mending shoes, he had his book before him, and while his hands were employed on the one, his mind was busy at the other, and

thus he acquired a knowledge of Greek, Latin, Hebre,
French, German, Italian, and other languages. When his-
employer died, Mr. Carey married the man's sister and continued his business. Unfortunately, his wife was an uneducated
woman who did not rise with her husband, and hence was a
hindrance rather than a help to him in the great work of
life.

While working at his trade, Mr. Carey was often seen
with a pack on his back, going to market to sell the shoes he
had made. He afterward exchanged his business for that of
school teaching, an occupation more in harmony with his
literary tastes. Before he became a missionary he was pastor
of the Baptist church at Moulton.

From books of history and travels, and especially from
Cook's ·voyages, he became acquainted with the degraded
condition of the heathen, and from the New Testament he
learned the Christian's duty toward them. While teaching
geography to the pupils in his ·school, he conceived the sublime idea of missions to the heathen. This idea grew in his
mind, and took possession of his heart, and filled him with
enthusiasm. He had a large map on which he wrote all the
information he could gain in reference to the people of each
country. To this map he devoted much study, and while he
mused, the fire burned. He felt, and felt it deeply, that what
the people of all these countries needed was the religion of
Jesus, and that the gospel was their only hope. Believing
that the Son of God died on the cross for all men, he was
ready to go to carry the glad tidings of salvation to the poor
heathens who were perishing in their sins. It was under the
impulse of these feelings that he wrote, in 1791, as we have
seen, on the conversion of the heathen, and in the following
year· preached his memorable sermon at Nottingham which
led to the formation of the Baptist Missionary Society.

It was remarked by Wilberforce, that "a sublimer thought can not be conceived than when a poor cobbler formed the resolution to give to the millions of Hindoos, the Bible in their own language." But what is most surprising is, that Mr. Carey at first found so little sympathy among his own brethren in the ministry. It is related that, at a meeting of ministers held at Northampton, Mr. Carey proposed as a topic for discussion, "The duty of Christians to attempt the spread of the Gospel among heathen nations ;" when the venerable Dr. Ryland sprang to his feet to denounce the proposition. "Young man," said he, "sit down ; when God pleases to convert the heathen, he will do it without your aid or mine." Even Mr. Fuller was at first startled by the novelty and magnitude of the proposal, and described his feelings as resembling those of the infidel courtier of Israel who said : "If the Lord should make windows in heaven might such a thing be."

Mr. Carey's discouragements were very great. He met with opposition not only from his brethren but even from his own household. His wife was not at first in sympathy with his views, and when he was appointed by the society as a missionary to India, she refused to go. All efforts to induce her to accompany her husband seemed unavailing, and the time was appointed for his departure with Mr. Thomas, when they were providentially delayed, and Mrs. Carey at last consented to go.

Mr. Carey felt that the cause was one of the highest importance, and he was determined that nothing should turn him aside from his noble purpose. Many difficulties had been overcome and new ones would be met at every step. Now that they were ready to enter upon their chosen work, the East India Company refused to give them permission to go to India as missionaries.

The East India Company carried on a large trade with India, and they feared that the work of missions would interfere with their business. When the missionaries found that they could not gain the consent of the company, they determined to go without it. So they went to India in a Danish vessel. On arriving there, they were without friends, and for a time were exposed to great hardships. Mr. Thomas proposed to support himself by practicing medicine, while Mr. Carey went to work at clearing the jungles, at the same time, keeping out of the way of the company for fear of arrest. In 1794, Mr. Carey took charge of an indigo factory, and Mr. Thomas took charge of another, and through their employer, they obtained permission to remain in the country. Marshman, his co-laborer in missions, gives a sad picture of the distressing circumstances to which Mr. Carey was for a time subjected : "He was in a foreign land, without a friend and without a farthing, except as he could wring it from Mr. Thomas, and it required all the strength derived from a firm confidence in the Divine promises, to keep him from being overwhelmed with despondency. His wife, who had accompanied him to India with great reluctance, was constantly upbraiding him with their wretchedness, and contrasting their indigence with the comparative luxury in which Mr. Thomas was living. His family, consisting of seven persons, was crowded into a small, ill ventilated house, without any of the conveniences requisite for the European constitution in an Eastern climate, and his wife and two of his children were attacked with dysentery, from which they recovered but slowly. Driven to distraction by this accumulation of troubles, he resolved to remove to the Soonderbuns, where he was offered the occupation of a small house, and proposed to take a grant of land and cultivate it for the support of his

WILLIAM CAREY, D. D.

See page 303.

family. But amidst all these difficulties, he never lost sight of the great object that had taken him to India."

We are reminded, at this crisis, of one of the celebrated sayings of the Duke of Wellington. A young clergyman once asked him if he did not think it almost useless and extravagant to preach - the gospel to the Hindoos? The duke replied : "With that you have nothing to do. Look to your marching orders ; Go, preach the gospel to every creature." Mr. Carey must have looked well to his marching orders.

He had determined to obey and to leave results with God, and his faith and patience had their reward. In 1796, Mr. Fountain came to the help of the missionaries, and, in 1799, four others joined the work; Marshman, Ward, Grant, and Brunsdon. But the East India Company, to their everlasting shame, refused to allow the missionaries to remain under their dominion. So, in the year 1800, they all removed to the Danish settlement of Serampore, where they enjoyed the protection of the Danish governor.

During these years of trial and suffering Mr. Carey had been busy in translating the Bible into the Bengalee language. When the new missionaries arrived, the whole work was completed and ready for the press, except two books of the Old Testament. Mr. Ward set the types with his own hands, and on the eighteenth of March, 1800, the first sheet of the New Testament was presented to Mr. Carey with feelings of exultation.

But great as was the joy of the missionaries at the completion of this important work, a still greater joy awaited them. In November, 1800, a native came to Dr. Thomas with a dislocated arm. After attending to the man's arm, the doctor spoke to him very fervently of the folly of idolatry and told him about the great truths of Christianity. The man was deeply affected and wept. He came again to hear, and forsaking idolatry he embraced the Christian religion and asked to be baptized. He openly renounced his caste by sitting down to eat with the missionaries. This act caused great excitement among the heathen, and he was seized by a mob and brought before a magistrate. But no criminal charge being brought against him he was released. This was the first Hindoo convert, and the first fruit of seven long years of missionary labor and suffering. His name was Krishnu. On the twenty-eighth of December, 1800, Mr. Carey walked down to the Ganges with his eldest son on one side, and Krishnu on the other, and baptized them both in the river. This interesting scene was witnessed by the governor and several Europeans, a large body of Portuguese, and a dense crowd of Hindoos and Mohammedans. The governor is said to have shed tears at the affecting scene.

This was the beginning of better days. From this time. converts, and churches, and missionaries, began to multiply, and the operations of the missionary society were extended to other countries besides India.

Thus, from small beginnings, the work advanced so rapidly that in a few years the converts from heathenism to Christianity were numbered by thousands.

The success of the missionary cause was its best vindication. Success did much, also, to secure to Dr. Carey the honor which he deserved. His name stands pre-eminent, not only as a zealous pioneer in missionary work, but, also, as a man of genius, a scholar and philanthropist. In translating the Scriptures and giving the Bible to the heathen in their own language, he performed a most glorious achievement and erected for himself a monument of unfading splendor. It will give us some idea of the magnitude and importance of his work to state that, in 1806, Dr. Carey and his associates were engaged in printing the Scriptures in six different languages and translating them into six more. In 1819 they were printing and translating the Bible in twenty-seven languages. And, altogether, they circulated 200,000 copies of the Scriptures translated into forty languages spoken by 270,000,000 of people. And, besides this, Dr. Carey, by learned labors at Calcutta, Dr. Marshman, by his school at Serampore, and Mr. Ward, by his printing press, each contributed more than five thousand dollars a year to the mission.

They had given themselves to the cause of missions, and when they had the opportunity to make money, they delighted to give that too.

The services of Dr. Carey became very valuable to the government, from which he received a large salary. Dr. Marshman had a school which brought him a large income, and Mr. Ward's printing offices brought him a large sum, and thus they were enabled to carry on the missionary work, and, at the same time, to contribute largely to the good cause.

The missionaries, on account of their valuable services, were highly esteemed by the officers of government, and began to be invited into the very best society. The daughter of Dr. Marshman became the wife of the distinguished Christian soldier, General Havelock, himself a Baptist, whose name became so illustrious in connection with the Afghan war, and the Sepoy rebellion. The Christian warrior, when dying, surrounded by distinguished men, called his son, saying ; " Come, see how a Christian can die." It is related that on the occasion of a public dinner given by Lord Hastings, the Governor General of India, a pompous officer

impertinently inquired if Dr. Carey were not once a shoe-·
maker? Dr. Carey happened to overhear the question, and
stepping up among the circle of brilliant officers, replied,
very much to the confusion of the questioner, " No Sir, only
a cobbler."

While seeking only the honor which comes from God,
they gained the respect of the world, at last, and their names
have been enrolled among the heroes and benefactors of the
race. The name of Dr. Carey will ever stand in unfading
luster at the head of the list of noble men who have devoted
their lives to the work of modern missions.

After a life of eminent usefulness, this great and good
man went to his heavenly reward on the ninth day of June,
1834.

His dying bed was peaceful. During his last hours he
spent most of the time in praise and prayer, and in view of
his approaching departure, he uttered these memorable
words ; " I have no raptures, and I have no fears ; for the
cross and atonement of Christ are my all-sufficient ground of
hope and joy."

From small beginnings have come marvelous results.
The society formed at Kettering now enjoys an income of
$300,000 annually, and has pressed out its lines, not only in
Italy, but to China, to Australia, to Africa, to the West Indies,
and to other places, so that now, in the English colonies, alone,
including the Canadas, there are over eight hundred ministers,
one thousand churches, and one hundred thousand members.
Besides, there are other Baptist societies, supported by separate
funds for foreign missions, among them those of Christian
women, to send the gospel to their heathen sisters. In
addition, the General Missionary Society was formed, 1816,
which is doing noble work among the benighted.

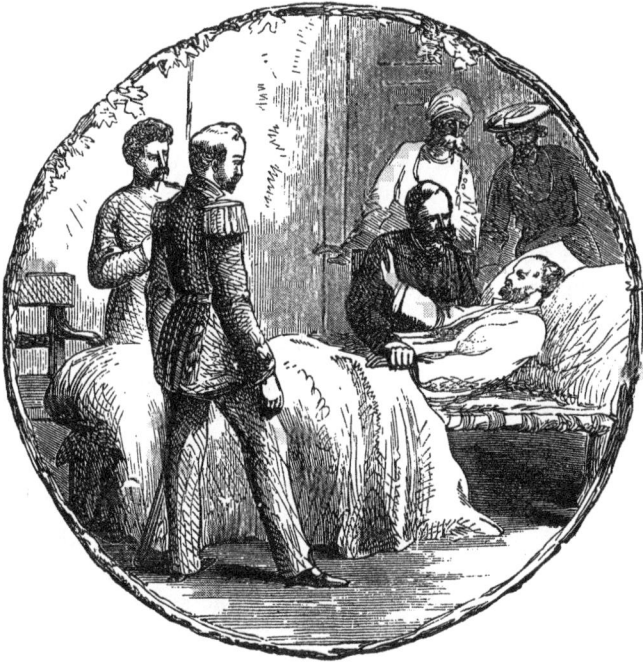

DEATH OF GENERAL HAVELOCK.

See page 317.

The missionary spirit in the churches has had its influence in quickening every branch of the work at home. Only five years after the foreign missionary society was formed at Kettering, the Baptist Home Missionary Society was organized—1797, to furnish the destitute towns of England, Wales, Scotland and Ireland with the gospel. Just before the great missionary awakening, there was a decline among the Baptists in the United Kingdom, but from that period on, there has been growth and progress. In 1763 there were but two hundred Baptist churches in England, but now, in England, alone, there are one thousand nine hundred and thirty five churches, one thousand four hundred and eight ministers, and two hundred and ten thousand, seven hundred and eighty seven members. Besides, which is very remarkable for so small a territory, there are, in Wales, five hundred and twenty six churches, three hundred and ninety seven ministers, and sixty-eight thousand, seven hundred and eighty five members, and they practice strict communion.

The English Baptist year-book is a model of its kind, with its cuts of churches, its four hundred pages, and its low price of fifty cents. While contributing for foreign missions the large sum of one dollar, per member, a year, and sustaining societies for building church edifices, for publishing Bibles, tracts &c., our English brethren have not neglected the intellectual and bodily needs of man. In this they are true followers of Christ. Societies have been formed for educating ministers' children, and students for the ministry, for aiding active pastors, for the support of the infirm, the aged, the widows, and the orphans, and many other such laudable objects. Contributions are freely made, often without solicitations, and some are largely endowed. Mr. Spurgeon need not ask any one, except the Lord, for money for his enterprises. The Baptists united in efforts for man's moral and spiritual good with their Pedobaptist brethren, and their endeavors began before the work of foreign missions was taken up, but they were greatly quickened afterward. Besides schools of high and low grade, they have one university in London, and several colleges and theological seminaries. Spurgeon's church is in the centre of a large circle of Christian labors, the influence of which is felt all round the world. The orphanage, the college, and the multitudinous works of the church, are the wonder of the world. With Mr. Spurgeon, the foremost preacher and Christian worker of his age, at their head, the English Baptists have the assurance of future success.

BIRTHPLACE OF WILLIAM CAREY.   See page 310.

CHAPTER XXVII

JUDSON.

N the 19th of February, 1812, four American missionaries embarked in the brig "Caravan," from Salem,
Mass., for Burmah. They arrived at Calcutta, June
17th. Two of them were Adoniram Judson, and
his wife Ann H. Judson. He was born in Malden,
Mass., August 9th, 1788, and was educated at Brown University. He entered the Theological Seminary at Andover,
in 1808, and was converted soon afterward, and joined the
Congregational church.

While at Andover, he and a few other pious students
turned their attention to foreign missions, and, impressed
with the wretched condition of the heathen, resolved to
devote themselves to the work, and presented themselves to
their older brethren in the ministry and the churches, as
ready to be sent abroad for that purpose. This led to the
formation of the " American Board of Commissioners for
Foreign Missions," in June, 1810. And Judson and wife,
with others, were sent to Burmah by the board.

The long voyage to Calcutta was partly occupied by Mr.
Judson in examining the subject of Christian baptism.

There were two reasons for this special study. First, he hoped to have conversions among the heathen, and what to do about the baptism of children and servants he did not know. Then he was going to reside for awhile among the Baptist missionaries at Serampore, and expected that they would introduce the subject of baptism, and that he would be called upon to defend his views.

Hear the result in his own words: "I could not find a single intimation in the New Testament that the children and domestics of believers were members of the church, or entitled to any church ordinance in consequence of the profession of the head of their family. Everything discouraged the idea. When baptism was spoken of, it was always in connection with believing. None but believers were commanded to be baptized, and it did not appear to my mind that any others were baptized."

"I knew that I had been sprinkled in infancy, and that this had been deemed baptism. But throughout the whole New Testament I could find nothing that looked like sprinkling in connection with the ordinance of baptism."

He felt that he had never yet received Christian baptism, and that his only consistent course was to join the Baptists. This plunged him into great difficulty and distress, and it cost him a struggle to decide.

"Must I, then," he asked, "forsake my parents, the church with which I am connected, the society under whose patronage I have come out, the companions of my missionary undertaking? Must I forfeit the good opinion of all my friends in my native land, occasioning grief to some, and provoking others to anger, and be regarded, henceforth, by all my former dear acquaintances as a weak, despicable Baptist, who has not sense enough to comprehend the connection between the Abrahamic and the Christian system ? All this was mortifying ; it was hard to flesh and blood. But I thought, again, it is better to be guided by the opinion of Christ, who is the truth, than by the opinion of men, however good, whom I know to be in an error."

"If I quieted my conscience in regard to my own personal baptism, and concluded that, on account of my peculiar circumstances, it was best to consult my own convenience, rather than the command of Christ, still the question would return, with redoubled force : How am I to treat the children and domestics of converted heathens ?" Mrs. Judson, in a letter to a friend, said : " An examination of the subject of baptism commenced on board the Caravan. As Mr. Judson was continuing the translation of the New Testament, which he began in America, he had many doubts respecting the meaning of the word baptize. After arriving at Burmah, he continued the examination of the foundation of the Pedobaptist system. The more he examined, the more his doubts increased ; and, unwilling as he was to admit it, he was *afraid* the Baptists were right and he was wrong. I felt afraid he would become a Baptist, and frequently urged the consequences, if he should. I always took the Pedobaptist side in reasoning with him, even after I was as doubtful of the truth of their system as he. We procured the best authors on both sides ; compared them with the Scriptures, examined and re-examined the sentiments of Baptists and Pedobaptists, and were finally compelled, from a conviction of truth, to embrace those of the former."

They requested baptism at the hands of the Baptist missionaries at Serampore, who were "extremely surprised," for nothing had been said upon the subject by either party. They were baptized on the 6th of September, 1812, in the Baptist chapel at Serampore. Luther Rice, who was ordained with Mr. Judson, and who arrived in India a short time afterward, also joined the Baptists. The effect of the baptism of Judson and his companions, upon the Baptists of America, was truly startling.

"It came," says Dr. Caldwell, "like a voice from heaven, laying almost a divine command upon them to go up and possess the land." Missionaries, competent and on the ground, were provided at their hand, whom they must take, or fly in the face of duty, and Providence itself. They were confronted by an unexpected opportunity, obligation even, to begin at once, and in earnest, a mission in the East. The fields and the pioneers had been selected for them.

There was no organization for foreign missions at the time among them, and no society able to undertake the support of a mission in India. The missionary spirit, even, was slumbering among them. There was something done at home, and a little abroad. Mr. Carey acknowledged the receipt of $6,000 from America, in 1806 and 1807. The Baptists numbered two hundred thousand, but the country was involved in war with Great Britain.

And now God calls them to sustain a mission in a foreign field ! "Such calls and such opportunities," says Dr. Caldwell, "have sometimes come and found no response. But now that seemed impossible. The Baptists in earlier days had suffered depressions and disabilities ; they had conflicts to maintain, which, possibly, contracted their sympathies, and, certainly, their ability, to engage in remote enterprises. But from these they were emerging. They stood, with all sects, equal before the law, having themselves had a large show in the honor of their victory. They were increasing, and feeling the courage of their numbers as well as of their principles. Their spirit and their sympathies were expanding, and the

ADONIRAM JUDSON, D. D.

See page 322.

opportunity which had come so suddenly both for concentration and diffusion, equally to consolidate them into unity, at least of co-operation, and to take them out of themselves into the grander movement of the evangelization of heathendom."

The first missionary society was formed in Boston, which assumed the support of the missionaries until the denomination in all the states could take action. "The General Missionary Convention of the Baptist Denomination in the United States for Foreign Missions," was formed in Philadelphia, May 18th, 1814. Rev. A. Judson, was appointed the missionary of the body to India, and Rev. Luther Rice to visit the Baptist churches of America, to interest them in the cause of missions. Thus it was that the first general foreign missionary society originated amongst the Baptists of this country.

The very first difficulty Judson encountered was from the English, who had possession of the country under the name of the East India Company for trading. They were opposed to any effort to evangelize India, and resisted Carey and his companions. Mr. and Mrs. Judson, and Mr. Rice, were ordered to England. They were permitted, however, to go to the Isle of France. Mr. Rice went home, and the Judsons first went to Madras, but compelled to flee again by the only available vessel there. They finally reached Rangoon, the principal seaport of Burmah, July 13th, 1813.

"A mission to Rangoon we had been accustomed to regard with feelings of horror," wrote Mr. Judson; "We must either venture there or be sent to Europe." They here found a home in the English Baptist mission house of Felix Carey. This same man, then driven about, the English people and government were to learn to honor, and love. The field was soon left to the American Missionaries.

It took them a long time to acquire the difficult language of Burmah, which was necessary for preaching to the people, and translating the Scriptures. And when some at home, growing tired, began to wonder and ask, "What prospect of ultimate success is there?" Judson wrote to Luther Rice, "Tell them, as much as there is an Almighty and faithful God, who will perform his promises, and no more. If this does not satisfy them, beg them to let me stay and try it, and to let you come, and to give us *bread*; or if they are unwilliug to risk their bread on such a forlorn hope, as has nothing but the WORD OF GOD to sustain it, beg of them, at least, not to prevent others from giving us bread ; and if we live some 20 or 30 years, they may hear from us again."

On the 15th of October, 1816, Mr. Hough, another American missionary, arrived ; and in September, 1818, Messrs. Coleman and Whitlock, and their wives came. A press and Burmese types were given them by the brethren at Serampore. Thus equipped, they could publish the Word of God in the language of the native heathen.

Having begun public worship in the Zayat built for the purpose, in April, 1819, on the 4th of May, Dr. Judson announced the first Burmese convert to the Lord Jesus Christ. Moung Nau asked baptism, and as all the misssionaries were corvinced of the reality of his religion, his wish was com-plied with. Dr. Judson thus records the event : "June 27, Lord's day. There were several strangers present at worship. After the usual course, I called Moung Nau before me, read and commented upon an appropriate portion of Scripture, asked him several questions concerning his *faith, hope* and *love*, and made the baptismal prayer, having concluded to have all the preparatory exercises done in the zayat. We then proceeded to a large pond in the vicinity, the bank of which is graced with an enormous image of Gaudama, and there administered baptism to the first Burman convert. O, may it prove the beginning of a series of baptisms in the Burman empire, which shall continue in uninterrupted succession to the end of time. July 4. Lord's day. We have had the pleasure of sitting down for the first time to the Lord's table with a converted Burman."

It was seven years, almost to a day, after Mr. Judson landed in India before the first Burman was converted to Christianity. In November, two more were baptized : This time in still and solemn night; and on Lord's day, the 14th, in the evening, THE THREE CONVERTS HELD A PRAYER MEET-ING, of their own accord, in the zayat.

The object of the missionaries had now come to be understood by the Burmese government, and the people, fearing the authorities, ceased their visits to the zayat. A visit to the capital, Ava, to lay the matter before the emperor, and obtain his permission, asking toleration for the Christian religion being determined on, Mr. Judson and Mr. Coleman, set out for Ava, in December. Their appeals were, of course, unheeded, and danger seemed impending, but the three converts stood firm, when upon the return to Rangoon they were made acquainted with the state of affairs.

The little church, despite persecution, grew slowly ; and under date of June 4, Mr. Judson writes ; " I have this day taken Moung Shua-ba (whom he had formally baptized) into the service of the mission. He bids fairer than any other member of the church to be qualified, in due time, for the ministry." Thus did God provide the first native assistant, now numbering 1000, in preaching the gospel.

In 1822, Mrs. Judson visited the United States, on account of her health, and the next year she returned to Burmah, accompanied by Rev. Jonathan Wade and wife. The mission had further been re-inforced by Rev. Jonathan Price, a missionary physician.

In 1822 Mr. Judson set out with Dr. Price for Ava, whither the latter was summoned by the emperor, on account of his medical skill. Mr. Judson, having secured a place for his mission in the capital, returned to Rangoon to await Mrs. Judson s arrival from America, and to prepare for removing, by invitation of the king, to Ava. While thus tarrying at Rangoon, he finished the translation of the New Testament in the Burman language.

Mr. Wade and Mr. Hough, with their wives, were to remain in charge of the little church there, which now numbered eighteen native converts who all seemed to be living for Christ.

Upon the arrival of Mrs. Judson, Mr. Judson hastened with her to Ava. But they knew not to what trials and sorrows they were hurrying. It was not yet God's time for opening Ava to the gospel, though the missionaries were plainly following the leadings of Providence. War was just beginning between the English and Burmah. The Judsons passed the Burman army on their way to Ava, where they found they had lost favor with the king, and that all foreigners were regarded with suspicion. Mrs. Judson thus describes the arrest of her husband, in 1824, on suspicion of giving information to the enemy.

" On the 8th of June, just as we were preparing for dinner, in rushed an officer, holding a black book, with a dozen Burmans, accompanied by *one*, whom, from his spotted face, we knew to be an executioner and a 'son of the prison.'

GIRLS' BOARDING SCHOOL, MAULMAIN.

See page 367.

Where is the teacher ?' was the first inquiry. Mr. Judson presented himself. You are called by the king said the officer—a form of speech always used when about to arrest a criminal. The spotted man instantly seized Mr. Judson, threw him on the floor, and produced the small cord, the instrument of torture. I caught hold of his arm. ' Stay !' said I : ' I will give you money.' ' Take her, too,' said the officer, ' she also is a foreigner.' Mr. Judson, with an imploring look, begged that they would let me remain till further orders. The scene was shocking beyond description. The whole neighborhood had collected, and the hardened executioner, with a kind of hellish joy, drew tight the cords, bound Mr. Judson, and dragged him off, I knew not whither. In vain I begged and entreated the spotted face to take the silver and loosen the ropes; but he spurned the offers and immediately departed. When a few rods from the house, the unfeeling wretches again threw their prisoner on the ground and drew the cords still tighter, so as almost to prevent respiration.''

Mr. Judson was committed to "the death-prison," while his tender wife spent a night of almost indescribable anguish. " A guard of ten ruffians" was placed around the house, who tried to force an entrance into it, and spent the night in dreadful carousing and almost diabolical language. But the anguish of that night was to be prolonged and intensified for months. Both husband and wife were doomed to suffer terrible indignities and cruelties before release came.

With all the white prisoners, Mr. Judson was confined in the death-prison, with three pairs of fetters, each, and fastened to a long pole to prevent them moving. Mrs. Judson, after effecting her own release, was hardly permitted to alleviate the sufferings of her husband. But with true womanly fidelity, she attended upon all the prioners, as far as she was allowed, by paying a fee to the keepers, preparing their food, and encouraging them. "In the midst of these trials, her little daughter Maria was born to the lonely woman." For seven long months this bitter imprisonment continued. Mrs. Judson often walked from the prison to her house, two miles distant, after nine o'clock at night, alone, fatigued and anxious. More than once, as Mrs. Judson afterwards learned, the execution of the captives had been ordered.

One day she found the prisoners all gone. She feared the worst. After many efforts she at length found out where they had been taken, as it was presumed, to be put to death, and she followed. Sick and exhausted with fever, Mr. Judson had been seized, and hatless, and shoeless, with a rope around his waist, and tied to another prisoner, he had been hurried with the others across the burning sands, miles away. The soles of his feet became blistered, and the skin peeled off. He would have fainted by the way, and been left to his fate, but a kind friend at hand helped him to Oung-pen-la, the end of the terrible journey. The prison-pen was wretched here, but Mr. Judson was allowed some liberty, immediately. Mrs. Judson administered to the necessities of the prisoners, but sickness laid her low in her wretched, little room. Before this, that terrible scourge, the small pox, entered the family, and two of them, May and the baby, had it. Now, little Maria, deprived by Mrs. Judson's illness of her nourishment, was carried daily in the arms of her manacled father to the women of the place, who had babies, that she might excite their compassion and be fed by them with their own milk.

At length the victorious English army was marching upon Ava. Gladly did the king send forth the outraged missionaries, and plead with them to make terms for him with the approaching foe, and spare the capital. Returning good for evil, Mr. Judson acted as embassador to secure peace. Even at this time, when complete release from their troubles seemed at hand, Mrs. Judson was stricken down again with disease, the spotted fever at Ava, which nearly terminated her life. The English demanded as one condition of peace, the unconditional release of all the prisoners. Mr. and Mrs. Judson soon found themselves on their way to the camp of the English.

Mr. Judson says : "It was on a cool, moonlight evening, in the month of March that, with hearts filled with gratitude to God so overflowing with joy at our prospects, we passed down the Irrewade, surrounded by six or eight golden boats, and accompained with all we had on earth. We now, for the first time for more than a year and a half, felt that we were free, and no longer subject to the oppressive yoke of the Burmese. And with what sensations of delight, on the next morning, did I behold the masts of the steamboats, the sure presage of being within the bounds of civilized life." Mr. and Mrs. Judson were invited at once by Sir Archibald Campbell, the English commander, to his head-quarters. A tent was provided for them near the tent of the general, and they were invited to eat at his table. The English officers seemed to vie with one another in showing the missionaries distinguished honors. "Their conduct towards us," says Mr. Judson, "formed a striking contrast to that of the Burmese. I presume to say that no persons on earth were ever happier than we were during the fortnight we passed in the English camp. *What shall we render to the Lord for all his benefits towards us ?*"

They reached the mission house at Rangoon after an absence of two years and three months.

After her husband's arrest, Mrs. Judson buried the manuscript of the Burmese New Testament, with some silver coin, under the house, but took it out for fear of mould, and sewing it up in a mean looking and hard pillow, so that even the jailers would not want it, Dr. Judson took the charge of it himself in the death-prison. Only a part of it had then been published.

When Dr. Judson took the fever his wife secured permission for his removal to a lion's pen in the prison yard. Sometime before the war, some one had presented the king with a noble lion. When the Burmans were defeated by the English, some superstitious persons spoke of the lion in the British flag. This was enough. The lion was supposed to have something to do with their defeat, and was removed to a strong iron cage in the prison yard, and suffered there to die of starvation. The prisoners had seen men die from want of food and water, but the agony of the poor beast was beyond all they had seen. When he died, Mrs. Judson asked to take her sick husband into this pen, which afforded better accommodations than the prison, and attend him. There he lived till sent to the prison hole far away. All that belonged to him was taken by the Burmese attendants. The man to whose lot the pillow fell, uncovered the mat, which he kept, and threw what he deemed the hard, worthless pillow away. "Some hours after, Moung Ing, stumbling upon this one relic of the vanquished prisoners, carried it to the house as a token, and several months from that time, the manuscript that now makes a part of the Burmese Bible was found within, uninjured."

Failing to secure toleration for Burmans at Rangoon, and finding the little church scattered, Mr. Judson moved to Amherst, within the territory conquered and retained by the English. Hoping yet to secure religious toleration in Burmah,

RANGOON.

See page 327.

Dr. Judson went as one of the English commissioners to Ava, but again failed. The money he received for his services he turned over to the missionary society.

But while away on this important mission, a sad blow of affliction overtook him. On the 24th of October, 1826, while he was away from home, Mrs. Judson died. They buried her near the spot where he first landed, under the far famed Hopia tree, or tree of hope, and put a small fence around the spot to protect the grass. Mr. and Mrs. Wade arrived about a month after the death of Mrs. Judson.

It was not long after, Mr. Judson, stricken in heart, returned to his desolate home, that he laid little Maria, his only child, by the side of her mother.

On the 27th of April, 1827, Mr. and Mrs. Boardman joined the mission. The mission was removed to Maulmain, in November, 1827. The work was now to be commenced anew, but under more favorable circumstances than before, at Rangoon. And it was not long before a flourishing church was established, which still remains. At this point the work deepened and widened, entering far and near as more missionaries appeared upon the field. Dr. Jones went to Siam, Mr. Brown to Assam, and Mr. Boardman to Tavoy, each to found a mission. Mr. Boardman died on the field as the fruits of his labors, among the Karens, were coming in. A few hours before his death, he was carried to the river bank, where he witnessed the baptism of thirty-four of that people.

Eight years after his death, April 10, 1834, his widow was married at Tavoy to Dr. Judson, and henceforth became known as Mrs. Sarah H. Judson. After eleven years of labor, and on account of Mrs. Judson's declining health, and in hopes of her restoration, Mr. and Mrs. Judson sailed for home. They reached St. Helena, where she died, Sept. 1, 1845, and was buried. Her bereaved husband and children

continued on the way. He says : " For a few days, in the
solitude of my cabin, with my poor children crying around
me, I could not help abandoning myself to heart-breaking
sorrow. But the promise of the gospel came to my aid, and
faith stretched her view to the bright world of eternal life,
and anticipated a happy meeting with those beloved beings
whose bodies are mouldering at Amherst and St. Helena."

He arrived at Boston, Oct. 15, and remained in this
country nine months. His name had become a familiar
word. " He was the only missionary remaining in the
heathen land, of those who had first left America for India,"
thirty years before. The generation that knew him had passed
away and another had arisen, of which, probably, not more
than fifty had ever seen him. " The desire to see him was
intense." " A spontaneous tribute of homage, love, and ven-
eration, awaited him in every village and city that he visited."
" The manner of his reception was wholly unexpected to
him. When he arrived in Boston, before coming on shore,
he was much troubled with the apprehension that he should
not know where to look for lodgings. The idea that a hundred houses would at once be thrown open to him, and that
as many families would feel honored to receive him as a
guest, never entered his mind."

For the full particulars of his life and work, read his
biography, by Dr. Wayland, which I have frequently quoted,
or the later one, by his son, Edward Judson, D. D.

Mr. Judson was again married, July 11, 1846, on the eve
of his departure, to Miss Emily Chubbuck, and embarked
with his wife for Maulmain. It was with delight that he resumed his work.

It was not many years, however, that he was permitted
to labor. Being seized with the fever of the country, he was
advised to take a sea voyage in hopes of his recovery, but
was compelled to leave Mrs. Judson behind. Mr. Ranney,

of Maulmain mission, went with him, and their destination
was the Isle of France, which, however, Dr. Judson never
reached His disorder increased, till, on the 12th of April,
1850, it terminated in his death. He was buried the same
day at sea.

Mrs. Judson, in a letter to his sister, says of him ;
" There was something exceedingly beautiful in the decline
of your brother's life—more beautiful than I can describe,
though the impression will remain with me as a sacred
legacy, until I go to meet him where suns shall never set,
and life shall have no end. He had been, from my acquaintance with him, an uncommonly spiritual Christian, exhibiting
his richest graces in the unguarded intercourse of private
life ; but during his last year, it seemed as though the light
of the world on which he was entering, had been sent to
brighten his upward pathway. Christ was his all."

Before embarking, he said to her : " Death will never
take me by surprise. *I feel so strong in Christ.*" Thus died
" the apostle to the Burmese." He went to India a pioneer
missionary ; when he died, after thirty eight years of toil, the
fields were already white to the harvest. Having given the
gospel to the Burmese, he entered upon his eternal reward.

We have now traced the origin of American Baptist
foreign missons. Many deeply interesting facts remain untold about the spread of this work. The untold benefit to
the heathen was not the only good result. It was the very
best for the churches at home. One has well said : Dr.
Judson " threw himself for support on the then feeble body
of American Baptists, who, in their effort to sustain and
re-enforce him, were led to the surest possible means of
strengthening the spirit of piety and philanthropy among
themselves at home, and may date, from their zeal in his
behalf, the dawn of their own rapid enlargement and cul-
minating prosperity. '

w

CHAPTER XXVIII.

ONCKEN.

E now reach the subject of American Baptist missions in Europe. Oncken has been all to the European missions that Judson was to the mission in India.

In the graveyard of the Welsh Tract Baptist meeting-house, near Newark, Delaware, repose the mortal remains of Captain Calvin Tubbs. He was a New Englander, by birth, and came to Delaware, where he was baptized, upon profession of his faith in Christ, into the fellowship of the Welsh Tract Baptist church, in May, 1815. He married Mary, the daughter of Gideon Farrell, who was pastor of that church from 1802 to 1820. In 1830 he became a member of the Sansom Street Baptist church, Philadelphia, but retained his membership there but for a short time. He was a sea captain by profession, and commanded the brig "Mars," owned by the late John Welsh, of Philadelphia. In the winter, probably, of 1830-31,[*] he was ice-bound with his vessel at Hamburg, Germany, where he boarded in the the lower part of the city, in the family of a pious German Pedobaptist, who used the English language, fluently. This

[*] Early and Later Delaware Baptists, pp. 63 to 71; Baptist Tract Magazine, September, 1831.

J. G. ONCKEN. D. D.

man was what became the celebrated John Gerard Oncken, D. D., the head of the great Baptist movement in Germany, and leader in the wonderful work for the renewal of evangelical religion on the continent of Europe, and in whose conversion to Baptist views, Capt. Tubbs was instrumental.

Oncken was born in the town of Varel, in the Grand Duchy of Oldenburg, January 26th, 1800 or 1801. In early life he went to England, where he married, and where he was converted, and commenced preaching. There he imbibed something of the spiritual nature of the religion of Jesus, and of the sanctity of the Lord's day. He returned to Germany to preach the gospel as the missionary of the British Continental Society, in 1823, in whose employ he labored till 1828, when he was appointed agent of the Edinburg Bible Society, which position he filled until appointed by the American Baptist Missionary Union, in 1834. He was, up to this period, a member of the English Independent church, Hamburg, with whose pastor, Matthews, he co operated for ten years in evangelical effort in the city.

J. G. Warren, D. D., kindly placed in our hands his copy-book, containing letters written while in Germany, in 1867, on a tour of inspection of the American Baptist mission stations there. His wonderfully graphic sketches were taken down on the spot, from facts furnished him by the principal mover in these events, the great German apostle, Oncken, himself.

" He, Oncken," says Dr. Warren, " pointed out to us in the lower part of the town, quite down to the wharf, the house in which Matthews lived, and the chamber in which he himself commenced his work, where the common people gathered to the utmost capacity of the place to hear the gospel, and the Holy Spirit came in convincing and converting power. You cannot tell how the good man's eyes brightened as he told us of those early displays of sovereign grace."

"These things being noised abroad, the pressure of the authorities was brought to bear on the principal actors, and they found it necessary to hold their meetings in another place. In an alley, narrow and dark, not far away, was pointed out to us the chambers, reached by an open stairway, where, to use Mr. Oncken's own words, the Baptist church was born. The rooms were occupied by a tailor, in very moderate circumstances, who was among the earliest converts. Here the disciples met, and prayed, and sang praises, and strengthened one another. Here Oncken preached to the crowds that flocked to hear him. 'Here,' I observed he remarked with peculiar emphasis, 'I formed a Bible class, and we, together, studied the word of God.' Here was formed into harmony of sentiment and fellowship of the Spirit, the group of believers subsequently baptized by Dr. Sears. This was the humble beginning, and very humble it was. These things were transpiring during the years from 1830 to 1835."

"Before leaving this general locality," says Dr. Warren, "I must mention an important link in the chain of events that, during this time, Mr. Oncken, engaged in business, *and also made the acquaintance of the first American Baptist.*"

The better to enable him to proceed to his work, he opened a small book-store, in 1828, in a part of his house. The business taken up reluctantly, as a matter of necessity, to secure him citizen-rights of use to him, became the means of great good to him and the cause. Without its income he never could have done the work he has accomplished ; while it has grown into a large and comprehensive agency for the printing and circulating tracts, Bibles, Testaments, hymn-books, and all sorts of work for the inculcation of the truth, and the exposition and vindication of Baptist sentiments. It is now a source from which light is shed all over Germany. Owing to the efforts of Drs. Griffith and G. W. Anderson, it has become the great Publishing House of the Baptists in Germany, with P. W. Bickel, D. D., at its head.

"While living in this house, an American seaman, Capt. Tubbs, a member of the old Sansom Street Baptist Church, Philadelphia, being ice-bound, was compelled to spend the winter in Hamburg. Oncken took him into his family, and during the long winter evenings they talked over the doctrines and practices of the Baptist churches in the United States, prayed together, and together went to the 'upper room' and worshiped God in company with the band of believers. When he returned home, Captain Tubbs told his pastor, Mr. Dagg, and afterward Dr. Cone, what a treasure he had found in Hamburg, and how his late 'host' was looking for some one to baptize him. God always has some way to bring to pass His grand designs. Soon after, correspondence was opened between America and Germany, and results, whose fame is in all the churches, followed in rapid succession."

It was, doubtless, this acquaintance that led Oncken not only to embrace Baptist views, but to form that alliance with the Baptists of this country that has resulted in reproducing, in the German Baptists " the American Baptists over again." " In all the grand fundamentals of faith and practice, in faith and church order and discipline, in forms of worship, and in administration of the ordinances of baptism and the Lord's Supper, they are one with us." As Hase puts it, they are formed after the " American type of Christianity."

* "Early and Later Delaware Baptists," A. B. Pub. Society.

Says Dr. Warren, in a private letter to the author : " Capt. Tubbs wintered with Oncken, and was, unaware to himself, even, sowing the primary seeds of what is destined to be a religious revolution in all Germany."

On the 22nd of April, 1834. Oncken and six others were baptized in the Elbe, opposite Hamburg, at Altona, by the Rev. Dr. (then Prof.) B. Sears. They did not dare to have this baptism at Hamburg, nor by the light of day, for fear of the authorities. The following day, the First Baptist church of Hamburg was organized, and Oncken ordained a minister of the gospel.

Dr. Warren thus details the event : " In 1833 we find Mr. Oncken, with his family, residing in a plain, comfortable brick house at No. 7 *Englische Planke.* It is removed several streets—eight or ten it may be—from his former residence, and stands amidst houses occupied by a better class of people." Not far off, round the corner, stand the old and new Baptist chapels. " To the lower front room of his new residence, Mr. Oncken removed his book store. In the room immediately in the rear of the store, the two men, Oncken and Sears, met for the first time in the autumn of 1833, opened their hearts to each other, bowed in prayer before the throne of the heavenly mercy, and entered into consultation with reference to plans for the future. In the chambers over the store is seen the spot where the Baptist Church, in Hamburg, was organized, April 23, 1834 of seven members and where Dr. Sears, by solemn prayer and the laying on of hands, formally set apart his own *brother,* Oncken, to the work of the gospel ministry and the administration of the ordinances of Christ's church."

" To No. 4, *Bohmken Strasse* (around the corner) the meetings were, about the same time, removed. Here, also,

SECOND BAPTIST CHURCH, WILMINGTON,
DELAWARE.

See page 257.

the work of translation and printing commenced, and here was established the store-room of the Bible and Tract Societies. Here, also, at a subsequent day, were our brethren assailed by the mob, when at worship, the windows and doors smashed to pieces, and other acts of violence committed. Thence was Oncken hurried away by officers of the law, taken before the magistrates, and then thrust into prison. Standing with us before the window where the little church was formed, and where he himself was ordained, pointing upward, while emotion too strong to be concealed choked his utterance, the good man exclaimed : ' To all Eternity, we, here, in Germany, and you, the churches in America, will have occasion to thank God for what was done in that chamber.' "

The events that followed the baptism of these few devoted believers, and the formation of this little church, is thus related by Oncken himself, and recorded by Lehmann : " The event caused a great sensation wherever Oncken's name was known. On account of his meetings and preaching, he had already suffered much persecution, which now rose to an unusual height. In an address, Oncken communicated the following concerning it :

' Scarcely had it become known to the clergy of Hamburg that these meetings were being held, when the persecution at once began. Threats and stringent prohibitions followed, so that I was obliged to discontinue these meetings in my house, and to transfer them to an attic, in a court. In a very short time, this place was crowded. Then the threats were renewed. Therefore, I was compelled, continually, to look around for new places. In this manner, it happened that Satan was taken in his own snares. For thus I was obliged to flee from one parish to another, and even to preach in parts of the city where the word had not as yet been proclaimed. The threats became yet more severe. I hold here in my hand, eighteen or twenty of the many citations, by which I was incessantly ordered to appear before the bar of the police, and which have cost me much distress, many sighs and throbbings of heart. Generally, one was served upon me each week, and I was obliged to wait almost the whole morning upon the police, until I was admitted before them. The threats only gave me a greater impulse. The longer I reflected the more I understood what kind of men they must be who could incite the authorities to forbid a man's preaching the gospel, whereby souls could be saved. They now imposed fines upon me. Naturally, I never paid them. What I lost, they were obliged to seize.'

"If, now, religious meetings had already stirred up such enmity, it was in the nature of things that, after our baptism had taken place, the measures against us would become more stringent, and so it was. But Jesus has all power in his hands. It happened that the Senator Hudtwalker, who, at that time, stood at the head of the police, was an esteemed Christian, who, although no Baptist, considered my religious activity as fraught with blessing. He was chosen of the Lord to be our guardian angel. The Lord reward him at that day! He was pressed hard to proceed against us, but he was not able to reconcile with his conscience the persecution of Christ in His members. But his successor in office (who, however, afterwards became our friend, and has shown us much kindness,) declared to me, at that time, that he would make every effort to exterminate us. When I reminded him that no religious movement could be suppressed by force, and said to him: 'Mr. Senator, you will find that all your trouble and labor will be in vain,' he answered, 'Well, then it will not be my fault, for as long as

I can move my little finger, it shall continue to move against you. If you wish to go to America, I will give you, together with your wife and children, a free passage, but here, such sectarianism will not be endured.' "*

With the growth of the church these threats multiplied. Each year from twelve to twenty-nine persons were baptized. Finally the senate determined to resort to force. One Wednesday evening the police forcibly entered their place of worship, and amid the boisterous mirth of the rabble, drove the members into the street. Oncken was arrested, and brought to the police prison in Winserbaum, where he was treated as a common prisoner and placed under lock and key. He was unaccustomed to the unpliant straw mattress and hard pillow, yet he felt happy to suffer for the name of Jesus. After a few days he was sentenced to four weeks imprisonment, which he was now compelled to endure. In addition to this, on other occasions, he was subjected to fines, and when, in obedience to his conscience, he refused to pay them, his valuables were seized and sold. In prison he was comforted by the presence of the beloved members of his church, on a bridge in the neighborhood, whence, full of longing desire, they locked up towards his grated window, threw him kindly greetings, pointed toward heaven, and, in similar sign-language, conversed with him, while he enjoyed the richest blessing in communion with the Saviour, and ever heard the comforting words : "I am with thee." "I uphold thee." "I will not leave thee nor forsake thee."

"If you ever go to Hamburg," writes Dr. Warren, "some one may take you through 'the valley of the shadow of death,' a deep, dark passage protected by heavy iron doors at either end of the building, secured for worship and other purposes sometime after they were driven out from No. 4,

* Dr. Warren's Letters.

Bohmken Strasse. It was on their entrance here that God wrought marvelously in their behalf, and, by means of the great fire of 1842, taken in connection with their own generosity in offering an asylum for the houseless, broke the power of their persecutor. The Government could not avail itself of the charitable deeds of those men, and, at the same time, oppress and imprison them. On the occasion of your visit, some other friend may take you to ' the ramparts' at the South-west corner of the old town, and over-looking the valley of the Elbe for a great distance, when you will look down on scores of ships, and beyond these see the island, a mile or two in length, at the Eastern extremity of which the famed 'seven' were baptized by 'brother Sears' on the night of the 22nd of April, 1834, a few hours before the church was constituted. At different points in all those waters you now see, the ordinance of baptism has since been administered scores of times, now in one place and then in another, to escape the notice of Government officials, now in the dominions of Hamburg, then in those of Hanover, and then again in those of Denmark, all of which could be reached in an hour or two. 'When they persecute you in one city, flee ye to another.' In the centre of the town on the most frequented streets, stands the Government House or City Hall, as we would call it, within which justice is supposed to be dealt, both to disturbers of the peace and other offenders against the well-being of society. With this building, and especially with the police court rooms, our hero became well acquainted. One day as we walked by, he suddenly stopped, and, pointing up, said: 'There I have been called scores of times, and scores of times before I had got accustomed to the smell of gun-powder I stood trembling, awaiting my turn for a hearing, the passer-by, in the meantime, spitting on me and crying out that I

CROZER THEOLOGICAL SEMINARY, UPLAND, PA.

See page 379.

ought 'to be hung.' The old prison, whose apartments were made sacred by the presence of these men, still stands. I looked on its dingy walls. Oncken and Kœbner were both at my side. They recounted to each other the incidents of their imprisonment. It was to me a moment of strange emotion. 'My room,' said one, pointing, ' was there, and out of that window I looked and saw the brethren and sisters as they came and stood where we now do, and, by their presence, sought to comfort us in our confinement.' 'I had my abode *there*,' responded the other, pointing to another part of the prison ; ' after all, it was not so bad, as I had nothing to do but to read my Bible and pray.' "

It was now time for the Baptists of America to take charge of this German mission, thrust upon them unsought and unexpectedly, as the Burman mission was before. On the 25th of September, 1834, Mr. Oncken became the missionary of the American Baptist Missionary Union.

" The results of Oncken's conversion to Baptist views were great and far-reaching. He was already well known in Germany, and, being a man of extensive influence, the light which began to break forth in Hamburg, was not confined within that city, but streamed forth in all directions. Here and there little groups of churches sprang up, which in like manner reproduced themselves in the regions beyond." And now tens of thousands, through him, rejoice in the truth as it is in Christ, and maintain the ordinances as commanded in the New Testament Scriptures. May 13th, 1837, Oncken baptized G. W. Lehmann, and five others at Berlin, which was the beginning of the work there. For fifty years Lehmann was pastor of the church at Berlin. The Triennial Conference was formed in 1849.

The truth has spread over Germany, Denmark, Sweden, Switzerland, Poland, Russia and Turkey.

Drs. Warren and Oncken, (in 1884,) and G. W. Lehmann, (in 1882,) have all gone to their reward in heaven, but Christ is with us and the work goes on.

It would give us pleasure to follow this great tidal wave of truth and of evangelical religion in its course over Europe, and trace, especially, the work of grace in Sweden, but we must be content to refer to books in which may be found full accounts of these glorious events. Even in America has this gracious influence been felt, not only in stirring up the Baptists of America to missionary effort in Europe, but in planting upon American soil, among others, German Baptist churches. These German Baptists, in America, are a devoted band of brethren, who, with true missionary spirit, are giving even beyond their means for the maintenance of the gospel at home and abroad, while they put the whole force of their teaching and example against transplanting the German Sabbath, and other hurtful German customs on our shores. Some of them are finding homes in American Baptist churches, while others are collected in German-speaking churches, where Germans who can be reached in no other way, are persuaded, in their native tongue, to be reconciled to God.

Before the conversion of Oncken to Baptists views, the American Baptists began, in 1832, their missions in Europe, and labors have, since then, been put forth in France, Spain, Greece, Italy, and other countries with more or less success, but none of these have been so successful as the movement in Germany, and none so far-reaching in blessed results.

CHAPTER XXIX.

SOCIETIES, OR METHODS.

THE Baptists have societies for Christian work, such as associations of neighboring churches for fraternal and missionary purposes; state conventions in nearly every state for state evangelization; organizations for building churches, for distributing tracts and Bibles, for caring for the poor, the sick, the aged, and the orphan; for the education of students for the Christian ministry, and for every other Christian activity. There are also general societies that seek to extend the kingdom of Christ at home and abroad.

None of these societies have any power over the churches, but are presumed to be their servants, or agents to conduct the work of the denomination. Each Baptist church is independent in government, acknowledging only Christ as head, and selecting its own officers which are only of two orders—pastors and deacons.

The names of the principal general societies of the Baptists North, are; The "American Baptist Missionary Union," the "American Baptist Home Mission Society," and the "American Baptist Publication Society." The members of these societies are the pastors and delegates of contributing Baptist churches, and individuals paying a stated sum. Besides there are the Woman's Societies for home and foreign missions. The annual meetings of these societies were last held at Detroit, Michigan, May, 1884, in the First Baptist church ; Z. Grenell, Jr., D. D., pastor.

The Baptists South, who constitute nearly two-thirds of the denomination in this country, do their home and foreign missionary work by a representative body, called the "Southern Baptist Convention," of which P. H. Mell, D. D., LL. D., is president, and Lansing Burrows, D. D., and Rev. O. P. Gregory, are (1884) secretaries ; and the "Southern Baptist General Convention," which is the missionary organization of the colored Baptists. The latter represents about one million communicants.

The Baptists South and the Baptists North, are the same in doctrine and practice, and are in sympathy and of one accord.

To attain its objects, the Southern Baptist Convention has two Boards, elected annually ; The Foreign Mission Board, Richmond, Va., J. L. M. Curry, D. D., LL. D., president, and H. A. Tupper, D. D, Secretary; and the Home Mission Board, Atlanta, Ga., Hon. Jno. D. Stewart, president, and I. T. Tichenor, D. D., secretary. The Convention met at Baltimore, May, 1884, with the Seventh church; Rev. T. D. Anderson, Jr., pastor.

A great work has been done through the Convention, both at home and abroad, and the work grows in magnitude and importance. In Africa there are ten, and in China fifty-seven, missionaries and native assistants ; while in Italy there are preaching stations at Rome, Naples, Venice, Milan, Modena, and other places, twelve in all. At Rome, a suitable building has been purchased in a most desirable

x

FIRST BAPTIST CHURCH, DETROIT, MICH.

See page 355.

location, near the Pantheon and the University of Rome, for mission purposes, for $25,000 in gold. At the head of the Italian mission is G. B. Taylor, D. D., whose father J. B. Taylor, D. D., was for many years the efficient secretary of the Foreign Mission Board. Missions are also maintained in Brazil and Mexico. In the latter place, the authorities have offered, through Governor Madero of Coahuila, the charge of education and valuable school property in that state, to the Baptists under Rev. W. D. Powell, missionary of the board, upon certain conditions. The Mexicans of all classes are represented as thirsting for light, liberty, and salvation, and as looking to the Baptists as their hope under God. *The Foreign Mission Journal* is an interesting and valuable publication edited for the board by Prof. H. H. Harriss.

There are, under the Home Mission Board, a Sunday-school department, an Indian mission, a mission to the Chinese in California, a church edifice building department, and mission work in many states among the whites and the colored people. The work among the Indians, under the late Dr. Buckner and others, was wonderful, and will be abiding. The board publishes *Kind Words*, a weekly, semi-weekly, and monthly Sunday-school paper, containing expositions of the International Series of Sunday-school Lessons. It originated with C. J. Elford and Drs. B. Manly and J. A. Broadus in 1864, and in 1870 was consolidated with the *Child's Delight*, published by S. Boykin, D. D., Macon, Georgia, who was employed as editor, which position he still retains. It produces, annually, for the Convention, a royalty of $1,000. The number of missionaries employed by this board is 144.

It was reported in 1884 that $86,625 97 had been contributed during the year for foreign missions, and $48,000 for home missions, the total of which is much more than double the amount raised in 1878. Special interest is manifested by Southern Baptist women, who have contributed, of themselves, in the past ten years, $75,000.

The American Baptist Publication Society is located at No. 1420 Chestnut street, Philadelphia, Pennsylvania. J. H. Deane is president, and Benjamin Griffith D. D., Secretary.

The origin of the society is given in the words of Geo. W. Anderson, D. D., the able book-editor of the society. " In 1823, the Rev. Noah Davis, of Maryland, wrote to his former classmate, the Rev. James D. Knowles, then living in Washington, D. C., in regard to the formation of a tract society." The idea was suggested to him by seeing a tract fall from the hat of another to the ground. "This letter led to a call for those who were favorable to the formation of a Baptist General Tract Society, to meet on the 25th of Feb., 1824, at the house of Mr. George Wood, a member of the Baptist church. At the appointed time there was a gathering of twenty-five persons, and a society was formed, which at once began its work. Its receipts for the first year of its existence were only $373,80 ; its issues amounted to 696,000 pp. 18mo. This was a small and unpretentious beginning, but the blessing of the Lord rested on the society, and it henceforth continued to grow. In 1826, it was transferred to Philadelphia." The society was put upon a firm basis at the start, by the labors of its secretary, Rev. Noah Davis. His life, however, was not spared long. The society had then no house, nor even " rooms ;" but one room in the third story."

It was not long before it was thought necessary to enlarge its work, so as to include the issue of bound volumes, and a care for Sunday-schools. The use of colporteurs was begun in 1840, and has continued to the present day. Its object is ; "To promote evangelical religion by means of the Bible, the Printing Press, Colportage, and the Sunday-schools." There are now three separate departments of the society ; business, missionary, and Bible; and the total receipts from all sources and for all purposes, for 1884, are $582,957.58 ; of this, $428,295 12 was received in the business ; $131,881.-94, in the missionary department, and $22,780.52 in the Bible department. And the issue for the year was 687, 695,-902 pages, 18 mo. There are one hundred and eighty-two missionaries and colporteurs of various classes employed among white and black natives, and foreign population at home, and in Germany, Sweden and Turkey.

Dr. Geo. W. Anderson says: " The Business Department is self-supporting, and is kept entirely distinct from the Missionary or the Benevolent Department. They have separate sets of books, and separate bank accounts. No money contributed to the Missionary work is ever, on any pretence, used in the Business Department." O. W. Spratt, A. M., is the business manager. Rev. G. J. Johnson, D. D., is missionary secretary.

Since May, 1883, it has been the accepted Bible Society of the denomination. The Bible Convention met at Saratoga, New York, May 22d, and 23d, 1883, composed of properly appointed delegates representing the Baptist denomination—at least in the North, (some were present from the South,) so decided, after mature deliberation, by an overwhelming majority. C. C. Bitting, D. D., was appointed Bible Secretary.

The Sunday School work of the Society deserves special mention. "Baptists were the first to establish Sunday-schools in the South, the first one being organized by the

WAYLAND SEMINARY, WASHINGTON, D. C.

See page 363.

Second Baptist Church of Baltimore, in 1804, and west of the Mississippi, at St. Louis.'' Says Dr. Warren Randolph, '' In 1817, Mrs. Betsy Baker carried, in a chest, and under her arm, the little library composing all the Sunday school books used in her school. Now think of such works as those written by Dr. Dyer, circulated by the thousand throughout the land. Dr. C. R. Blackall has charge of the Sunday school work, and Prof. H. F. Reed is Superintendent of the publishing department.

The periodicals of the Society published, as Sunday school aids, are numerous, and very well adapted to the purpose. We can but name them, and their editors. *The Baptist Teacher*, P. S. Henson, D. D.; *Our Young People*, and the *Senior Quarterly*, A. J. Rowland, D. D.; *Young Reaper*, and *The Sunlight*, B. Griffith, D. D.; *Bible Lesson Quarterly*, and the *Advanced Quarterly*, E. G. Taylor, D. D.; *Our Little Ones*, Miss May F. Kean ; *Intermediate Quarterly*, *The Primary Quarterly*, and the *Picture Lesson Quarterly*, Mrs. M. G. Kennedy ; *Baptist Superintendent*, Dr. C. R. Blackall; *Childrens' Picture Lessons* and *Merit Cards* ; and *The Year Book*, Lansing Burrows, D. D.

The issue of these publications reached the enormous total number of 24,219,468 for the year ending May 1884.

Here is an illustration of what the society is doing to disseminate the truth of the gospel. The sermon of H. H. Tucker, D. D., LL. D., on *Baptism*, preached at Saratoga, has been translated into Armenian, Turkish, Greek, Swedish and Spanish ; and is about to be translated into German, and, probably, into Portuguese. The three languages first named will take it into the region round about Mount Ararat, and to the Euphrates, and the Tigris, and I suppose nearly to the Persian Gulf, and starting from Constantinople will spread over all that part of Asia Minor, where Paul preached, and about the Black and Caspian Seas. The Swedish edition will reach, I suppose, nearly to the Polar Sea, and down to the Baltic, when the German will take it up, and carry it down the Danube till it meets the version from Constantinople. The Spanish edition is for Mexico, and the Portuguese, (if it is translated into the language,) is for Brazil. This is better than speaking with tongues ; for only a few can hear, but millions can read ; one reaches to the extent of a human voice, the other reaches half a world.

The marble publishing house of the society is unsurpassed, as a book store, by any in the world. To Dr. B. Griffith, and the Crozer and Bucknell families, is due the credit of securing such a house for our society.

The German Baptists of America, who originated with Rev. K. A. Fleischmann, have a publication society located at Cleveland, Ohio. The society owns its building, and has been largely instrumental in the growth of the German Baptists, in this country. From eight ministers, eight churches and four hundred and five members, in 1851, to one hundred and fifteen pastors, one hundred and thirty churches, nine thousand and twenty members in 1880, and who are now contributing towards the support of the gospel, nearly $10 per member. Rev. J. C. Haselhuhn, is editor, and H. Schulte, manager. With such men as Rev. J. S. Gubelmann, Rev. J. C. Grimmell, Prof. Rauschenbusch, as leaders, the success of the German Baptists is assured. Our German brethren have their own conventions, and are organized for work.

The first organizations for home mission work in this country, were local. The Baptist Missionary society of Massachusetts, formed in 1807, sent Rev. J. M. Peck to the far west, to labor. He became distinguished as a pioneer missionary in the then western wilds, and "the denominational leader in the Mississippi valley, in all departments of denominational enterprise." "To Jonathan Going, the Baptists of America are instrumentally indebted for that national organization in home missions which began its work as the scattering of a few handfulls of ' corn on the tops of the mountains,' yet whose fruit now ' shakes like Lebanon'."

The "American Baptist Home Mission Society" was formed in New York, April 27, 1832, with Jonathan Going as secretary.

The object of the society is, "The preaching of the gospel to every creature in our country," which object is so well expressed in its grand motto: "North America for Christ." It sustains missionaries, organizes and helps churches and Sunday-schools, and assists in building houses of worship, and in educating a colored ministry for their own race. The first year, over $6,500 was raised, while in 1884, $401,692.19 was reported from all sources. John B. Trevor is president, and H. L. Morehouse, D. D., secretary. The society has a conditional and permanent trust fund, aggregating $495,224.56 including a building loan fund. The educational department has in charge 15 schools, for the education of preachers and teachers of the colored race. One of them is the Wayland Seminary, Washington, D. C., Rev. G. M. P. King, president.

Besides these there are two other schools, Indian University, Tahlequah, Indian Territory, Professor A C. Bacone ; and the International School, Monterey, Mexico, Rev. Thomas M. Westrup. Some of these schools are very large, three of them requiring an annual expenditure aggregating $70,000. The total value of the school property of the society is $500,000. The teaching force in these schools is 82, and pupils, two thousand eight hundred and twenty-eight. Students, preparing to preach during the year, four hundred and three, and conversions of pupils, two hundred and sixty.

A great work is being done in the states and territories for the spread of the kingdom of Christ, and among English speaking people, Welsh, Germans, Scandinavians, French, Spanish, Indians, Chinese, and among the Mormons in Utah, and the Mexicans in Mexico. It is doing the work of three societies in one, and employs six hundred and forty four laborers. In fifty two years it has organized three thousand one huudred and thirty seven churches, and commissioned ten thousand one hundred and sixty missionaries, who have baptized nearly one hundred thousand persons. Some of the churches formed and helped by the agents of this society, are now among the best churches in many of the states. The *Baptist Home Mission Monthly* has a circulation of eight thousand.

The "American Baptist Missionary Union" is the foreign mission society of the Baptists North. The head-quarters of the society are in Boston, Tremont Temple ; Hon. J. Warren Merrill, is president, and J. N. Murdock, D. D., and A. G. Lawson, D. D., are secretaries. The object of the "Union" is "to diffuse the knowledge of the religion of Jesus Christ, by means of missions, throughout the world." It has been found that the teacher must follow the missionary, so that schools are established among the converted heathen, greatly to the advantage of the work, and among them, training schools for native students for the ministry. Of the formation of the society, we have already spoken. Here are some of the results, as given by Dr. Geo. W. Anderson : " The Missionary Union has established missions in Burmah, Siam, Arracan, Assam, China, Western Africa, among the Teloo-

WALNUT STREET BAPTIST CHURCH, LOUISVILLE, KY. See page 263

goos, and our own Indians, and in Greece. It has lately assumed charge of missions in Japan which were originated, and for many years carried on, by the Free Mission Society. It has also felt called upon to extend its aid to our feeble churches in France, Germany, Denmark, and Spain ; and assumed a few years since the care of the work of the Baptists in Sweden, which had been commenced in 1855 by the colporteurs of the American Baptist Publication Society, and had been eminently successful." And now the " Dark Continent," a way through which has been opened by Livingston, Stanley, and others, is inviting, with peculiar claims, evangelization, through American Baptists.

The " Livingston Inland Mission," on the Congo River, Africa, has been accepted by the society. The mission was established by English Baptists and has cost $150,000, up to this time. It consists of seven mission-stations, with twenty-six missionaries. One of the stations is on Stanley Pool, and from this point, with the mission steamer, " Henry Reed," brought from England, four or five thousand miles of navigable water of the Congo and its tributaries can be traversed, and fifty millions of people reached. This work is thrust upon us as was the work in Burmah, and in Germany. The report of the Union for 1884, is : Preachers in Europe and Asia, 1,682, churches 1,127, baptisms, 11,716, and members, 112,122. Of these, there are in Asia, 812 preachers, 586 churches, 4,679 baptisms, and 53,649 members redeemed from heathenism. $324,443.89 has been contributed during the year. The Teloogoos alone have averaged 2,000 conversions, yearly, since 1877 8, and now aggregate 25,000. The thrilling story of the " Lone Star Mission" and " Prayer Meeting Hill" is known to all.

The " *Baptist Missionary Magazine,*" now in its eightieth year, is the oldest Baptist periodical in America. Its editors are Dr. Murdock, and Rev. E. F. Merriam.

Many of the cuts we exhibit illustrating the condition of the heathen, with, as well as without, the gospel, and well known events, men, and places, in the history of Baptist missions, were kindly furnished by the society, and through the courtesy of W. G. Corthell, of Boston.

The "American Baptist Free Mission Society," mentioned, was formed in 1842, and was dissolved in 1872. It established missions among the Burmese in Bassein Provinces and Rangoon, and also in Hayti and in Japan.

Baptist Women's societies for both Home and Foreign missions, or woman's work for women, are in successful operation. By the formation of circles in churches, and weekly contribntions of two cents each, the ladies are raising large additional amounts for missions.

The "Women's Baptist Foreign Missionary Society" was formed in 1871. Missions are maintained in Europe, Asia, and Africa, and thirty-six missionaries are employed, eighty-six schools conducted, with three thousand two hundred and ninety-four pupils, forty-eight Bible women supported, one hundred and eighteen baptisms administered, and $54,301 84 raised for 1884. The president is Mrs. Gardner Colby, Massachusets, and the secretary, Mrs. O. W. Gates.

The "Woman's Foreign Missionary Society of the West," was formed in 1871. It covers the same general field abroad, and reported, in 1884, $23,081 99 raised ; twenty missionaries, forty-three Bible women, eighteen schools, with seven hundred and ninety-three pupils, and thirty-four native teachers supported, and fifty four baptisms. Mrs. A. J. Howe, Chicago, is president, and Mrs. A. M. Bacon, secretary. "*The Helping Hand,*" and the "*Little Worker,*" are joint publications.

"The Woman's Baptist Home Mission Society" was organized in 1877. Reported for 1884, $25,944 64 collected, and twenty-six missionaries, six missionary teachers, and ten bible women, employed among the Freed-people, Indians, Mormans, Germans, Scandinavians, and native whites. Mrs. J. N. Crouse, Chicago, is president, and Mrs. C. Swift, secretary. The society publishes the "*Tidings.*"

"The Woman's American Baptist Home Mission Society," was formed in 1878. Receipts for 1884, $10,324-77. Mrs. Thomas Nickerson, Massachusetts, president, and Mrs. A. S. Hunt, Maine, secretary.

The "American Baptist Historical Society," originated in a suggestion of J. M. Peck, D. D., while secretary of the Publication Society, in whose building it has a room, but since 1861 it has been a separate society. In 1861 its library consisted of but four volumes, and sixty-four pamphlets. Now it comprises over six hundred volumes. This remarkable growth is chiefly owing to the gratuitous services of Dr. Howard Malcolm, and to William Cathcart, D. D. H. G. Weston, D. D., is president, H. E. Lincoln, librarian and treasurer, and Rev. I. N. Ritner, secretary. Another "Baptist Historical Society" has been formed at Richmond, Virginia.

"The American and Foreign Bible Society" (Baptist) was formed in 1816, and received and expended, in Bible work, over $1,200,000, and circulated nearly three million copies of the Scriptures in our own and other lands; among them, Dr. Judson's Burmese translation, and Dr. Mason's Karen Bible. A Bible society for the Baptists is a necessity, since the Bible society, under Pedobaptist control, refused to print Judson's Burmese Bible, or any other pure translation of the word of God, although Baptists were contributing to the fuñds of the society. Being denied equal rights in a union organization, Baptists formed a Bible society of their own. Since the Baptist Bible Convention at Saratoga in 1883, the Pedobaptist society has even refused grants of Bibles to Baptists.

The "American Bible Union," was formed in May, 1850, in New York. "It owes its rise and support," says Dr. T. J Morgan, "mainly to the Baptists." Its object was, "for procuring and circulating of the most faithful versions of the sacred Scriptures in all languages." Some of the results are given in the language of an address issued in February, 1874, by Thos. Armitage, D. D., president, and Dr. W. H. Wyckoff, secretary at that time,

"One of the striking results of the perservering efforts of the Bible Union is, that general conviction of the faults and defects of the common English version which has induced the Convocation of Canterbury, the responsible representative of the Church of England, to attempt its improvement."

"We have circulated more than a million copies of the sacred Scriptures. Last year our gratuitous appropriations exceeded forty-nine thousand. We have aided in printing and circulating faithful versions in Karen, Siamese, Burmese, Bengali, Sanskrit, Armenian, Teloogoo, Chinese, and other Asiatic languages, have made versions of the New Testament in two Chinese languages, in the Spanish and the Italian, and aided in several others ;" and " have revised the English New Testament and a large part of the Old."

"To May, 1865, the number of Foreign Scriptures published, was 135,543, and the number of English Scrip·tures, 355,842. The Society had then received and expended, from its origin, nearly $873,000."

In view of all the missionary operations of the Baptists, how fitting that a Baptist, Rev. S. F. Smith, should give to the church its grand missionary hymn. Truly, now, since the spirit of missions has been revived in the church, can **we** sing,

" The morning light is breaking," etc.

RICHARD B. COOK, D. D.

CHAPTER XXX.

BAPTIST SCHOOLS.

T is an error into which some have fallen respecting the Baptists, that they are not the friends of education, in general, and especially of ministerial education. Our interest in educational matters now, the number of our institutions of learning, the ability of our present ministry, as well as the facts of our past history, prove the contrary.

Dr. Sprague, as quoted by Dr. Hovey, says: " Baptists have less credit as the friends and patrons of learning than they have deserved." And Dr. Hovey, himself, says; ''Though there have been, and are now, Baptists who think otherwise, yet, the denomination, as a body, has believed in a liberally trained ministry." He cites Dr. Chalmers as testifying to the learning and eloquence of the Baptist ministry of England, and Dr. Baird to the same effect as to that, of America. " They have always, however, insisted upon piety as of more importance to the ministry than learning, and that the latter was nothing without the former."

Baptists, however, should strive for leadership in education. Their very principles seem to require of them to be second to none in learning, and in zeal for the promotion of knowledge.

Y

As early as 1756, when the Baptists were but few and feeble, the Philadelphia Association opened an academy at Hopewell, New Jersey, for the education of youth for the ministry, and the Baptists of Georgia and South Carolina co-operated with those of Pennsylvania and New Jersey in the matter, and raised funds for the purpose. Isaac Eaton, pastor of the Baptist church there, was the principal of the school. This was the first attempt American Baptists made in this direction. The old school-house at Hopewell still stands, and is an object of great interest, for in it were educated, in part, some of the ablest Baptist ministers of that day, and among them the first president of Brown University, Dr. Manning.

The Academy declined when Brown University was established. Here we have both the Academy and the College, while as Dr. Hovey says ; "Schools of Theology began to be founded by the Baptists about the middle of the first century of the republic, and only in the last twenty-five years, gratifying progress has been made towards endowing several of them."

We have now (1884) in the United States, sixty academies, thirty-three colleges, and eight theological seminaries, besides a German Baptist theological seminary.

The total value of the property of all these Baptist schools, including endowments, is over $15,000,000, with a total income of nearly $1,000,000. "Most of them are in need of money, but some of them are well endowed, and among these is this large amount distributed."

Money is needed for educational institutions, because an education is expensive, and but few would otherwise get it. Every college in the land is endowed, and no one pays the actual cost of an education. The instruction alone costs from $200 to nearly $1,000 per year for each student in our theological seminaries, and that without books, board or clothing. The most of theological students, who are poor, could never get an education if they had to pay for it. Hence the need of endowments. Besides, we Baptists feel it to be our duty to support our own institutions, and to refuse all aid from the state. And the churches, not the students, should bear the expense, just as the nation at its own expense educates the men who are to be the leaders of its army and navy. It is right for the churches to bear the expense, and it is honorable for young men to accept the support.

Baptists prove their belief in education by planting schools, with liberal endowments, all over the land.

The oldest Baptist institution of learning existing in this country, is Brown University, Providence, Rhode Island, founded in 1764. The president is E. G. Robinson, D. D., LL. D. It ranks among the first as a university. From its walls have gone out hundreds to occupy and adorn the highest places in church and state. It was here, while president of the college, that Dr. F. Wayland wrote his famous text-books. Colby University, Waterville, Maine, G. D. B. Pepper, D. D., LL. D , president, was founded in 1820.

At Hamilton, New York, there is a double school, "a double star," shedding its light out into the world : The Hamilton Theological Seminary, founded in 1819, and the Madison University, in 1846, E. Dodge, D. D., LL. D., president. The Baptists of New York have another first-class school at Rochester, founded in 1850. It has three departments. M. B. Anderson, LL. D., is president of the University, A. H. Strong, D. D. of the Theological Seminary, and Prof. A. Rauschenbusch, D. D., of the German Theological department.

PEDDIE INSTITUTE, HIGHTSTOWN, N. J.:

See page 377.

The Columbian College, now *The Columbian University,* was opened in 1822, at Washington, D. C. Prof. S. M. Shute, D. D., says: "It was the result of that awakening movement in the denomination, which was coincident with the remarkable change of views of Judson and Rice, on the subject of baptism, and with the quickened consciousness on the part of the church, that they had failed in the solemn duty of carrying the gospel to the heathen. The object of placing the college at Washington was to have a geographical centre, and by bringing young men together at the Capital, to give them large and liberal views of men and things. James C. Welling, LL. D., is president. A Medical school has been connected with the College from its foundation. Several years ago, a Law School was organized, which has grown into one of the most flourishing and popular in the land. The Corcoran School of Science and Arts, named after W. W. Corcoran, LL. D., a most generous benefactor of the College, has just been opened, furnishing the most ample facilities for students, in all branches of the physical sciences. The original site of the College has been sold ; a piece of ground centrally located in the city purchased, and a most elegant and commodious building erected upon it, which, with the ample equipments of the Scientific School, has cost about $200,000. There is, also, a flourishing Preparatory School in connection with the University, occupying a beautiful and spacious building, and with a large list of instructors. The University has an encouraging prospect before it, under its new arrangements, and its numerous friends and patrons will rejoice in its widening prosperity." Robert C. Fox, LL. D., is treasurer.

The Newton Theological Institution, Massachusetts, Alvah Hovey, D. D., president, was founded in 1825, and is one of the very best seminaries for the education of ministers in the land. Shurtleff College, Upper Alton, Ill., was founded in 1827, and has a theological department which was originated in 1862 ; A. A. Kendrick D. D., is president. In 1829 the Georgetown College, Kentucky, was founded ; R. M. Dudley, D. D.,is president. At Chicago, Ill., the University of Chicago was founded in 1859, president, Galusha Anderson, D. D., and the Baptist Union Theological Seminary, in 1867, G. W. Northrup, D. D.

Other older institutions of learning, with their presidents, are : Dennison University, Granville, Ohio, Alfred Owen, D. D., 1831 ; Richmond College, Va., 1832, B. Puryear, LL. D. ; Wake Forrest College, N. C., 1833, Franklin College, Indiana, 1834, W. T. Scott, D. D. ; Mercer University, Macon, Ga., 1838, A. J. Battle, D. D., LL. D. ; Howard College, Marion, Ala., 1842, Col. J. T. Murfree ; Baylor University, Texas, 1845, W. Carey Crane, D. D., LL. D. ; the University at Lewisburg, Penn., 1846, Rev. D. J. Hill, LL. D. ; William Jewell College, Liberty, Mo., 1849, with its Verdeman School of Theology, 1868, J. G. Clark, LL. D.; Mississippi College, Clinton, 1850, W. S. Webb, D. D. ; Furman University, Greenville, S. C., 1851, Charles Manly, D. D. ; Bethel College, Russellville, Ky., 1852, J. H. Fuqua, A. M., ; Carson College, Tennessee, 1853, W. B. Goforth, D.D. ; Central University, Pella, Iowa, 1853 ; Mt. Pleasant College, Mo., 1854, A. S. Worrell, D. D. ; Kalamazoo College, Mich., 1855, Kendall Brooks, D. D. ; La Grange College, Mo., 1859, J. F. Cook, LL. D. ; McMinnville College, Oregon, 1858, Rev. G. J. Burchett, A. M. ; Waco University, Texas, 1861, R. C. Burleson D. D. ; Vassar College, New York, 1861, S. L. Caldwell, D D., LL. D. ; Ottawa University, Kansas, in 1866, Prof. M. L. Ward ; and

University of Des Moines, 1866, Ira E. Kenney, D. D.
All these were founded prior to 1867. There are others
of later date: Monongahela College, Penn., 1871, C. S.
James, Ph., D. ; California Collége, 1871; Judson University,
Ark., 1870, R. S. James, D. D., LL. D.; South Western
University, Tenn., 1874, George W. Jarman, LL. D.

In the *Year Book** are many institutions of learning,
modestly classed, by their own option, under the head of
acadamies, some of them deserving a higher designation.
We name several : Hollins Institute, Botetourt Springs, Va.,
1841, Prof. C. L. Cocke ; Peddie Institute, Hightstown, N.
J., 1867, Rev. John Greene, A. M. ; Shorter College, Rome,
Ga., 1873, L. R. Gwaltney, D. D. ; South Jersey Institute,
Bridgeton, N. J., 1869, H. K. Trask, LL. D.

It is remarkable how many good schools we have for
young ladies, and especially in the South. Many young
ladies in the North, bent upon obtaining an education, and
yet contending feebly against the rigors of a northern winter,
would find it to their profit to seek for what they want in
these southern Baptist schools.

The one school for the training of ministers for their
work, upon which southern Baptists are, for the most part,
concentrating their strength, is the Southern Baptist Theological Seminary, Louisville, Kentucky. J. P. Boyce, D. D.,
LL. D., is president. It has a large endowment and a most
efficient corps of instructors, among the very best in the
land. It was founded at Greenville, in 1859.

Among the youngest of our theological seminaries is
Crozer, at Upland, Penn., H. G. Weston, D. D., president.
It was founded in 1868. The family of the late John P.
Crozer, with Samuel A Crozer at the head, have given
grounds, buildings, and endowment, amounting to about

* J: G. **Walker,** D. D., editor, 1884.

WILLIAM JEWELL COLLEGE, LIBERTY, MO.

See page 396

$350,000. William Bucknell, in memory of his wife, a Miss Crozer, built Pearl Hall, the library building, and gave a large sum for books.

Baptist interest in education is shown by the liberality of our noble hearted men and women, of means, whose names and benefactions are too numerous to mention : The Browns and Ives to Brown University ; Nicholas Brown's subscriptions amounting to $160,000. Col. Albert Shorter, for Shorter College, Ga., $150,000. Gardner Colby, to Colby University, $50,000. Dr. Mercer, for Mercer University, Ga., $40,000. Gov. Abner Coburn towards the endowment of the four Baptist academies in Maine, $50,-000, and $100,000 to Colby University. James B. Colgate, for grounds, building and endowment of Colgate Academy, Hamilton, New York, $85,000, and Colgate and Trevor, for the same object, $30,000. Mathew Vassar, for founding Vassar Female College, Poughkeepsie, New York, $408,000, during his life, and by will, $150,000 more. Col. E. W. Cook, for establishing Cook Academy, Havana, New York, $123,000. Hon. T. B. Peddie, for Peddie Institute, Hightstown, New Jersey, $50,000. The Mulfords for South Jersey Institute, Bridgeton, New Jersey, $50,000. The Overholts, for Mount Pleasant Institute, Pennsylvania, $60,-000. The Hollins family, for Hollins Institute, Virginia, $19,000. Gov. C. H. Hardin, to Hardin College, Missouri, $40,000. Gov. J. E. Brown, Georgia, to the Southern Baptist Theological Seminary, $50,000 ; which amount has been increased, by others, to $200,000. Large amounts have been given to Rochester University, New York ; Hon. Hiram Sibley, $102,000, John B. Trevor, $113,000, John H. Deane, $100,000, Hon. Wm. Kelley and family, $38,000, Gen. J. F. Rathbone, $42,000, J. B. Hoyt, $27,000, Charles Pratt, $25,·

ooo, Jeremiah Milbank, $25,000, J. F. Wyckoff, $22,000, J. B. Colgate, $20,000, and many others. A. E. Dickinson, D. D., by noble efforts, has just (1884) raised nearly $100,000 for Richmond College, Virginia, as follows: $10,000 towards a scholarship-fund for ministers' sons; nearly $50,000 for the library fund; and over $40,000 for the south wing of the college building, called the "Jeter Memorial Hall," in honor of the late J. B. Jeter, D. D.

REV. H. M. WHARTON,   See page 394.

CHAPTER XXXI.

THE RELIGIOUS PRESS.

NE of the greatest instrumentalities in our growth, as Baptists, has been the denominational press. Like all else that is Baptist, it is independent ; it knows no master save Christ. There is a more important part for it to play in the future than in the past. If the evangelization of the world, and the discipline of the Baptist hosts for efficient service, and their development in spiritual life, be the work before us, and it is, then there was never greater need than at present for the powerful influence of the religious paper. And he who would help or lead in this great movement, whether minister or layman, must aid and use the press.

The *Christian Watchman* is the oldest of our Baptist papers, and was founded in 1819, at Boston, Mass., by James Loring, who, for many years, was editor and proprietor. It was a "folio of four pages," containing intelligence from the churches, communications on theological and practical topics, and a summary of secular news. It met the conscious wants of the people at the time. The more highly organized religious newspaper of the present day was not practicable, and would hardly have been appreciated. The *Christian*

Reflector was begun in 1839, at Worcester, by the Rev. Cyrus P. Grosvener, in the interests of anti-slavery. The *Watchman* was never pro-slavery, but conservative. The *Reflector* gained in circulation, rivaling that of the older journal. In 1848 the sentiment of the denomination had advanced so far in the direction led by the *Reflector*, removed to Boston in 1844, that the *Watchman* and *Reflector* were united, with J. W. Olmstead, D. D., and William Hague, D. D., editors. The *Watchman and Reflector* was the first Baptist weekly paper to enrich its columns by the pens of paid correspondents and contributors. The *Christian Era* was commenced at Lowell in 1850, and removed to Boston. In 1876, The Watchman Publishing Company was formed and acquired both journals, and thus *The Watchman* of to-day, combining the strength and representing in spirit its several predecessors, continues the mission begun in 1819. John W. Olmstead, D. D., is editor and manager; Lucius E. Smith, D. D., and Joseph C Foster, D. D., are associate editors.

The *Christian Index* is published at Atlanta, Ga. by Harrison, Wharton and Co. 16 pp. Editor, M. B. Wharton, D. D. Associates: J. S. Lawton, S. Henderson, D. D., D. Shaver D. D., and Paul Willis. It was originated in 1821, at Washington, D. C., as *The Columbian Star*. It was moved to Philadelphia and edited as *The Christian Index*, by Dr. W. T. Brantley Sr., who transferred it, in 1833, to Dr. Mercer, of Georgia, who presented it, in 1840, to the state convention. It was edited from 1833 to 1861, successively, by Rev. W. H. Stokes, Dr. J. S. Baker, J. F. Dagg, T. D. Martin, J. Walker, S. Landrum, E. W. Warren, and S. Boykin. It was removed to Atlanta in 1865 and edited in turn by Dr. D. Shaver, Rev. D. E. Butler, and Dr. H. H. Tucker.

Dr. Boykin writes, " The present firm acquired possession in 1883, and its management is such as to make it one of the most widely circulated and influential religious journals among Baptists. It is eminently sound and sensible in its denominational views, and a strong supporter of Baptist sentiments. Its chief editor is a man of power, and Drs. Shaver and Henderson are men of extensive learning, great ability and high literary distinction. It has exerted a wonderful influence in promoting the growth and prosperity of of the Baptist denomination in Georgia."

The *Christian Secretary* was first issued February 2, 1822, Rev. Elisha Cushman, Sr., editor. It was then 16 by 19, and is now 28 by 42 inches. Mr. Cushman was succeeded by Rev. Gurdon Robins, in 1824, and Mr. Robins by Deacon Philemon Canfield, in 1829. In 1837 it was united with the *Gospel Witness*, of New York, but owing to dissatisfaction, the publication of the *Secretary* was resumed in 1838, by its first editor. Upon his death, in October following, his son took charge till 1840, when Mr. Normand Burr became editor and proprietor, till his death in 1861. Rev. E. Cushman succeeded him until his death, January 4, 1876, when the paper passed into the hands of S. D. Phelps, D. D., who is still proprietor and senior editor. For some time his son, Dryden W. Phelps, was assistant editor. Mrs. S. E. Phelps and Rev. E. P. Bond, are now associate editors.

" *The Examiner*," published in New York, by Bright, Church and Company, is " by many thousands, the most widely circulated Baptist newspaper in the world." " It has always had a strong denominational character, and has fearlessly maintained the distinguishing doctrines of the old Baptist faith. Its aim has been to be as complete as it could be made in all the departments that belong to a first-class newspaper; to deal with the great questions of social and political, as well as Christian life ; to present the news, with comments, from a Christian stand-point ; and to do it with the fullness, freshness, and force, that ought to characterize the very best class of religious newspapers."

It originated in 1823, at Utica, in the *New York Baptist Register*, which was united afterwards with the *Recorder*. Edward Bright, D. D., and S. S. Cutting, D. D., bought the *Register* and *Recorder* in 1855, and became its editors, changing its name to *The Examiner*. It had a circulation of ten thousand, and was a four-page paper. The next year Dr. Cutting withdrew, leaving Dr. Bright sole editor, which position he has occupied ever since. In the first ten years of Dr. Bright's management, the circulation doubled.

In 1865 the *New York Chronicle*, owned and edited by Dr. P. Church, was united with *The Examiner* under the name of *The Examiner* and *Chronicle*. In 1869, it reached its present size, that of a seven-column, eight-page paper. The paper has resumed its former name of, *The Examiner*.

In 1825, the *Religious Herald* was established in Richmond, Va. Its projectors and editors were Eli Ball and Henry Keeling, and R. B. Semple, Andrew Broaddus, J. B. Taylor, and others, who were then the chief men among the Virginia Baptists. For over thirty years the *Herald* was owned and edited by Wm. Sands, a Baptist layman of great wisdom and excellence. A few months after the close of the war, the paper passed into the hands of Drs. J. B. Jeter and A. E. Dickinson. With their main purpose in view to make it "a common medium for the Baptists," they pushed their circulation in the North as well as in the South. Hence, Dr. Dickinson has attended, for the past eighteen years, most of the larger meetings of the Baptists at the North. The *Herald* has sought to unify the Baptist sentiment of the country, and has had the honor of making the two sections

know each other better. W. E. Hatcher, D. D., is now
associated with Dr. Dickinson in the editorial management
of the paper, and never in all its history has the *Herald* been
more prosperous than it is at present. It is read in almost
every neighborhood in the South, and has troops of friends
in the North.

Zion's Advocate is the organ of the Baptists of Maine ;
H. S. Burrage, D. D., is proprietor and editor. It originated
in 1828 with Rev. Adam Wilson. J. Ricker took charge
from 1838 to 1842, when Dr. Wilson resumed control, aided
by Rev. L. Colby. Prof. S. K. Smith became owner, and
issued it in 1848 as *Zion's Advocate and Eastern Watchman.*
The latter half of the name was dropped in 1884. Prof. J.
B. Foster edited it for eight years, when W. H. Shailer, D.
D., became editor and proprietor, assisted by J. W Colcord.
The office was burned during the great fire at Portland, in
1866. The paper had been already issued. The next week
a small sheet was published, and the week after that, the
paper appeared as usual. The *Advocate* came into the hands
of its present scholarly editor, in 1873, and became an eight-
column paper in 1877 It has had great influence in the
enlargement and elevation of the Baptist churches in Maine,
and with firmness, but courtesy, it has maintained " the faith
once delivered to the saints."

The Journal and Messenger was first issued at Cincinnati,
Ohio, July 22nd, 1831, as the *Baptist Weekly Journal of the
Mississippi Valley*, Prof. J. Stevens, D. D., editor. In 1850
The Christian Messenger, Indiana, was united with it and its
present name assumed. In 1856 the Central Baptist Press
Company was formed, and purchased the paper, and Rev. G.
Cole was editor till 1865, when Rev. T. J. Melish was in-
stalled. In 1872 J. R. Baumes, D. D., succeeded him. In
1876 G. W. Lasher, D. D., purchased all the stock and

property of the company, and became editor, proprietor and publisher, continuing in that relation until the present time. The paper is a large quarto, thirty-five by forty-seven inches, with fifty-six columns, and its circulation is exceeded by only three others of our denominational papers. Its special field is Ohio, Indiana, West Virginia, and the great and growing states beyond the Mississippi.

The *Biblical Recorder*, the organ of the Baptists of North Carolina, was established by Rev. Thomas Meredith in 1834. It has now 5100 regular subscribers, and its circulation while confined, principally, to the state, extends to all parts of the Union, and to the mission-stations of the Southern Baptist Convention. The paper is conservative, honest and outspoken, has little use for the new theories and issues, and vigorously contends for the old and established principles of Baptist churches. Rev. C. T. Bailey, D. D., is editor, and C. S. Farriss, associate. It is published at Raleigh, by Edwards, Broughton & Co., "never clubs with other journals, and publishes no immoral or quack advertisements."

The *Tennessee Baptist* was originated in Nashville, in 1835, with R. B. C. Howell, D. D., as editor. In 1843 J. R. Graves, LL. D., became proprietor and editor. Under his management, the paper prospered beyond precedent. It became a large folio. In 1861 its circulation was in all the southern states, and the largest of any Baptist paper in America. After the war, its publication office having been burned, and its assets ($52,000) destroyed, it was re-established and has since reached a circulation of 10,000. It is an unfaltering advocate of the old landmarks of Baptist faith and practice, of Christian education and missions. Its editor is the oldest editor in the United States, has had the longest unbroken connection with the same paper. The decided and consistent denominationalism of the south, it is freely admitted, is largely due to the influence of this paper.

The Michigan Baptists, with but slight interim, have sustained a denominational state paper for nearly half a century, known most of the time as the *Christian Herald.* Rev. M. Allen, Rev. G. W. Harris, Prof. Ten Brook, and O. S. Gulley, were familiar names connected with its early history, and later, Dr. E. Olney, and Revs. Curtess and Clark. In 1866, the latter, to the disappointment of many, sold the *Herald* to the Chicago *Standard.* The present proprietor, Rev. H. L. Trowbridge, began its publication in 1870, as an aid to educational work of the state, as carried on by the Kalamazoo College. The coming of a state paper to the homes of the Baptists of Michigan was so acceptable and their co-operation so hearty, that very soon the paper was published weekly, and was, by vote, made the official organ of the denomination. Its growth and usefulness, in promoting missions and education, have often been subjects of congratulatory resolutions. It is an eight-page, 56 column paper, and published at Detroit, in its own building.

Ford's Christian Repository and Home Circle, was established by Rev. J. L. Waller, LL. D., in Louisville, Kentucky, in 1852. S. H. Ford, LL. D., soon after became its sole proprietor and editor. In 1855 Dr. Ford married Miss Sallie Rochester, who became editor of the family department. She wrote the serial, "Grace Truman," published by Sheldon, whose influence has been very great. The *Repository* aims at combining the features of a review, a historic memorial, and a family magazine. It has absorbed *The Baptist Memorial, The Mothers' Journal,* and *The Home Circle,* and is now thought to be the most widely circulated religious monthly magazine in America. It was removed to St. Louis, Missouri, in 1871.

z

The Standard was established in Chicago, Illinois, in 1853, as *The Christian Times.* For three months it was conducted by J. C. Burroughs, D. D. Mr. Edward Goodman the present senior proprietor, became connected with it, as agent, from the first. In 1883 it was purchased by Rev. Leroy Church, and Justin A. Smith, D. D., who became joint proprietors and editors. Mr. Goodman and Mr. Church finally became proprietors, with Dr. Smith editor-in chief, which position he has now held continuously for thirty-one years. In 1875 J. S. Dickerson, D. D., purchased the interest of Mr. Church, and the firm of Goodman and Dickerson was formed. Dr. Dickerson's interest, at his death, in 1876, passed to his widow, Mrs. E. R. Dickerson. J. Spencer Dickerson is now one of the firm. The *Standard* is a Baptist paper of national circulation, but, especially, the organ for the denomination in the North-west. It now ranks second in the number of its subscribers and readers in the list of American Baptist journals.

The *Baptist Weekly*, New York, A. S. Patton, D. D., editor, and Dr. R. T. Middleditch, associate, is devoted to the promotion of Christianity, as held by the Baptists. The *American Baptist*, issued in 1857, Rev. W. Walker, editor, was the organ of the Free Mission Society. Dr. Brown first assisted Mr. Walker, and then became editor-in-chief, assisted by Rev. J. Duer. In 1872 Dr. Brown went to Japan. The paper under him was opposed to all secret societies, to clergymen receiving honorary titles, and to human slavery. Dr. Patton bought it in 1872, enlarged it to a quarto, and greatly improved it. He dropped the specialties, and made it broad in its scope. "It earnestly maintains the distinctive principles and practices of the Baptists."

In 1864 the minds of many prominent Baptists in the vicinity of Philadelphia became impressed with the necessity of a paper which should be issued in Philadelphia, and which should represent, especially, the interests of the denomination in Pennsylvania, New Jersey, Delaware, and the region of which Philadelphia is the centre. With this view a sum was raised, mainly through the efforts of Dr. B. Griffith, and placed in the hands of the American Baptist Publication Society as a basis for the paper. The publication of the *National Baptist* commenced, January, 1865. It is not impossible that the name of the paper reflected the prevailing sentiment of the times, and was meant to emphasize the fact that the United States was a nation. Its editors have been Geo. W. Anderson, D. D , Kendall Brooks, D. D., Lemuel Moss, D. D., and H. L. Wayland, D. D. Dr. Wayland became editor in 1872, and has remained in charge of the paper to the present time. He has rare qualifications for the manifold duties of an editor, has conducted the *Baptist* with marked ability, and has spared neither toil nor money to make it the first class paper that it is to-day. Among the assistant editors have been J. Stockbridge, D. D., J. Eugene Reed, A. M., and Rev. Philip Berry. At present, E. P. Anderson, A. M., is the literary editor, Mrs A. B. Bosson, editor of the family department, and Theo. Felsberg, business manager. With the beginning of 1883 the paper became an individual enterprise, having been purchased by Dr. Wayland. Its circulation is constantly increasing, having doubled within the last six years.

The *Texas Baptist Herald* has Rev. J. B. Link proprietor and editor, and Rev. O. C. Pope, D. D., as assistant. The close of the war found Texas practically without a Baptist paper. Rev. J. B. Link, by urgent request, issued the *Herald* first in December, 1865. It appeared occasionally until July, 1866, when it became a weekly. Irregular mails, scarcity of railroads, (there being not over 200 miles in the state,) Houston the head-quarters of the paper, a visitation of the yellow fever in 1867, and a small capital of only $200, were some of the difficulties to contend with. The paper has, however, paid its way, and yielded something besides. In 1883 it was moved to Austin, and has a circulation of 5000. A very large part of Baptist prosperity in the state can be ascribed to the influence of this excellent journal.

The Central Baptist, St. Louis, Mo., is the out-come of the Missouri *Baptist Journal* and *The Record*. Rev. A. A. Kendrick, editor of the *Record* suggested, in the interests of harmony, their consolidation which was effected in 1868, and the present name chosen. The Baptists united, and increased activity discovered itself in all denominational enterprises. The editor-in-chief, J. H. Luther, was assisted successively by Revs. Norman Fox, A. A. Kendrick, and W. Pope Yeaman. "No paper in the United States has made for itself a nobler reputation, as the champion of religious freedom, the advocate of mental and moral culture, and the defender of distinctive Baptist principles. In three years and a half its circulation had reached its eighth thousand. In 1875, W. Pope Yeaman, D. D., and Rev. W. J. Patrick became sole editors and for some two years it was published by the Western Baptist Publishing House. Mr. Patrick retired the same year, and Dr. Yeaman, in 1877, the latter having been assisted by Rev. Mr. Abbott and Rev. W. Ferguson. Mr. Ferguson became sole proprietor and editor, with Rev. J. C. Armstrong as associate. The paper was purchased in 1882 by Rev. W. H. Williams, since which time its influence and circulation have been steadily increasing. Rev. G. W. Hyde, associate editor, and Rev. Harvey Hatcher, field editor.

The Baptist Courier was established in 1869 under the name of *The Working Christian*, at Yorkville. It was removed in a year or two to Charleston, and afterwards to Columbia where it was published for several years. In 1877 the name was changed to *The Baptist Courier* and in 1879 it was removed to its present location, Greenville, where it has had an uninterrupted period of prosperity. Its circulation has steadily grown since it was purchased by its present senior proprietor, in 1878, and now has attained a circulation far beyond that which any Baptist paper has ever enjoyed in South Carolina. It is edited by James A. Hoyt and W. W. Keys, with Dr. James C. Furman, as associate editor.

The Alabama Baptist was established at Marion, in 1874, by the state convention. It was edited gratuitously by E. T. Winkler, D. D., with E. B. Teague and J. J. D. Renfroe, D. D., as associates. In 1877, Rev. J. L. West was appointed publisher and business manager. In January, 1878, the paper was moved to Selma. In 1879, it became the property of Rev. J. L. West, who is sole editor and proprietor. Under his earnest effort it has attained an extensive circulation in the state, and has proved a power for good, within its sphere.

In January, 1882, J. M. Robertson, D. D., of Alabama, bought the *Baptist Sun* and the *Baptist Beacon* and consolidated them under the name of *American Baptist* at Chattanooga, Tennessee. In July, 1882, Dr. Robertson purchased the *Baptist Reflector* established in 1874, and changed the name of his paper to the *American Baptist Reflector.* The combined circulation was then 3,500, while now it is 7,983, chiefly in Tennessee, Georgia and Alabama. E. T. Winkler, D. D., LL. D., was a regular contributor till his death, and others are, J. M. Pendleton, D. D., M. Hillsman, D. D., J. C. Hiden, D. D., Wm. Norton, of England, J. T. Christian,

A. M., Rev. R. A. Venable, Rev. W. M. Bridges, and Rev. Wm. Huff.

The American Battle Flag, St. Louis, Mo., D. B. Ray, D. D., editor and proprietor, is a large eight-page religious paper. It was first issued in 1877, and conducted at La Grange for over two years, then removed to St. Louis. It was first called the *Baptist Battle Flag*, but for five years has borne its present name. It was originated by Dr. Ray. The leading design of the *Flag* is to develop our points of denominational truth more aggressively than any other Baptist paper west of the Mississippi. The editor is a Baptist author, and church historian of note.

The *Baptist Record*, Clinton, Miss., was established in 1877, by the state convention. Prof. M. T. Morton was proprietor, and Elder J. B. Gambrell was elected editor. From the first, the paper was devoted to the unification and development of Baptists of the state. Good success has attended its efforts. It was the first paper in the state to advocate prohibition, and has always been an outspoken temperance advocate. Missions and education have been leading questions in its columns, as has also the elevation of the colored race. Now in its eighth year it enjoys a good patronage, and a steady growth. Rev. J. B. Gambrell and Prof. Geo. Wharton are proprietors and editors.

The *Baptist Review* is a quarterly, owned and conducted by J. R. Baumes, D. D., at Cincinnati, Ohio. In 1876, Dr. Baumes retired from the *Journal and Messenger*. In a year or two afterward he began the publication of the *Review*, intended for ministers and intelligent members. It has been a success. It has been conducted with ability, and has a paying list of subscribers.

The *Child's Gem* is a weekly Baptist illustrated Sunday school paper for primary classes, published and edited by S.

Boykin, D. D., Macon, Ga. It is now in its sixth year and has a large circulation. Few, if any, papers are better adapted to intelligent children from six to ten. It contains the International S. S. Lessons, and is handsomely printed.

In 1879, Rev. J. K. Richardson, urged on by his brethren who thought that there was need and that he was the man, issued a prospectus for a paper to be devoted to the interests of the Vermont Baptist Convention. The reception of the prospectus encouraged him to issue the first number of the *Vermont Baptist*, February, 1879, at Rutland, Vt. It has been regularly issued, monthly, ever since. Its aim has not been to supersede, but to supplement other Baptist papers, and in cases where others were not taken, and such cases are too numerous, to do a work that can only be done by a faithful, consistent Baptist paper. The paper therefore aims to present, in the most attractive and readable manner, such matter as will be likely to build up a strong Christian and Bible Baptist character and the Baptist churches of the state.

The *Arkansas Evangel* was started by a stock company February 8, 1881, with B. R. Womack, D. D., as editor, at Russellville. Mr. Womack had been editor and publisher of the *Baptist Reflector*, Nashville, Tenn. At the end of the year the *Evangel* was turned over to Dr. Womack. It is a four-page thirty-two column paper, devoted exclusively to Baptist interests in the state. It has built up state mission-work to three times what it was, and by its constant advocacy of foreign missions has increased the contributions of the people. Through it the denomination is aroused to the necessity of founding a state Baptist college. Baptist progress in the state during the last three years has been great, mainly through the influence of the *Evangel*. A. S. Worrell is associate editor.

The publication of the *Indiana Baptist* was begun at Indianapolis, September 1, 1881, by Rev. G. H. Elgin and

N. M. Chaille, both young, and natives of Indiana, and, from their conversions, deeply interested in Baptist progress in the state. The *Baptist* had its origin in a conviction on their part that a dollar paper devoted to the interests of the Baptists in Indiana would be encouraged. Their hopes have been more than realized. It is not yet three years old and has a *bona fide* circulation of four thousand, and gradually growing. It more than paid expenses from the very start. It has had, and still enjoys, the most hearty support of the entire denomination in the state, by which it has been adopted as the organ. Rev. H. E. Stetson is Mr. Elgin's assistant, as editor, and Mr. Chaille is business manager.

The *Kansas Baptist* is published and edited by L. H. Holt, at Clay Centre. It has been issued since September 1, 1882, received with favor and supported. It is a monthly, but the demand is so strong for a weekly, that arrangements are now completed to combine it with *The Nebraska Visitor*, and make it a weekly. The combined papers will be issued under the name of *The Western Baptist*, L. H. Holt and George Sutherland, editors and proprietors, and begin with a circulation of 2,500.

On the 1st of September, 1883, the first issue of *The Baltimore Baptist* appeared. It was the fruit of the conviction of Rev. H. M. Wharton, the editor, that a Baptist paper was necessary to the progress of the Baptist cause in Maryland. It was the successor of *The Baptist Nation*, edited at Washington, by Rev. M. C. Thwing, and Mr. Wharton's own church paper. Its circulation is 3,100 and extends mainly through Maryland, Delaware and Virginia. Rev. A. C. Barron is the able associate editor, and F. H. Kerfoot, D.D., is special contributor. The portrait of Mr. Wharton appears as the youngest Baptist journalist.

Among the other denominational papers in America, too numerous to mention, are the following: *The Western*

Recorder and also the *American Baptist*, A. C. Caperton, D, D., editor, Louisville, Ky., *The Banner of Truth*, Rev. G. W. Fears, Corinth, Miss., *The Baptist Beacon*, R. W. J. Crawford, Salem, Ore., *The Baptist Journal*, Rev. A. R. Griggs, Marshall, Texas, *The Baptist Messenger*, J. W. Cater, Tennessee, *The Baptist Messenger*, J. J. Spelman, Jackson, Miss., The *Blue Ridge Baptist*, D. B. Nelson, Hendersonville, N. C., *The Canadian Baptist*, E. W. Dadson, B. A., Toronto, Ont., *The Christian Messenger*, S. Seldon, Halifax, N. S., the *Christian Visitor*, J. E. Hopper, D. D., St. Johns, N. B., The *Georgia Baptist*, Rev. W. J. White, Angusta, the *African Expositor*, Rev. N. F. Roberts, Raleigh, N. C., the *Baptist Pioneer*, E. M. Brawley, Clinton, Miss., the *Herald of Truth*, G. S. Abbott, D. D., Oakland, Cal., the *Missionary Baptist*, C. C. Dickinson, Memphis, Tenn., *The Southern Baptist*, Rev. A. Greasett, Meridian, Miss., *The Texas Baptist*, Drs. Hayden and Anderson, Dalas.

The Baptist press of America is of a high order, and calculated to elevate and extend the churches of Christ. But this cannot be done unless the people read the papers. While the aggregate circulation is large, yet it is not half what it should be. There are scores of people who have no religious paper, while a denominational paper is indispensable in every family. It is useless to plead poverty, all are able. It is worse to plead " pressure of business" and " no time to read." There are some things for which time must be taken, and this is one. There are things not to be neglected even for business, and among them, the cultivation of the mind and heart. The Religious Press is one of the most important of auxiliaries to the accomplishment of this grand purpose. If the church is more important than the world, and if eternal things are of more moment than temdoral things, then, at least, one religious paper should be weekly read and digested.

CHAPTER XXXII.

FUTURE PROSPECTS AND PRESENT OBLIGATIONS.

THE Baptists throughout the world number (1884) 33,007 churches, 20,620 ministers, and 3,000,389 members. The greater part of these are in the United States: 27,913 churches, 17,327 ordained ministers, and 2,474,771 church members. There have been 111,932 baptisms in the last year in this country, where the annual average number of baptisms for the last ten years has been about 100,000.

This enumeration does not include those denominations that immerse, and that may be considered, for this and other reasons, as branches of the Baptist family. For example: Free-will Baptists, (open communion,) 76,706 ; Disciples, or Campbellites, 846,300 ; * Seventh day Baptists, 8,606 ; Tunkers, 90,000 ; Adventists, 114,141 ; Six-principle Baptists, 2,075 ; Church of God, or Winebrennerians, 45,000, in all, 1,182,828 ; and with the Regular Baptists, a grand total of 3,657,599 in the United States, or a number larger than the population of the country at the time of the war for Independence.

Besides a large number in Pedobaptist churches who hold our views in reference to baptism in practice or in theory, and our principles are gaining ground.

* According to their own estimate.

The first Baptist Sunday-school for religious instruction was established in the Second Baptist church, Baltimore, Md., in 1804. Now, 1884, there are in the United States 15,939 Sunday-schools, with 134,395 officers and teachers, and 1,118,129 scholars, reporting for the year 14,216 baptisms, and $6,996,105.66 contributions.

Baptist people and principles have already exerted a blessed influence far beyond the limits of their own denomination. The Baptists have laid the world under incalculable obligation, and truths held by them have been like leaven in the midst of Papal and Pedobaptist errors. Baptist authors have adorned every branch of literature. The doctrine of civil and religious liberty once contended for by the Baptists almost alone, is now maintained as well by other denominations of Christians, has become the heritage of many nations, and the hope of the oppressed in all the earth. Baptists were the first to inaugurate the great missionary movement among Protestants, and to arouse Christians to engage in this glorious work. They have taken a prominent part in the translation of the Bible into the languages of the nations of the earth and in its general distribution both at home and abroad. They were the leaders, says Dr. Philip Schaff, in the great work of modern Bible revision. A Baptist minister, Joseph Hughes, first suggested the idea of a society for the circulation of the Bible throughout the world. John Canne, a Baptist minister, was the first to prepare and publish the Bible with scriptural reference in the margin, throughout.

If so much has been accomplished in the past, by a few, hindered by severe persecution and opposition, how much more should be achieved to-day with our increased abilities, and great opportunities !

Some one has made the curious calculation that since the Baptists in this country increased from 25,000 in 1776 to 1,800,000 in 1876, that they will number in 1976, at the same rate of growth, 130,000,000. Such an estimate is almost incredible, but, when we hear Joseph Cook discourse upon the vast extent and boundless resources as well as the glorious future prospects of our country, teeming with an immense population, such a growth of the Baptist denomination is not to be regarded as improbable. It is only necessary for our denominational growth in the future, to be as in the past, in order to realize it all. There are evidently great possibilities before us as a denomination. Dr. W. R. Williams says that Krummacher remarked to an eminent American Baptist that the Baptists had "a future." It is to be greatly hoped that our "future" may be worthy of the glorious past.

But whether this prospective greatness will be realized depends, under God, upon present fidelity to the sacred trusts committed to us by Christ, and upon our promptness in seeing and seizing our opportunities. Vast responsibilities rest upon us. Great dangers beset us. We have, first of all, great need of humility, of self-distrust, and of dependence upon God. While, on the one hand, there are elements of strength found in us, as a denomination, yet, on the other hand, there are seeds of weakness. There are, however, no perils threatening our denominational prospects that may not be averted, and each danger suggests a present obligation.

One danger is opposition to Baptist principles, and calls upon us to be firm and united, true to each other and loyal to Christ. It is sometimes remarked that there is no need for the separate existence of the Baptist denomination. Such a declaration proves that our work is not yet done.

What reason is there for the separate existence of any denomination? We uphold and practice truth too important for the world to lose. If the world can be made better for our lives and our principles, then there is not only abundant reason for our denominational integrity, but also for the determined maintenance of our views. We cannot leave the truths we hold, for safe keeping to those who wish our dissolution on account of our principles. It is sometimes presumed that the only Baptist principle assailed is our views on the communion question. This is an error, for there is not one unopposed. The great question of to-day is as to the supreme authority of the Bible. To this is the main assault of the infidel directed. There are only two tenable grounds; its total rejection, or its entire acceptance. The position taken by Baptists is the only safe one for all Christains; the Bible, only, the standard rule of faith and practice. Every other question turns upon this. And as to our other distinctive principles, there is not one that is not assailed. Our opponents will not be satisfied when we give up one position, but will press on and drive us from another. If we admit the unbaptized to the Lord's Supper, then we must receive them to church membership, or we are " inconsistent," " bigots," and " uncharitable." The assault is along the whole line of our faith and practice. Our views as to the subject, mode, design and order of baptism; the separation of church and state; the purity of the church; independent church government and indeed all we hold dear for Christ's sake is, to-day, called in question. The oldest weapons are reburnished and used against us. If, what we hold is the Bible truth, then we are right and must stand firmly for it. And many noble minded Pedobaptist brethren will applaud us for our consistency in so doing.

It is no time to give up when Professor Trail calls separa-

MEMORIAL BAPTIST CHURCH, PHILADELPHIA.

H.M. SNYDER

See page 256.

tion of church and state " Atheism ;" when it is shamelessly asserted that immersion is not baptism ; when Presbyterians formally condemn a minister of that body for immersing a believer ; when infants are boldly proclaimed to be members of the church ; and when, in some quarters, Bible baptism is as unpopular as the blood of Jesus.

Those who oppose us will never be satisfied until, in the language of the Sea Grove resolutions and prayers,—the day " when each evangelical church shall recognize the validity and Christian character of the ministry, ordinances, certificates, and sacraments of every other church." Jesus prayed for no such union as this ; a union in error and not in the truth as it is in Christ,and which conciliates men by disloyalty to the Saviour himself.

Another danger may arise from relaxation of effort, and this reminds us of our duty to grow. The same ceaseless energies that have characterized the past, are still necessary not only for continued advancement, but even to prevent decline. The word must be preached by pastor, evangelist and people, and souls gathered to Christ by ones, by families, and by thousands, as in the days of the apostles. Every disciple is a preacher. And not until the whole church goes to the whole world will the whole earth rejoice in Christ and his salvation.

Our country is rapidly filling up. The coming immense population will need the gospel, and it is our part as Christians and as Baptists to give it to them. We are not true to Christ if we fail in this, and are craven if we leave it to others. The perpetuity of our country—its institutions, and its liberties, rests upon the fidelity with which the gospel is preached in the growing and the destitute portions of the land. The conflict for liberty, once waged honorably and successfully here, is now going on in the old world, but this country is to be the theatre of another longer and severer conflict—between capital and labor. And there is nothing to prevent it, or to mitigate its horrors except the gospel, which comes teaching the brotherhood of man and the Fatherhood of God, harmonizing all things by the blood of the cross, and making all men one in Christ. The Baptists have ever been the friends of humanity and the advocates in all ages of the rights of man, and hence, have the ears of the people, and it is, therefore, for them to do the utmost in their power to bring to Christ the thousands that seek a refuge on our shores. But we must grow in numbers, or we can never meet the demands made upon us by the rapidly increasing millions of our population.

But this is not all. We have a duty to perform in other lands and to other nations. Never has any portion of God's people been more highly favored with opportunities to reach the heathen and success in missionary labor. As yet, our missionaries have but effected a landing upon the shores of Asia and Africa, while those great continents lie undeveloped before them. We have prayed for the doors of Japan to be opened, for the walls of China to be razed, and the Dark Continent to be explored, and lo! all is as we asked, and the opportunity is ours. Shall we now hesitate to go up and possess the land with all our force? Ah! we must grow for the sake of the nations and the glory of our God in the earth. We have a great work to do. It has been asserted that while we have been the most highly favored of all Christians in our missionary operations, that we have given less for missions than any others. If this is true, and we greatly fear it is, let us take away this reproach, and henceforth lead all other denominations in our contributions for saving perishing souls. Dr. B. Sears says: " The downfall of heathenism is certain ; it is decreed in the historic march of human events, as it is in the counsels of heaven. The only question that remains to be settled is, shall it be superseded by some species of philosophical unbelief, or by the Christian faith? What an argument is this for renewed and vastly increased activity in our work."

Another peril arises from rapid numerical growth, and this admonishes us to be careful in the reception of members, and in the training of converts. We should grow, but grow wisely.

Numbers may be an element of weakness. Tacitus said that the Roman Empire was in danger of breaking down from its own greatness; and so, in our rapid increase, we may lose the strength and vigor of earlier years.

Yet the cry is for more, and some churches think they are not progressing unless receiving accessions. There is a craving, in many quarters, for the feverish excitement of large ingatherings, and for pastors who will " draw," and " fill the pews," and " pay." Hence, the pastor, in a large degree, is prevented from steadily laying solid foundations for the spiritual house, and finds himself almost unconsciously drifting with the popular current, seeking to please, laboring for present effect, and securing, it may be, large, but superficial results. In the efforts for increasing numbers, the training of converts and the seeking of the wandering are too apt to be neglected. If this goes on we will become an untrained mob, rather than a skillfully directed organization.

I apprehend that our method is wrong. There is a kind of church-growth that ought to be sought first in order of time, as it is first in importance. We speak of development which is internal not external, spiritual instead of material, in quality

2A

rather than in quantity, in knowledge, in grace, and in Christian activity. Progress in this direction may be slow, like the advancing hour-hand of the clock, or the maturing child, but it is steady and sure. Let this inward growth be manifest to "those without" by the broadest distinction made in theory and in practice between the church and the world, and nothing be done by Christians in the pursuit of pleasure or of business that is a reproach to Christ ; and mark the result. Attention thus given to that part of the commission which requires "teaching them to observe" and observing ourselves, the "all things" "commanded ;" will not fail of best success. The church that attends faithfully to its own spiritual prosperity will be too active to cease to grow from without. It is spiritual strength that the churches most need ; and which mere numbers cannot give. When persecution ceased upon the conversion of Saul, and the churches had "rest," then were they first "edified," and consequently "multiplied." Now is the period of "rest." This is our opportunity. How long it may last we know not, but while it does, let us grow.

"Every creature" to whom we are sent, whether child or adult has mind and body as well as a spiritual nature. The work of sowing the seed and of gathering the harvest, from pulpit, in Sunday-school, and from house to house, is not all that the Christian has to do. We are to provide for the creature's intellectual and bodily wants. The body must be fed, clothed, sheltered and nursed. The best care should be taken of God's poor, whom it is a privilege to have with us. As a denomination we have not fully done our duty in this regard. We have left too much to other denominations the care of suffering humanity. We have too few homes or hospitals for the aged, sick, afflicted, young, poor, and homeless, among us. Christ went about

MEMORIAL BAPTIST CHURCH, PHILADELPHIA.

See page 256.

doing good to the bodies as well as the souls of men. His work for man's temporal and physical good was very prominent. The Lord approached men to do them good through their bodies. To be wise winners of souls we must imitate him in this respect, as we have in others, and go seek the neglected and destitute with the word of God upon our lips, and also with food and raiment in our hands.

If we are to succeed, our ministerial supply must be kept up. A great multitude will need a host of competent leaders. There is a fear, in some minds, that our little churches are suffering, because young ministers are trained away from them. This may be true, and we may need an uneducated class to do a work for God's poor that ought to be congenial even to a highly cultivated Christian ministry. Nevertheless, men are needed to go before us, and many of them, with every natural ability and acquired advantage. Safe leaders are more needed than brilliant preachers, in order that our course may be steady and sure. We cannot afford to lose the counsel and guiding hand of experienced and aged ministers, who ought to be put to the front along with younger leaders. Ministerial supply threatens to be inadequate to our needs. Rev. Dr Heman Lincoln, of Newton, Mass., remarked to us that there are not as many young men now in our classical schools, studying for the Christian ministry as there used to be; and also, that, while formerly there were frequent revivals in such institutions and many conversions of students who went to swell the ranks of the ministry, there are few heard of at the present.

It is also true that those entering the ministry are chiefly from the class unable to pay for their education. This is not said to their detriment, but to show how limited the source of supply. Our pulpits should be supplied from all classes of society. It is right that the student for the ministry should accept a support while preparing for his work. From the time a young man begins his preparation for the ministry down to old age and death, the churches owe him and his family, large or small, an adequate support.

There are over 10,000 more churches in our denomination, in this country, than there are ordained ministers. Ministers are required for present as well as future needs, and young men should be urged to consider the claims of God upon them, in reference to the Christian ministry. But there are difficulties to be removed before the want is supplied. The large number of pastorless churches, the many ministers without charge, and the rush for vacant pulpits, are evidences of unrest in the ministry. And the cause of this unrest may account for the falling off of ministerial supply. The shortness of pastorates in general, shows the same unsettled condition. While the pastoral relation is so brief and uncertain, young men will avoid it. As far as the fault is with the ministry, they should correct it. Before entering the sacred calling, one should count well the cost, and resolve to do and suffer for Christ. But the churches are, in part, to blame for the unrest and insecurity named. It is for the church to make the pastor feel settled. It is wrong to keep him on trial, as some do, from his first appearance among them until his last. Pastor and people would find it far better to regard their union as sacred and permanent, not to be easily ruptured, but to be cherished and cemented. The feeling should be ; "What God hath joined together, let not man put asunder." The strong churches are those that insist upon stability in the pastorate, and successfully use all proper means to secure it.

We are told that the honors and pecuniary inducements the world offers to young men, are keeping many from entering the gospel ministry. In one sense this is an unworthy reason. Those who enter the sacred office should not do it for worldly gain. But there is another side to this question. If a young man surrender all hopes of worldly success and riches for the gospel, there is no reason why he should also give up all expectation of a necessary support. If the support is precarious, and insufficient, then high-minded men will stay out. What is just and fair should be paid without any hesitation, and without solicitation.

It is charged by some, that the country pastor is not the only pastor underpaid ; but that the salaries of many city pastors are too low. However this may be, it is still true that a right minded man will, if his people are poor and self-sacrificing, help them to bear their burdens. It is noble for any pastor to deny himself, when his flock are denying themselves to give to the objects of humanity and of religion. Why, however, ministers should not be paid as other men, I fail to see. If this, now, be one of the difficulties in the way of an adequate ministerial supply, then let the noblest sacrifices be made to remove it. Let the support of the pastor, in city and country, be fair and liberal, and in proportion to the means of his people, and the manner in which he is expected to live.

Baptists ought to be the most liberal givers for the support of the gospel at home and abroad, for churches, missions and all denominational institutions and enterprises. If the gospel be worth more than all else, then let us pay for it the highest price. Let there be no close bargaining for the things of the kingdom of Jesus. Jewing should not be known among Christians, at least when bargaining for the gospel of Christ. We glory in our sublime doctrines, and we do well, but let us be sublime in our living and doing for our Redeemer.

In all this we speak for others rather than for ourselves. In two pastorates, extending over nearly twenty years, God, by his grace, has given us, frequently, large ingatherings, and we have labored with a good and liberal people—among the best in the land ; so that we can truly exclaim : " The lines are fallen unto me in pleasant places."

Let us avoid all these dangers that threaten, and aim to secure the bright future that seems to be within our reach.

It is sometimes asked whether all Christians will become, eventually, one. In an essential sense they are one now—spiritually. Uniformity in external things, or consolidation of the churches under one government, or one man, is not necessary to Christian unity. The union that our Lord prayed for, was the oneness of all Christians in mind, in heart, in purpose, in life, in works, in the truth, in Christ. When thus united the world will believe in Jesus. It is not necessary that we go to others, or that others come to us, but that we all go to Christ. Each individual church can be separate and independent, and yet, all truly unite in singing the familiar hymn, written by John Fawcett, a Baptist minister :

> " Blest be the tie that binds
> " Our hearts in Christian love,
> " The fellowship of kindred minds
> " Is like to that above.

Let us, who are Christians of whatever name, grow in grace and in the knowledge of our Lord and Saviour, Jesus Christ, " till we all come, in the unity of the faith, and of the knowledge of the Son of God, unto a perfect man, unto the measure of the stature of the fullness of Christ."

SECOND BAPTIST CHURCH, ST. LOUIS, MO.,
W. W. BOYD, D. D., PASTOR.

THE COLORED BAPTISTS.

A SUPPLEMENTARY CHAPTER.

THE STEAMER "HENRY REED," UPPER CONGO.

THE COLORED BAPTISTS.

HE Island of Jamaica, W. I., first belonged to Spain, and then to England. The Indians were driven off and the island populated with slaves from Africa by Spaniards and English. Baptist missionary work was begun there by black men from America, and not by missionaries from England. "The Voice of Jubilee" says that when the English Baptist missionaries arrived at Jamaica, in 1814, they found that Christian black men from America had already been preaching the gospel there and found a people prepared to hail them in their coming, receive their message and co-operate with them in their ministry.

In 1783, George Lisle, a Baptist of Virginia, went to Jamaica. He first preached in Georgia in 1777, during the Revolution. The church having called him to the gospel ministry, he went to Jamaica from Savannah, Ga., as the slave of an English officer, at the close of the war, and was left free upon the death of his master.

Arrived at Kingston he was touched by the ignorance and vice of his own race, and preached to them at the race-course and in his own hired room. He gathered a church of four members, who were refugees from America, like himself, supporting himself by his own labor. He spread the gospel

413

among bond and free on neighboring plantations and to distant parts of the island, personally and by his own converts, so that in about seven years he had baptized five hundred believers. In 1793 he built the first dissenting chapel in Jamaica. But he and his brethren were subjected to every species of insult and persecution. He was thrown into prison for preaching sedition; "loaded with irons and his feet fastened in the stocks, not even his wife or his children were permitted to see him." He was tried for his life and acquitted, but afterwards was imprisoned more than once.

Among those who labored in the gospel with George Lisle were George Gives and T. N. Swingle, who collected a second church of 700 at Kingston, and Moses Baker, a converted drunkard, who formed a church at Crooked Spring. Another of these devoted men, whose name is not given, was hung for preaching and baptizing. From 1805 to 1814 a law forbidding preaching to slaves was rigidly enforced.

August 28, 1833, England emancipated the slaves of Jamaica.

It was the correspondence of George Lisle, Moses Baker and others, with Drs. Ryland and Rippon of England, that led finally to the sending out of the English Baptist missionaries.

The mission undertaken by the English Baptists not only became self-sustaining, but, in 1842, there were 45 missionaries to leave Jamaica for Africa, to take the gospel to their brethren at home.

"Perhaps you will be made slaves by the heathen, if you go," said some one; when they replied:

"We have been made slaves for men; we can be made slaves for Christ."

After this a Baptist named Keith sold what he possessed, bought a few clothes only, left a beloved companion for two years, "and worked his passage out to Africa to proclaim—and he did proclaim, on the very spot where he had been stolen—the gospel of salvation."

There are now in Jamaica 142 churches and 31,000 members, reporting 2,140 Baptisms for the year.

Rev. W. H. Brooks has published a sketch of George Lisle, entitled: "The Black Apostle."

In 1835 Rev. W. C. Monroe, an educated colored man, was ordained in New York and sailed for Port-au-Prince, Hayti. He met with such discouragments that he was forced to abandon the work. It has since been resumed. There are six churches and five ministers in Hayti; and in all the West Indies 189 churches, 109 ministers, and 37,564 members.

AFRICAN MISSIONS.

Rev. Lot Cary was the first missionary from America to Africa, and was very properly of African descent. He was a slave in Richmond, Va., but by application to business was enabled to buy the freedom of himself and his two children for $850, in 1813. He had, in 1807, united with the Baptist Church. He took an active part in the formation of the African Missionary Society in Richmond, in 1815, which in five years raised $700 for missions in Africa. This was one of the earliest missionary societies in the land. Another society was formed in Georgia soon after. Cary and Rev. Colin Teague, both colored, and of Richmond, began their labors among the Bassas at Monrovia, Liberia, where there was an American colony, in 1822. There they founded a church. Six were baptized in 1823, and in the following year nine more. Cary became the pastor. Teague returned to Sierra

Leone, where they had landed at first. Cary extended the mission to Cape Grand Mount, among "the Veys, one of the most powerful and intelligent tribes on the coast." He maintained missions at both places, and "manifested much energy and faithfulness in his labors, great sagacity in civil affairs, and remarkable power and earnestness as a preacher." He was Vice-Governor of Liberia, and active Governor during the absence of Governor Ashmun. While preparing to lead the forces of the colony against hostile natives, he was suddenly killed by the accidental explosion of powder, November, 1828.

It was thought that no white man could live on the western coast of Africa, hence the mission was reinforced by Rev. A. W. Anderson, Rev. J. Lewis and Rev. H. Teague, son of Rev. C. Teague, all colored. Rev. J. Vonbrunn, a native Bassa, kept up the mission after the death or departure of the white missionaries that had been sent out.

In 1846 the Southern Baptist Convention "sent two colored missionaries to Africa, Rev. J. Day and Rev. A. L. Jones. From 1846 to 1856 others were appointed, and churches and schools were established in fourteen villages in Liberia, and two in Sierra Leone. In 1860 there were 24 stations and churches, 18 pastors, 1258 members, 26 teachers and 665 pupils." The mission was, by orders from home, closed in 1875, by Rev. W. J. Davis and Rev. W. W. Colley, who then resumed work in Yoruba, where they were hailed with delight as "God's men." Thousands had been converted while the work went on, and "many godly men and women of the African race were developed."

Rev. J. Day was born in Virginia, went to Liberia in 1830, resigned a judgeship and was elected Lieutenant-Governor in 1847. He became, in 1854, pastor of the church in Mon-

rovia, where he founded and presided over a high school, in which were departments; elementary, classical and theological. As superintendent of the mission he made extended preaching tours, and reported "a Sunday-school in every village and the word preached statedly to more than 10,000 heathen."

The Yoruba Mission was founded by Rev. J. T. Bowen, in 1850. Other missionaries were sent out in 1853. "Stations were opened, residences and chapels were built, and schools and churches established. Rev. S. Cosby was sent out in 1878 by the colored Baptists of Virginia, and was the first missionary under appointment by a colored board. He was the associate of Rev. W. W. Colley for Missionary David, who had returned home. Mr. Bowen opened the way for colored missionaries.

In 1879 the colored Baptists of South Carolina sent Rev. H. N. Bouey as their missionary to Africa, who was placed in charge of the Missionary Church at Royeville, where he labored three years and returned home. He was successful in organizing churches and associations on a permanent basis. Rev. J. O. Hayes also labored as a missionary in Africa.

There are in Africa, including Western, Southern and Central Africa, where the Congo Mission is, three associations, 81 churches, 55 ministers and 3012 members. The sentiment of the colored Baptists is, Africa for Christ!

The Livingston Inland Mission, on the Congo, Africa, is conducted by the American Baptist Missionary Union. A picture of the missionary steamer, built in England, and the gift of one lady, after whose late husband it is named, is given.

ORGANIZATIONS.

Rev. R. L. Perry, Ph.D., writes: "The million colored Baptists in the United States maintain their own churches, associations and missionary conventions. Their early history in the South was interwoven with the history of the white churches, but since emancipation they have made their own independent record in the South, just as they were doing in the North before the war.

" They began in the North about 80 years ago—that is, the Joy Street church, Boston, Mass., was constituted in 1805 ; the Abyssinian church, New York, in 1808, and the First African church, Philadelphia, in 1809. From these as mother churches, others were established, till, in 1840, there had been such an increase in churches in Pennsylvania, Connecticut, Rhode Island and Massachusetts, that they then formed themselves into a Missionary Convention, for work among their own race.

" The work of this body was confined to the North, excepting an effort to establish a mission in Africa, till peace, in 1865, enabled them to enter the South, to which their whole attention was then given. At their 26th anniversary, at Richmond, Va., August, 1866, this body united with the Northwestern and Southern Convention. The united bodies took the name of the Consolidated American Baptist Missionary Convention, and did a grand work in the South. Some difference of opinion arose as to jurisdiction and management at Richmond, in 1877, which indicated approaching disruption. This Convention still exists, but the fields it once occupied are now worked by new organizations: the New England Baptist Missionary Convention, in the North ; the Baptist Foreign Missionary Convention of the United States, in the South ; and the Baptist General Association of the Western States and Territories, in the West.

" In each quarter of the United States—North, South, East and West—there are some strong churches and able men, who

2B

take the lead in mission work and denominational action in their respective societies.

"The Foreign Missionary Convention of the South, and the General Association of the Western States and Terrritories, have Foreign Mission Stations in Africa, while the Consolidated Convention has a mission station, and owns good mission property at Port-au-Prince, Hayti."

There are churches in the South, as we shall see, that antedate those above named; besides, among the older churches, are the Ebenezer, New York, 1825, and the Union, Cincinnati, 1827.

Dr. Perry is the author of a learned publication entitled, "The Cushite."

GENERAL MISSIONARY SOCIETIES.

The Baptist General Association of the Western States and Territories was organized in 1873 and enlarged in 1880. Rev. R. De Baptiste writes: "In 1853 a movement was begun in the Wood River Association, Illinois, to reach wider and more needy parts of the West, which resulted in the formation of the Western Colored Baptist Convention, which, in 1864, was still further widened into the Northwestern and Southern Baptist Convention. The latter was consolidated in 1867 with the American Baptist Missionary Convention, operating in the Eastern and Northeastern States, the new body taking the name of the Consolidated American Baptist Convention, which continued its work at home and abroad till 1879, as a united body, when the Western churches withdrew and formed their own association. A weekly journal, established in 1883, is now published at Keokuk, Iowa, and called the *Western Herald.*

The officers for 1887 are: Rev. W. H. Howard, M.D.,

Moderator; Rev. J. W. Crushshon and Rev. J. H. Oden, Assistant Moderators; Rev. J. L. Cohron, Recording Secretary; Rev. T. L. Johnson, Corresponding Secretary, and Rev. R. De Baptiste, Treasurer. The income for the year was $5,163. Rev. T. L. Johnson, London, Eng., and Rev. J. W. Polk, at home, are agents for collecting funds for the African Mission.

Great interest has been awakened in the Congo Mission, Africa, and the association appointed, in 1886, Rev. J. W. Ricketts and T. E. S. Scholes, M.D., as missionaries to the Congo Valley. Miss L. C. Flemming goes as a missionary also to the Congo country, whence her father was brought as a slave to this land. She is a graduate of Shaw University, and will be accompanied by Miss Faulkner and Miss Hamilton. They go out under the Women's Societies of the East and the West, which have already been doing a work among the women of the South through female teachers and missionaries.

The New England Baptist Missionary Convention was formed in 1875. Its field of operation is in the Northern and Eastern States. The minutes for 1886 show a list of 43 churches—one in Delaware, six in Pennsylvania, nine in New York, nine in New Jersey, four in Connecticut, two in Rhode Island, eleven in Massachusetts and one in Virginia. The main object of the Convention is to send out missionaries into destitute regions and to plant and build up churches within its reach. Its officers for 1887 are : President, Rev. R. D. Wynn ; Vice-president, Rev. B. T. Moore ; Recording Secretary, Rev. T. D. Miller, D.D. ; Corresponding Secretary, Rev. W. T. Dixon ; Treasurer, Rev. R. A. Motley ; General Agent, Rev. R. L. Perry, Ph.D.

The Baptist Foreign Missionary Convention of the United States was formed in 1880. Its officers are : Rev. A. S. Jack-

ON THE CONGO, AFRICA.

P. 422

son, President; Hon. J. J. Spelman, Secretary; Prof. J. E. Jones, Corresponding Secretary; Rev. R. Wells, Treasurer; and the location of the Executive Board, Richmond, Va. The Convention has divided the country into districts for foreign mission work: 1st. Virginia; 2d. the territory covered by the New England Convention; 3d. South Carolina, Georgia and Alabama. The receipts for 1886 were $4,473. Six missionaries were sent to Africa in 1883: Rev. J. H. Presley and wife, Rev. W. W. Colley and wife, Rev. J. J. Coles and Rev. H. McKinney. An account of their labors and trials in the establishment of the Baptist Vey Mission is given by Rev. J. J. Coles in a book entitled, " Africa in Brief." In 1886 the Convention sent to the Vey Mission Rev. J. J. Coles, who had returned to America, Mrs. Coles, Rev. and Mrs. E. B. Topp and Rev. J. J. Diggs. Mrs. Diggs was soon to follow. The Foreign Missionary force now consists of four ordained ministers, four native helpers and two women. The field of operations is in the Vey country, West Central Africa. There are three divisions: Bendoo, Jundoo and Mississippi, with six out stations. There are two churches and 150 members. In two years and a half there have been 100 baptisms, and for the year 20. The Convention, through its corresponding secretary, publishes a paper—*African Missions.* " Be it ever remembered," says Rev. J. J. Coles, " that out of the Virginia Baptist State Convention came the Baptist Foreign Missionary Convention of the United States."

The American National Baptist Convention. In pursuance of a suggestion made by Rev. W. J. Simmons, D.D., and of a call signed by prominent Baptists throughout the land, the First National Convention of colored Baptists convened August 25, 1886, at the First Baptist church of St. Louis, Mo., Rev. J. R. Young, pastor. Rev. Dr. W. J. Simmons called the Convention to order, and a temporary organization was effected by calling Rev. W. J. Shelton to the chair, and selecting W. H. Steward, Secretary. Seventeen States were represented by 600 delegates and visitors. Among them " were graduates in law, medicine and theology ; professors of philosophy, German, French, Latin, Greek and Hebrew ; a number of State ex-representatives, and ex-senators ; two ex-lieutenant-governors, editors and teachers not a few ; a Baptist senator from Mississippi and a Baptist missionary from London, Eng." Rev. W. J. Simmons, D.D., was elected permanent President ; Rev. J. R. Young and T. L. Johnson, Vice-presidents ; Rev. S. T. Clanton, D.D., and W. H. Steward, Secretaries ; Rev. R. De Baptiste, Corresponding Secretary ; Rev. D. A. Gaddie, Treasurer, and Miss L. W. Smith, Historian. A constitution was adopted and the body made permanent. The Executive Board, Rev. Dr. Simmons, Chairman, is located at Louisville, Ky. One of the main objects of the Convention is to unify the denomination in mission work. Rev. T. L. Johnson, one of the speakers, said : " Knox lifted up Scotland, Luther lifted up Germany, and it is for us to lift up the heathen of the land of our fathers." The meeting of the Convention for 1887 will be in August, with the Third Baptist church, Mobile, Ala., Rev. A. F. Owens, pastor.

SCHOOLS.

There are in the South at least 26 Institutions of higher learning for the education of preachers and teachers for the colored people. The following have colored presidents and for the most part colored teachers, and are under the control of the colored Baptists.

The State University, at Louisville, Ky., was founded in 1873, and has for President Rev. W. J. Simmons, D.D., and six assistants, of whom two only are white. There are three departments—college, normal and model school, with 171 students. Property valuation, $18,000. A class was graduated in 1886, in the degree of A. B.

Natchez College, Natchez, Miss., 1877, Prof. P. A. Wardlaw, President, has three instructors, and 165 students.

Selma University, Selma, Ala., 1878, Rev. C. L. Purce, President, has seven instructors, and 353 students, male and female, and property valued at $15,000.

Brazoria Institute, Brazoria, Tex., 1867, Prof. S. H. Smothers, President since 1868, has trained more than 60 teachers.

Seguine Academy, Seguine, Tex., has property valued at $14,000.

Hearne Academy, Hearne, Tex., 1881, Prof. W. F. Smith, A.M., Principal, has three instructors, 32 students, and property valued at $4,000.

Western Union Institute, Asherville, N. C., 1884, Rev. E. H. Lipscombe, A.M., President, has four teachers, 200 students, and property valued at $5,000.

There are several other academies in North Carolina: Winston Academy, Rev. C. S. Brown, A.B., Principal, costing $2,000 ; Garysburg High School, Rev. R. J. Walden, A.M., Principal, worth $1,500 ; High School at Warrenton, Rev. J. A. Whitted, A.B., Principal, valued at $5,000 ; Cedar Grove Academy, Rev. R. H. Harris, Principal ; and at Goldsboro a lot has been purchased for a school site on which buildings will soon be erected.

At Coalsmouth, W. Va., a school property, formerly Shelton College, has been purchased worth $25,000, and a school of high grade will soon be opened with Rev. C. H. Payne as President.

The colored Baptists of Lynchburg, Va., have bought a lot

on which to erect a building and open a school preparatory to Richmond Seminary.

At Little Rock, Ark., a school was opened 1886, under "a very scholarly and competent President, Prof. J. H. Garnett."

The first, third and last of the above schools, as well as those that shall follow, are under the fostering care of the AMERICAN BAPTIST HOME MISSION SOCIETY. Dr. Morehouse says, "The colored Baptists have raised apart from the Society's efforts, about $50,000 for property and teachers, chiefly for the schools at Selma, Live Oak, and Marshall, Texas."

It is estimated that 8,000 students have gone out from the HOME MISSION SCHOOLS alone; and those who go forth from all are strong advocates of temperance and missions.

The Roger Williams University, Nashville, Tenn., 1864, was the first school of the kind in order of time. President, W. H. Stifler, D.D. There are 8 assistants and 126 young men and 87 young women students. The property is valued at $85,000.

Wayland Seminary, Washington, D. C., 1865, G. M. P. King, D. D., President, has six teachers, 121 students, 72 male and 49 female. Value of property $10,000. For 18 years Dr. King has been training preachers and teachers, many of whom are now among the foremost workers in the denomination.

Shaw University, Raleigh, N. C., 1865, H. M. Tupper, D. D., President, has a faculty of 20, and 402 students, male and female. The work of Dr. Tupper, from a small beginning 22 years ago, is remarkable; the smallest part of it is seen in the many fine buildings now in service. The University building, Estey Hall, Leonard Medical building, Chapel and dining hall, Medical dormitory, and residences costing in all $125,-

MAIN BUILDING, SHAW UNIVERSITY, RALEIGH, N. C.

P. 427

ooo. The medical faculty is composed of the best white tal. ent in Raleigh, while the theological department is in charge of Rev. Dr. T. E. Skinner, for years pastor of the First white Baptist church, in Raleigh, who says : " The work is itself an inspiration. The deportment is good, and far beyond any I have seen. The desire to learn is a most encouraging feature to the teacher, the ability to learn is fully equal to that of the white people, where the advantages have been the same."

The Richmond Theological Seminary, Richmond, Va., 1867, has had from the start as its President, C. H. Corey, D. D. Two of its faculty of four are colored. There are 62 attending its course of instruction. "A former student, now a Professor in the Institution, is Grand Chief Templar of the Grand Lodge, (Dual), of Virginia. He is also President of the Third District Temperance Alliance, by the voice of the white as well as of the colored people of the State. In view of his distinguished services in the cause, the lodges of Richmond and vicinity, recently presented him with a magnificent regalia."

Atlanta Seminary, Atlanta, Ga., 1867, S. Graves, D.D., President, has 5 teachers and 153 students. Value of property $20,000. Dr. Graves feels the need of a new site and new buildings. ·

Leland University, New Orleans, La., 1870, Rev. M. C. Cole, acting President, has a property valued at $85,000. It has eight instructors and 221 students, is self-supporting and has an endowment of $95,000.

Benedict Institute, Columbia, S. C., 1870, Rev. C. E. Becker, President, has property valued at $40,000. Prof. Becker has four assistants; there are four departments—theological, academic, musical, and industrial; and 218 students—119 male and 99 female.

Jackson College, Jackson, Miss., founded at Natchez, in 1877, but not to be confounded with the present Natchez College; Rev. C. Ayer, President, with four assistants and 251 students, and property valued at $30,000.

Florida Institute, Live Oak, Fla., 1880, Rev. J. L. A. Fish, President, with 6 teachers, 96 students, and property valued at $7,000.

Bishop College, Marshall, Texas, 1881, Rev. S. W. Culver, President, with 5 assistants and 156 students; one of the faculty is a graduate of the school. It has always been under the charge of President Culver. It is named after the late Dr. Nathan Bishop, whose widow has liberally endowed it.

Spelman Seminary, Atlanta, Ga., 1881, Miss S. B. Packard, and Miss H. Giles, Principals, is for females only. It has 250 boarders, and in all 555 scholars, and 20 instructors.

Hartshorn Memorial College, Richmond, Va., is also for females, and has 96 pupils, was founded in 1884, and its President is Rev. L. B. Tefft. The property is valued at $35,000.

The Creek Freedman School, Tullehasse, I. T., 1883, Prof. G. E. Burdick, Ph. D., superintendent, has three teachers, six pupils, and property valued at $6,000.

In the Home Mission schools alone there are 23 colored teachers, 2,739 scholars, 437 preparing to preach, 963 preparing to teach, 35 desiring to go to Africa as missionaries, and 38 medical students. Of the pupils 1200 are young men and 1500 young women. 150 pupils were converted during the year.

COLORED BAPTIST NEWSPAPERS.

African Expositor, Rev. Prof. N. F. Roberts, Raleigh, N. C.; American Baptist, Rev. W. J. Simmons, D.D., and W. H. Steward, Louisville, Ky.; Arkansas Baptist, Rev. E. C. Morris, Little Rock, Ark.; Arkansas Review, Rev. J. T. White, Helena, Ark.; Baptist Advocate, Rev. A. S. Jackson, and Rev. S. T. Clanton, B. D., New Orleans, La.; Baptist Beacon, Rev. W. R. Boone, B.D., Springfield, O.; Baptist Messenger, Hon. J. J. Spelman, Jackson, Miss.; Baptist Preacher, Rev. A. R. Griggs, Dallas, Tex.; Georgia Baptist, Rev. W. J. White, Augusta, Ga.; Baptist Signal, Rev. G. W. Gayles, Greenville, Miss.; Living Way, Rev. W. A. Brinkley, Memphis, Tenn. ; Memphis Watchman, J. T. Turner, Memphis, Tenn.; National Monitor, Rev. R. L. Perry, Ph. D., Brooklyn, N.Y.; Western Herald, Rev. R. De Baptiste, Rev. A. Johnson,' Rev. R. M. Duling, Rev. T. L. Smith, Keokuk, Ia.; Richmond Planet, J. Mitchell, Jr., Richmond, Va.; West Virginia Enterprise, Rev. C. H. Payne, Charleston, W. Va.; Weekly Sentinel, Rev. R. R. Wright, and Rev. E. K. Love, Augusta, Ga.; Baptist Watchtower, W. H. Anderson, Evansville, Ind.; Mountain Gleaner, Rev. E. H. Lipscombe, Asherville, N. C.; Baptist Pilot, Rev. L. G. Jordan, and Elder F. G. Davis, Waco, Tex.; Baptist Tribune, Rev. E. M. Brawley, D. D., Columbia, S. C.; Baptist Leader, Rev. A. N. McEwen, Montgomery, Ala.; Herald, J. C. Duke, Montgomery, Ala.; African Missions, Prof. J. E. Jones, Richmond, Va.; The Caret, Rev. C. D. Cooley, Newport News, Va.; Marion Head Light, J. L. Fleming, Marion, Ark.; Pioneer Press, J. R. Clifford, Martinsburg, W. Va.; Golden Epoch, G. H. W. Stewart, Helena, Ark.; Baptist Banner, J. W. Browder, Columbus, Kan.; Texas Pioneer, Prof. S. M. Smothers, Brazoria, Tex.; Seven Mansions, N. O. Bryant, Calvert, Tex.; Busy Bee, F. J. Jones, Greenville, Miss.; Baptist Review, (magazine,) Rev. E. Carter, Atlanta, Ga.; Missouri Baptist Standard, G. H. McDaniel, Palmyra, Mo.; Pulpit and Desk (Quarterly), Rev. Bird Wilkins, B. D., St. Paul, Minn.

Some in the above list are secular papers with Baptist editors. Drs. Brawley and Perry think there are at least as many more papers secular and religious as are contained in the list given.

The Mount Olivet church, West 53d street, New York City, was organized in 1878 with 21 members and with five dollars in the treasury. They then worshipped in a hall and were under the care of the Fifth Avenue Baptist church. It flourished under the pastor-elect, Rev. D. W. Wisher, of Norfolk, Va. The church was recognized and the pastor ordained May 30, 1878, Rev. Dr. Armitage preaching the sermon. At once the hall became too small for the people that crowded to hear the gospel. Over 500 were added to the church by baptism, 250 by letter, and 300 by experience, and there was in 1886, an active membership of 700, besides, $40,000 has been raised for church expenses, $6,000 for missions at home and abroad, and $16,000 for repairs and interest. In April, 1884, with the aid of the Southern New York Association, this church purchased the splendid granite church edifice it now occupies and which was the church of the Rev. Dr. Cheever, valued at $125,000, seating 2,000 persons, and with an organ costing $5,000. The dedication services began Sunday, June 15, 1884, when Rev. Harvey Johnson preached in the morning, Dr. Armitage in the afternoon, the dedicatory sermon, and Rev. T. D. Miller, D.D., at night. The prayer was made by Rev. H. Williams, Jr. On Thursday the venerable Dr. Cheever delivered an address of most thrilling interest, and a letter from the poet, J. G. Whittier, was read. God raised up for them many friends of means, among them, Rev. H. F. Barnes, S. S. Constant, B. F. Judson, who each gave from $500 to $8,000. J. D. Rockefeller gave one-fourth of the entire cost of the property.

A colored Baptist preacher gathered a few Baptists in a private house in Baltimore, Md., 1818, but not until 1836, was the first church organized. Moses Clayton, a slave in Vir-

UNION CHURCH, BALTIMORE, MD.

p. 432.

ginia, came to Baltimore in 1834. He could read and write and speak with fluency. He made his living at his trade as carpenter, and preached on Sunday. " He began a school with three children, two of them his own. Often he preached to an audience comprising his wife and two or three others, and spoke with as much earnestness as if addressing a thousand." A church was formed with 8 or 10, and he ordained pastor. Rev. L. Hicks, pastor, collected money for a house of worship in 1865, into which they removed from the old schoolhouse. In 1880, a larger house was built in an eligible location, costing $16,500. The pastor is Rev. J. C. Allen.

The Union Church, Baltimore, was organized in 1852, with 57 members. The first pastor was Rev. J. Carey. They now exceed 2,000. " Rev. Harvey Johnson, the pastor, stands high in the community as an Evangelical leader." He is a graduate of Wayland Seminary, and became pastor in 1872, when the church numbered 278 members. In 1876 they entered their new house of worship which cost $20,000, which they themselves paid for, excepting $500, in four years. It seats 1200. The pastor was mainly the originator of the Baptist State Convention. His sermon on " The Equality of the Father and the Son," was published.

The above facts are from " The History of the Baptist Churches in Maryland," published by J. F. Weishampel, Jr.

There are in the State 20 churches, 6,000 members, 15 ministers, and $150,000 worth of church property.

Rev. Walter H. Brooks writes : " The Baptists of Washington, D. C., organized their first church, and erected their first meeting-house at the corner of 19th and I streets, in 1802. There were six constituent members, all white. In process of time many colored persons were received as members. The house of worship had in 1833, become too small for the congregation and the old house was abandoned for a new one on 10th street. The colored people were encouraged to continue in the old building. Finally the property was sold to the colored Baptists of the district. They had then, 1833, no church organization. They were members of the church on 10th street, although they had their separate place of worship, and a Sunday-school for their children. A number of colored Baptists who had come to Washington formed themselves into a Baptist church in 1839 The church numbered four, of whom one, Emily Coke, still lives. As soon as the church was formed the colored members of the church on 10th street united with the new body and the property on 19th street passed into their hands. In 1846 they numbered 202, from 1865 to 1873 they increased from 370 to 1191, and in 1876 the membership was 1200, but a revision of the roll reduced it to 1086, the present number. The first pastor was Rev. S. White, and the present one is Rev. W. H. Brooks. From this church has gone out: The Second, Fourth, Fifth, Salem, and Berean churches. Since 1860 other Baptist churches have sprung up that are not off-shoots of the First church. There are to-day in the district between 20 and 30 colored Baptist churches, many of which have a membership of between 1000 and 1800. They own some valuable church property, such as that of the Shiloh, First, Liberty, Fourth, Fifth, Berean, and others too numerous to name, which shows to what good use thousands of the money of this people have been put.''

Revs. Brooks, Walker, Lee, Johnson, Howard, of the Zion church, preach to large congregations.

The First white Baptist church, of Richmond, Va., was organized with 14 members, in 1780, when Richmond was a village of 1800 inhabitants, one-half of whom were Africans.

THE LOWER CONGO, AFRICA.

P. 435

" Since 1863 the colored Baptists have constituted themselves separately, and have their own associations." The colored people throughout the South generally were members of the same churches with the whites. The First African church of Richmond, existed before the war. Rev. R. Ryland, D.D., President of Richmond College, was the pastor of this church for twenty-five years, and during his pastorate there baptized over 3800 persons. Their house of worship was built between the years 1790 and 1800, and set apart for the use of the colored Baptists when the white Baptists erected a new church in 1841. The old house was historic, and published in the list of places to be visited by the stranger in the city, who took Sunday for the purpose, to hear the excellent music. Within its walls some of the most important meetings have been held and the most distinguished men have spoken. The Virginia convention of 1829–30 met here. Madison and Marshall were there. It was the last time that these distinguished men held a seat in a public assembly. In April, 1861, " the largest meeting ever held in that church took place in behalf of the Union, the Constitution, and the Enforcement of the Laws." In 1864, a famous meeting took place there, the object of which was to urge the people to renewed resistance of the Federal Army then thundering at the gates of Richmond. Addresses were made by Jefferson Davis, J. P. Benjamin and others. Here, too, was held after the surrender a meeting of the freedmen—" The first ever held in the South." In those days such men as Horace Greeley, Gerritt Davis, Henry Wilson, and Gen. Howard addressed the multitudes in the old church. " The African Church" was the place both before and after the war for all great gatherings, and a large price was charged for its use. It was demolished in 1876, to make way for the present elegant structure which cost $40,000, seats 2500 people and has an organ that cost $2500.

Rev. J. H. Holmes, the present pastor, took charge in 1867, when the membership was 3,000. Since then 5,000 have been added to its membership, and eleven other churches been organized of material from this church. The present number is 3040. The Sunday-school has in it 600 pupils. The church collections amount to $4,000 annually. Rev. J. H. Holmes was born in 1826, and came to Richmond in 1835, where he professed faith in Christ and united with this church. He was ordained in 1867. Though born a slave, he has through his own efforts obtained an education, and is now a power for good and of great service to his race. In June, 1878 he baptized at one time 268, another day 598, and at one time this year 200 believers. The Second church has a membership of 3,000. The venerable church at Portsmouth, Va., has a remarkable history, and dates back to 1798.

The First church, Manchester, Va., held its meetings apart from the whites for the first time in 1821, at the house of Mrs. Nancy Rasfield. Then they were few in number, and a branch of the Spring Creek church. They grew under their white pastors, until about 1825, when they purchased ground on which they built a frame meeting-house. Their white pastors were assisted by colored preachers. About 1854 a brick meeting-house was erected. Rev. R. Wells was the first colored pastor, and took charge in 1865. Rev. A Binga, Jr. became pastor in 1872. He has baptized 908 persons. In 1869 they entered their present house of worship, which seats 1400, and cost $18,000 The membership is 1512. Three churches have gone out from this church in 15 years.

The Fourth church, Rev. E Paine, pastor, numbers 1,400; Ebenezer, Rev. R. Wells, 1600; and Second, Rev. W. Troy, 3,000. Rev. John Jasper also preaches to a large congregation. Rev. H. Williams, Jr. is preparing a history of the colored Baptists of Virginia.

The officers of the State Convention are: Rev. J. M. Armistead, President; Rev. A. Gordon, Rev. A. Truatt, Rev. A. H. Lewis, Rev. H. W. Dickerson, Vice-presidents ; Rev. H. H. Mitchell, Corresponding Secretary ; Rev. A. Binga, Jr., Recording Secretary ; and J. E. Farrar, Treasurer. Six missionaries have been employed, about $3,000 raised for missions and $2,250 actually paid to missionaries in Africa during 1886. Rev. J. A. Taylor is Secretary and Agent of the Foreign Mission Board.

A fine lot has been purchased for $1,800 by the colored Baptists of Lynchburg, Va., which overlooks the city, and on which a denominational school of high grade will soon be established.

Ten years ago there were less than 500 Baptists in West Virginia, while now there are over 1800 members, 25 churches, 3 associations, and one State convention. The Executive Board of the Convention has purchased a school property and will open an academic, normal, theological and industrial school. Rev. C. H. Payne, the originator of the scheme, was assisted in it by other leading men of the State. The *Religious Herald* says that " he is an educated man and a good preacher, and will probably take charge of the school."

The 17th Annual Session of the General Association of Kentucky was held at Danville, in 1885. Officers :—Moderator, Rev. P. Johnson ; Assistant Moderators, Rev. D. A. Gaddie, Rev. P. H. Kennedy ; Recording Secretary, W. H. Steward ; Corresponding Secretary, Q. B. Jones ; Treasurer, Rev P. Alexander ; Chairman of the Executive Board, Rev. A Heath ; Chairman of the Board of Trustees, W. H. Steward 287 churches and 46,902 members were reported.

There is a State Baptist Women's Educational Convention. President, Mrs. A. V. Nelson ; Secretary, Mrs. M. B. Wallace; Chairman Board of Managers, Miss L. C. Crittenden.

The State University, Louisville, is the result of efforts put forth by the colored Baptists of the State to educate their preachers and teachers. The President, Dr. Simmons, is also pastor, editor, President of the National Press Association, of the State Teachers' Association, and of the National Baptist Convention. Educated and energetic, he is an indefatigable worker and a leader of men. He is writing a history of the Kentucky colored Baptists. Rev. A. Allensworth, A. M., Chaplain U. S. A. is a member of the Board of Trustees.

W. H. Steward says "The Fifth church, Louisville, formed in 1839, has the finest building and largest congregation in the State. Rev. J. H. Frank is pastor. The membership is 1500. It is a model church and has the best choir in the South. The colored Baptist denomination is the largest in the State."

Dr. Everts says: "The colored Baptists are sharing the progressive spirit of the white churches, and have increased to fifteen churches, with almost five thousand members in Louisville."

Rev. C. C. Stumm says that Rev. G. W. Dupee is the Nestor of the Kentucky Baptists.

The State Convention of Tennessee held its 14th anniversary at Winchester in 1886. Its officers are : President, Rev. R. B. Vandervell, D D.; Vice-presidents, Rev. C. C. Russel, Rev. J. Bransford, Rev. I. Trimble ; Secretary, Rev. B. Frierson ; Corresponding Secretary, Rev. B. A. Franklin ; Treasurer, Rev. A. Buchanan. The annual sermon was by Rev. S. M. Dickinson, and addresses were made by Rev. H. Woodsmall, Rev. D. A. Franklin. There are 10 associations and over 35,000 members in the State. There is a church at Memphis, for which $100,000 cash was paid. The First church, Nashville, has a membership of about 2500, and a handsome church edifice costing $26,000, and seating 1300.

LEONARD MEDICAL SCHOOL, SHAW UNIVERSITY.   p. 440

Rev. Prof. N. F. Roberts writes: " The State Convention of North Carolina was organized in 1866. Then the colored Baptists had but few churches in the State, and most of these had neither house of worship nor pastor. There are now 500 ministers, 850 churches, 110,000 members, and 850 Sunday-schools, 3500 teachers and 75,000 scholars. There are several academies of high grade preparing youth for Shaw University. During the last 20 years God has greatly prospered us. Our preachers have planted churches in many destitute fields and the people are hearing the word with gladness. Over 8,000 were baptized last year. Many brethren of other denomina-nations have learned the truth as we hold it and have united with us. Within the past year many of the Churches have provided themselves with comfortable houses of worship."

The officers of the North Carolina State Convention are: Prof. Roberts, President ; Rev. A. M. Conway, Vice-president ; Rev. W. T. H. Woodward, Recording Secretary ; Rev. J. O. Crosby, Corresponding Secretary ; Rev. A. B. Williams, Treas-urer ; Rev. G. W. Holland, Auditor.

The Baptist Educational, Missionary and Sunday-school Convention of South Carolina is doing noble work and its Secretary, Rev. J. J. Durham, M.D., asks for $5,000 this year for missions. President I. P. Brockenton says : " The Con-vention is one of the great levers for lifting our people ; it has done a great deal towards raising our ministry to its present height. One of its grand objects is to give to our churches an educated ministry." Rev. J. C. Butler is Vice-president, Rev. S. B. Stratfoot, Treasurer, and Rev. E. M. Brawley, D.D , Historian. Dr. Brawley, late President of Selma Theological Seminary, has removed to Columbia, where the Benedict In-stitute is, and where he edits the *Baptist Tribune*. He is thoroughly educated, being a graduate of Bucknell University, Pennsylvania.

There are 100,000 colored Baptists in the State.

The officers of the Georgia State Convention are : President, Rev. J. C. Bryan ; Vice-president, Rev. U. L. Houston ; Secretary, J. H. Brown ; Assistant Secretary, Rev. T. J. Hornsby ; Treasurer, Rev. J. T. Tolbert ; Corresponding Secretary, Rev. C. H. Lyons. At the 16th anniversary meeting in 1886, sermons were preached by Rev. C. T. James, Rev. F. M. Simmons, and Rev. C. C. Terry. There are in the State 42 associations, 1301 churches and 134,489 members, which is claimed as the largest colored Baptist membership in any State. Two missionaries are employed by the Convention and over $1,000 expended. The First church, Savannah, Rev. E. K. Love, pastor, has 4,000 members. It was founded in 1788, by Rev. Andrew Bryan, who was baptized by Rev. George Lisle before he went to Jamaica. He suffered for Christ's sake, and died in 1812. The Second church was organized in 1803. There is a church at Augusta with 5,000 members.

The officers of the General Convention of Florida, for 1887, are : President, Rev. J. N. Stokes, Vice-president, Rev. T. Lancester ; Recording Secretary, Rev. G. P. McKinney ; Corresponding Secretary, Rev. J. B. Hankers ; Treasurer, Rev. P. S. Sommers. The Convention was called to order by Rev. J. A. Potter, and Rev. J. Felder and Rev. J. G. Ross preached. The latter is pastor of Bethel Church, Jacksonville, which has built a $2,000 parsonage, and sent Miss L. C. Flemming to Africa. Lawyer Fairfax says that there are 27,000 colored Baptists in the State. Over $1300 was given in 1885 for Florida Institute. The officers of the Sunday-school Convention are : President, A. Dallas ; Recording Secretary, D. H. Brown ; Corresponding Secretary, J. W. Benton ; Treasurer, Rev. M. Wiggins.

In Alabama there are 50 associations, 700 ministers, 800 churches, and 85,000 members. The State Convention, organized in 1868, is an active missionary body. The value of church property is $250,000. The officers of the Convention for 1886 are : Rev. M. Tyler, President; Rev. J. A. Foster, Vice-president; C. W. White, Treasurer ; N. R. Nickerson, Clerk.

Hon. J. J. Spelman says that "Mississippi has a State Convention, besides a General Association, having over 38,766 communicants, and a paper edited, and its whole mechanical department managed by colored men. They have also a college at Natchez worth $20,000, without a dollar of debt, with a president and faculty, all colored, and 165 students."

The officers of the General Association are: Moderator, Rev. H. W. Bowen; Vice-moderator, Rev. A. Reed; Corresponding Secretary, Rev. J. H. Nichols; Recording Secretary, Rev. H. M. Thompson ; Statistical Secretary, Hon. J. J. Spelman ; Treasurer, Rev. A. Durham ; and of the State Sunday-school Convention are: President, Hon. J. J. Spelman ; Vice-presidents, Rev. H. Watson, Rev. H. M. Thompson ; Corresponding Secretary, Rev. T. L. Jordan; Recording Secretary, Rev. J. H. Nichols; Treasurer, R. L. Shepherd.

Over $400 were raised in the Association in 1886 for African Missions, and farewell addresses were made by two of its members, Rev. E. B. Topp and wife, under appointment as missionaries to the Veys, Africa. The introductory sermon was by Rev. G. W. Cohran, doctrinal sermon by Rev. J. F. Boulden, educational sermon by Rev. T. L. Jordan, temperance sermon by Rev. R. Ramsey.

Hon. J. J. Spelman is writing a history of the colored Baptists of the State.

The first Baptist preacher to enter Louisiana was Joseph Willis, a mulatto, in 1804. He organized several churches, and the Louisiana Baptist Association, of which he was elected moderator, in 1837. Henry Adams, a colored Baptist preacher, came into the State and formed a church at Mount Lebanon, of which he became pastor. He had some education, and the church was one of the most active in the State.

Rev. S. T. Clanton, B.D., writes: "The first colored Association was the Louisiana Southern, formed in 1865; the State Convention was organized in 1872, and the State was subdivided, in 1883, into thirteen district associations, making sixteen in all. Immense moral and intellectual progress and advance in Christian work have, in these years, been made. The American Baptist Publication Society is an acknowledged agency in this great revolution for good. There are 500 churches connected with the Convention, and others unassociated; 70,000 members; 650 ministers, and 350 Sunday-schools."

The officers of the State Convention are: President, Rev. J. Marks; Recording Secretary, Rev. A. S. Jackson; Corresponding Secretary, Rev. S. T. Clanton; Treasurer, Rev. A. Hubbs; and of the Sunday-school Convention: President, Rev. C. J. Hardy; Vice-president, Rev. A. L. Reese; Corresponding Secretary, Rev. S. T. Clanton; Recording Secretary, Rev. H. K. Barrett; Treasurer, Rev. B. Dorsey.

Rev. A. R. Griggs writes: "The colored Baptists of Texas began as an independent people, with the ordination of Elder J. J. Reinhardt, in 1866, by the white Baptists. In the same year they ordained Elder S. Cobb, at Waco, and organized the First colored Baptist church. In 1867 Elder I. S. Campbell came to Texas as missionary of the Consolidated Convention, and organized the First church of Galveston in 1867,

BISHOP COLLEGE, MARSHALL, TEXAS.

P. 445

and within a few months some 50 or 60 churches were formed by him, and the Lincoln Association, organized in 1867, at Houston. In 1880 this Association numbered 150 churches and 12,000 members. There are now 25 associations, 795 churches, 664 ministers, and 69,950 members. The State Convention was organized in 1872, and the Sunday-school Convention in 1880. The first denominational school for colored people originated at Dallas, in 1867, in the Northwestern Association, through the efforts of Rev. A. R. Griggs. It is still in operation at Brazoria. Bishop College and Hearne Academy are both Baptist institutions. The latter was established by the colored State Convention, and to the former the colored Baptists contributed the lot, costing $2,500 and $3,500 cash. The late T. Hill, of Austin, a colored man, bequeathed $6,000 to Hearne Academy. Seguine Academy was founded by the Guadalupe Association, through the efforts of Elder W. B. Ball. The first colored newspaper was started by Rev. A. R. Griggs, in 1867, and is now known as *Baptist Pilot*, at Waco. To Elder I. S. Campbell, more than to any other man, is due the credit for the formation of the present organizations in the State. In 1887 he celebrated his fiftieth year in the ministry and his twentieth year as pastor at Waco, where he has nearly completed the best brick colored church in the State. There are in the State 19 women's missionary societies, and there has been collected for the year $13,474. The value of church property is $250,000."

The officers of the State Convention are: President, Rev. W. Massey; Vice-president, Rev. F. Hooks; Secretary, W. F. Smith; Treasurer, A. Terrell; Corresponding Secretary, Prof. D. Abner, Jr.; Superintendent of Missions, Rev. A. R. Griggs; and of the Sunday-school Convention: President, Rev. J. Toliver; Secretary, Hon. J. H. Stewart; Treasurer, M. Dudley; and State Evangelist, Rev. A. R. Griggs.

In Arkansas there are 19 associations, about 300 ministers, over 500 churches and 30,000 members.

Rev. R. De Baptiste writes: "In Illinois the first organization of colored Baptists was among the colored farmers, near Alton. They were free people, some of whom owned their farms. The oldest colored Baptist church in the State is the Salem, Wood River, near Alton. In 1838 the four or five colored Baptist churches, so far formed, mostly through the labors of the pioneer, Rev. J. Livingston, organized the Wood River Association, probably the oldest colored association in the United States. From this has grown two associations— the Wood River, with 48 churches, 3500 members and 40 ministers; and the Mount Olive, with 45 churches, 2,000 members and 29 ministers. Rev. De Baptiste was pastor for nearly 19 years over one of the strongest churches in the Wood River Association, and instrumental in collecting and organizing six churches. A movement originated in the Wood River Association in 1853, that led to the formation of the Western Baptist Convention, in whose organization the colored Baptists of St. Louis, Mo., took part. Seizing the opportunity afforded by the liberation of their race, to extend their labors among the colored people South, the Convention issued a call, which eventuated, in 1864, in the formation of the Northwestern and Southern Baptist Convention, and from this the work of organization and consolidation went on.

The Olivet Church, Chicago, had Rev. R. De Baptiste as pastor, from 1863 to 1882, during which time the membership increased from 100 to 600, about 1600 persons having united with the church—over one-half by baptism. They have a neat house on a lot which alone cost $13,000. The Bethesda church went out of this church in 1883, with 43 members, while Rev. J. A. D. Podd was pastor, who went with them.

Rev. R. De Baptiste writes: "Probably the oldest Baptist

church in the West or Southwest is the First church, St. Louis, Mo., organized about 1830. For years its pastor was Rev. J. B. Meacham. He died in 1854 or '55, and was succeeded by Rev. E. Cartwright, who was laid aside in 1873. From this church a large number went out and formed the Second or Eighth Street church, now the Central. Its first pastor was Rev. J. R. Anderson, who was, perhaps, the leading Baptist minister of his race at that period, at least, in the West. He was educated, and learned his trade in the printing office of Rev. E. P. Lovejoy, Alton, Ill. He was pastor till his death, in 1863."

Rev. R. H. Brown writes: " The Central church, St. Louis, was organized 1846, with 25 members, and now numbers 800. It has received 1941 members, and expended for the gospel, at home and abroad, $108,512; value of property, $30,000. Rev. S. P. Anderson is serving his second pastorate with this people, and his father was pastor before him. The Second church, Kansas City, Mo., was organized by Rev. C. Moore, pastor, and twelve others, in 1866. Several times their house of worship has been torn down to make room for the growing congregation. Rev. H. Roberson has been their successful pastor. The present membership is 475, and value of property, $50,000. The Pleasant Green church, of Kansas City, was formed with eight members, in 1881. Rev. J. Morgan became pastor. Their house cost $3,300, and the membership is 283. The Berean Church, of the same city, was organized in 1882, through the efforts of Rev. R. H. Brown, who was born in Richmond, Va., baptized by Dr. Ryland and educated at Howard University. After great labor in building a house of worship and in collecting a church and Sunday-school, the house was demolished by a tornado. They hope soon to have a property worth $3,000.

STATISTICS.

Rev. R. De Baptiste writes: "The following facts are gathered from reliable statistical reports. There are now 1,071,902 colored Baptist church members in the United States, organized into churches and associations. Of the 311 associations organized, 255 reported 9,079 churches; 218 reported 4,590 ordained ministers; 90 reported 2,603 Sunday-schools; 94 reported 143,832 Sunday-school pupils; 58 reported $1,334,092.00 valuation of church property; 153 reported $181,063.41 contributions for religious and educational work; 168 reported 39,151 baptisms.

Rev. Dr. Simmons, who has written and published an illustrated book of 750 pages, entitled: "Men of Mark—Eminent, Professional and Rising," says: "I claim that there are in the United States more colored Baptists than white Baptists, and more colored Baptists than all Pedo-baptists together."

SECOND BAPTIST CHURCH, WILMINGTON, DELAWARE.

See page #57.

INDEX.